DJENANE NAKHLE, PHD

FINDING HOME

A Memoir

**From
Cairo
to
New York**

Cover design by Kari Brownlie
Book design by Asya Blue Design
Back cover photo by Rob Greer Photography

ISBN 979-8-9905477-2-8 Paperback
ISBN 979-8-9905477-0-4 Ebook

To Joelle and Sabrina
&
Serena, Sierra, Samson, Lazer, and Zahra

Not all wounds are visible.
Not all challenges meet the eyes.

— Djenane Nakhle, PhD

"You may encounter many defeats,
but you must not be defeated.
In fact, it may be necessary
to encounter the defeats,
so, you can know who you are,
what you can rise from,
how you can still come out of it."

— Maya Angelou

AUTHOR'S NOTE

The content of my memoir is based on my recollection of reported events and a diary labeled "my life," where I documented essential dates as they unfolded.

To protect confidentiality, I have changed some names and events.

I strived to be as authentic as possible in telling my story.

1

CAIRO, EGYPT, 1951

From an early age, I felt great pride in the heritage and beauty of Cairo, my hometown. My bedroom's balcony was my haven. I often found myself lost in the splendor before me. In the foreground, the Nile River symbolized abundance, while in the background, the pyramids represented our majestic Pharaonic ancestry. The immaculate gardens of the British Embassy in front of me complemented the spectacular view that extended from the Nile to the pyramids on the horizon.

The sky was always bright blue and the sun sparkling gold. On a breezy day, the scent of jasmine from the street vendors filled the air and made the view even more enchanting. I enjoyed resting my elbows against the railing, taking deep breaths of the delightful fragrance while admiring the panorama.

As I looked out, I noticed a man wearing a flowing *jillaba* (robe) standing on the stern of his sailboat. The white mast trembled in the day's drift, with its bow slightly raised as ripples danced on the surface of the Nile.

Fascinated by the sight, I wondered where the man was headed—perhaps sailing upstream toward Upper Egypt? Would I ever sail somewhere, some day? If so, where would I navigate? Probably close to home, to my balcony with its boundless perspective of my world.

"Djenane...Djenane..." Mom's calls disrupted my reverie. I was too busy to answer.

Political volatility cast a shadow on my seven-year-old worldview. On the evening of January 26, 1952, a series of conflagrations, known as the Cairo Fire, erupted across the city. Dad came home early to be with Mom and me. He walked in silently and, with a somber expression, asked Mom to follow him. He then carried me on his shoulders to the roof of our apartment building.

A few hundred meters away, I could see unbridled mobs rioting, looting, and burning structures in retaliation against the previous day's attack on an Egyptian government building by British army troops. Thousands of people hurled their wrath. Flames raged from floor to floor, filling the air with black smoke and an acrid smell. Mom choked and coughed.

I held my two hands tighter to Dad's head and clasped my knees against his temples, still not fully grasping the reason for the insurrection. The silence was untenable. I hoped one of the two, most likely Dad, would decode the scene.

I looked at Mom and saw tears streaming down her face. Dad then said solemnly, "Things are not well. We must leave the country." (*Ça ne va pas. Il faut qu'on quitte le pays.*) French was our home language, with occasional words in Arabic to spice up the conversation.

In response, Mom yelled, "I won't leave! This is my country." (*Je ne vais pas quitter! C'est mon pays.*)

Dad kept silent. He didn't want to upset Mom and tended to follow her will.

Political rumblings followed the January 1952 upheaval. In July of that year, the Egyptian Revolution, or coup d'état, broke out under Gamal Abdel Nasser. Egypt's political, economic, and social changes became overpowering and far-reaching. Land redistribution and nationalization of the Suez Canal Company were the first steps.

We stayed despite Dad's warning and the political turmoil. He may have had second thoughts about leaving. His finance and commodity business thrived. He signed commercial agreements on our Nile view terrace between Egypt and European and Asian countries. He negotiated the Aswan Dam project at the highest level.

My balcony continued to be my view of enthralling beauty. The British Embassy maintained an immaculate dark green lawn with multicolored flowers, sprawling to the Nile riverbank. Sailboats resumed trailing waves on the otherwise calm surface of Egypt's lifeline. At a distance, the pyramids symbolized everlasting majesty and immortality.

One afternoon, I saw Nasser, Nehru, and Tito about to embark on a Nile cruise. It made my day and animated my conversations with anyone who would listen. Observing three influential world leaders helped me realize the importance of being open to the multicultural world and its experiences.

By October 1952, everyday life resumed in Cairo. The stark contrast between the tumultuous turmoil and my peaceful view surfaced in my mind. The revolution infiltrated our family conversations. Change and instability seeped insidiously through our lives and worldviews.

2

CAIRO, UP TO JULY 1, 1961

As a daughter and an only child in a strict, Middle Eastern, patriarchal society, my daily activities, as those of my female friends, revolved around parents, friends, and school, not necessarily in that order.

Mom and Dad formed a caring and loving unit, each with specific expectations. Mom doted on me but had high demands for rules and a low tolerance for nonessentials. In addition to fostering learning and life lessons, Dad understood an occasional frivolous wish. Both made me feel secure. I knew my parents loved each other. And I knew they loved me.

Mass attendance was a non-negotiable requirement on Sundays. Afterward, merriment filled the day at home, at one of my friends' homes, or preferably at the Gezira Sporting Club, a private, multisport complex where we knew other members. We gathered in groups of ten or twelve, carefree, seeking a friendly get-together, usually having a good time, occasionally playing a sport. Parents monitored outings. A script preceded my ability to step out the door. "Where are you going? With whom?" They sometimes consulted with other parents. They all knew each other.

My school behavior didn't reach the Pink or Blue ribbon (*Ruban Rose* or *Ruban Bleu)* level granted to those who followed all the rules of the Sacred Heart Catholic School. I was OK with it. Chatting with my classmates was more enjoyable than wearing that badge of exemplary conduct.

I performed well academically and knew I could excel if I put my mind to it. Intellectual curiosity sparked my motivation and learning. In high school, I found subjects more exciting and wrote longer papers in French and Arabic. Spring 1960 marked the peak of academic momentum. I could only think of the French Baccalaureate (*le bac*) looming on the horizon. I prepared well and was self-confident, especially after the results of le bac blanc, a mock exam in preparation for the real one.

In the weeks leading up to the bac, Dad discovered I had a boyfriend, a platonic relationship that he deemed inappropriate for his fifteen-year-old daughter. He threatened the terrified young man with retaliation if he came near me and spoke to his parents in no uncertain terms. The vociferations did not deter my boyfriend and me from seeing each other and hooking up for the first and last time. It was our farewell, filled with mutual sadness at the breakup.

The end of my first relationship and my father's wrath made it difficult for me to concentrate on my studies. I missed my bac by half a point. Shame ensued. That half-point weighed heavily on my mind. It symbolized my double loss.

Mom and Dad were not as harsh on me as I was on myself. "You're fifteen years old, too young to take the bac. If you put your mind to it, you can do it next year." They repeated this to no end, encouraging me to reflect, to become aware of my academic capabilities. I nodded, barely hearing them. In my mind, they were doing what Mom and Dad do.

Repeating the year did not yield the anticipated result in June 1961. My focus continued to wobble. High grades seemed unattainable. I misplaced my energy, hiding my feelings behind camouflaged smiles, keeping my chin up, rather than delving into my books.

The second bac result shattered my academic self-confidence. I did not realize then that ability and performance are not always positively correlated. Many variables interfere with the results. Still, deep down, I kept thinking, One day, I will earn an academic degree. One day, I will succeed.

3

CAIRO, JULY 1961–APRIL 1962

In July 1961, while grappling with my bac result, Nasser nationalized privately owned companies, including Dad's. Nasser's ambition for a government-controlled economy escalated in October 1961 when he seized (sequestered) the private properties of my parents and their peers, including real estate, bank accounts, safes, furniture, and cars. Asset-based rulings were applied to all, regardless of ethnicity, religion, or age.

These decrees led my parents and most of their dispossessed friends to try to flee to Europe or America. Emigration became the norm. Politics planted uncertainty and insecurity in our lives.

Dad was on a business trip in Geneva when sequestration occurred. Mom immediately called him through the operator (known as Trank in those days). "Things have changed. The government has sequestrated our assets," Mom said.

"..."

"Djenane is still a minor, yet the government took over the funds and real estate property your father bequeathed to her," Mom continued.

"Try to get exit visas (government authorization to travel) for the two of you," Dad said.

"You better stay where you are," Mom said.

"I'll apply for a *permis de séjour* (equivalent to a Green Card in the US) for the three of us."

"I advise you to stop the conversation here before you say too much," interrupted the Trank mandated to listen in to international phone communications. "Say goodbye. I will disconnect you afterward."

4

CAIRO, MARCH 1962

With respect to emigration, my parents considered their plan to be the most feasible. Due to his status as a sequestered businessman, Dad would have had a hard time obtaining an exit visa. Had he been given one, unwarranted attention might have resulted if the three of us left altogether.

Dad's Swiss business contacts knew of Egypt's political turmoil. A few days following his application, Dad received residency in Lausanne, a top destination for Egyptian immigrants. Obtaining visas to travel out of Egypt took much longer. The procedure was demanding and time-consuming. Mom prepared responses to questionnaires required for her daily visits to the Mugamma, a government building on Liberation Square *(Midan el Tahrir)* in Cairo. Each time, officials promised to complete a three-month Swiss visa the next day, tomorrow *(bokra)*. Nine months later, she received a permit valid for only two weeks in Geneva.

Mom's sadness at leaving Egypt overshadowed her relief at receiving our visas. In a phone call to Loulou, her younger sister and my godmother, she said, "We got the visas."

"Great!" Loulou said.

"My heart is broken. I'm leaving my parents, you, and my brothers behind. My home… I'm leaving my home."

"You can no longer afford to live in your home. You lost everything. With the meager government assistance you receive, you can't even cover a small part of your monthly expenses."

Our close family came to say goodbye on the eve of our departure. Family jokes and laughter, mixed with hugs and tears, animated the reunion. After dinner, Mom said, "I have one request," pointing at two gold and brown leather-bound books on the upper left of the living room bookcase. "These two books are important to us—my father-in-law's dissertation on international law from Montpellier University and my brother-in-law's dissertation on philosophy from Sorbonne University in Paris." She then looked at two family members and added, "Please take these two books home until you can forward them to us."

She continued, "The furniture remaining in the apartment is yours. You decide amongst each other who takes what."

"Are you sure?" was the family's response.

"Yes," Mom said. "The secret service's surveillance recorded every move we made. We had to smuggle items out of our apartment at changing shifts or under the pretext of sending furniture for repair."

"I felt scrutinized as I was coming up. It made me feel uncomfortable," Loulou said.

Her comments resonated with other family members who had felt the same. Politics had changed. Social interactions did, too.

5

CAIRO, APRIL 1962

On Departure Day, Mom and I went to the airport accompanied by the thirty-two pieces of luggage she had packed. She didn't want to attract attention to our undeclared permanent departure, as if the number of bags was not glaring enough. The airport passport security officers questioned Mom about our trip. She said with a casual tone and stern facial expression, "My husband is there on business. A week or two..."

"A week or two with all this luggage?" the officer burst out.

Before Mom could answer, the officer said, "Have a pleasant trip" (*Te rouhou wa tergaoo bel salama*) and stamped our passports, to which Mom bashfully mumbled, "Thank you." (*Shoukran.*)

Mom and I boarded a Swissair flight to Geneva less than an hour later.

My life as I knew it ended on April 1, 1962. My way of living that I loved and already missed had been taken away. Above all, my friends were about to be scattered around the globe.

Egypt's political and economic turmoil triggered my journey as a sixteen-year-old seeking an anchor and an identity out of Cairo. A closed-eye view of my bedroom was all I had left—unaware of the lasting impact it would have on my life.

6

LAUSANNE, SWITZERLAND, APRIL 1962

Since my early childhood, my parents and I summered in Switzerland as tourists and enjoyed it. We stayed at Hotel Richmond by Geneva Lake. Its view of the lake in the foreground and the Alps in the background was magnificent. Dad and I met in the late afternoon at a particular spot in the hotel lobby he called his headquarters. He greeted me with a beaming smile and a glass of Evian on ice. "I want to tell you about life, about my experience in life," Dad often said. "Knowledge you will learn at school. I am sharing with you my experience, know-how."

Dad conducted most of his commodity deals in Geneva and Lausanne. He enjoyed telling me that he was a self-made man. He learned to plow along and keep his chin up at age twenty-four. As soon as he earned his MBA, his father, whose means allowed him to do otherwise, told him, "I bought you a car and filled its tank. Here is $250. You're on your own. Manage."

Dad did it and succeeded.

During the vacation years, I didn't grasp the essence of Dad's message, but I appreciated his sharing.

Immigrating from Egypt to Switzerland was remarkably different from vacationing there. It was a double-edged sword. The country welcomed us. We appreciated its hospitality. But Switzerland wasn't home. "Home" was a label we stuck on our resettlement "over there" while our home was foregone "back there."

Dad had lost his companies, deals, and business status when we moved to Switzerland. Then forty-seven, he found himself in an adoptive country, in the same predicament his father had put him in twenty-three years earlier. Keeping his chin up while focusing on our relocation and his commodity trading, Dad restarted his career.

Alienated from her family and roots, Mom had to recreate our home. Unlike Dad, she felt better getting thoughts and feelings off her chest. She longed for the days when life was sweet, before the upheaval (*abla el dawcha*). All too often, Mom repeated, "At home in Egypt" (*Chez nous en Egypte*). looking at me and expecting a reaction from me as if she were saying it for the first time.

For Mom, our ancestral homeland was preferable to Switzerland, whereas Dad disagreed with her. He shook his head and said, "Not anymore," and continued by saying, "Why are we whining about the loss of a birth country that stripped our belongings and pushed us to leave when we had no intention to do so beforehand?"

I consoled myself thinking that Lausanne would be an interim stop. I didn't like complaining or whining. Dad ingrained in me the "chin-up" behavior model. Anyhow, to whom would I have expressed myself? My parents were struggling with the relocation even more than I was. Close friends were no longer around at an age and a stage when social interactions revolved around them.

Whenever I met someone new, they asked about my cultural background. Feeling uncomfortable, I synthesized it until I devised a compact, user-friendly edition.

No one could pronounce my name correctly. The considerate ones said, "Please say your name for me," and stumbled across it, "Je…Dge…" I enunciated it for them. Again uncomfortable, I yelled at my mother, "With a name like this, I wasn't meant for export."

There were times when I felt at my wit's end. I would walk along the lake on a sunny day or sit at a window on the next rainy day—finally understanding people's grumbles about the unpredictable weather. No one ever wondered about the weather in Cairo. It was a daily given.

To boost myself, I closed my eyes. A vivid memory of the everlasting blue-sky view from my childhood balcony greeted me. It revitalized my mind and spirit.

While contending with our relocation, I enrolled as a non-matriculated student in the Political Sciences Department at the University of Lausanne, hoping to become a full-time student after passing a few exams in the new educational system.

Politics was a passion of mine, even though I knew I didn't have the skin of a politician. American history was also a course I took. I cheered myself, thinking I would one day live in the United States. That meant being independent, feeling free, and leaving everything behind.

I will choose a city that I can call my own. Hopefully, that city will adopt me, too, and I will feel at home again.

7

LAUSANNE, APRIL–JULY 1962

Estrangement from our homeland led me to consider the primary impact of immigration on our lives. Home had become a concept, a memory, a movable physical location—no longer a specific spot, a visceral geographical anchor where generations lived. Country became an attraction, an attachment, and a source of growing identification.

Our experience as immigrants implanted instability at the core of our beings. As our lives became unreliable, we weren't surprised when people became unreliable, too. Comforting predictability was lost. Life could change at any time. We learned to be ready for it.

Despite longing for their native country, my parents didn't return to Egypt. Their violation of the strict visa allowance put them at risk of severe repercussions. Yet, they left part of their hearts and souls there—Mom much more than Dad, who was ready to leave ten years before we did. The visual memory of the Nile remained vivid in their minds.

Being out of Egypt was a primal loss for me. Politics stripped away both my emotional and material roots. I had been transplanted. The need to adjust for survival screened the search for identity. I had to adapt to where I was and smile, whether my new habitat fit me or not.

Dad's enthusiasm for sharing his experience with "chin-ups" became clear to me. It inspired me to maintain a positive attitude toward most aspects of life, often smiling.

No one leaves their birth country without a reason. Emigration shaped who I, and many of us, evolved to be today.

8

BEIRUT, LEBANON AUGUST 1962

Two months after we immigrated to Switzerland, a classmate and close friend, Mira, invited me to her wedding in Beirut and asked me to be her maid of honor. At nineteen years old (an appropriate age for marriage in Middle Eastern cultures), she married a distant cousin of hers from a family branch based in Lebanon.

That was what I needed—a change of scenery. I ran to ask my mother about attending the wedding. She said, "Ask your father," doubting he would agree.

Dad was on a business trip. He called a few minutes later.

"Dad, my classmate is getting married and wants me to be her maid of honor."

"Good."

"Her wedding is in Beirut."

"Good."

"Can I go?"

"Yes, why not? Your maternal uncle and his wife will be there. You'll stay at the same hotel."

His answer stunned me. It was a first. Such a trip hadn't occurred before.

My mother responded using hindsight, "What got into him? I wouldn't have let you go."

I ignored her answer and called my friend. "Dad agreed. I'm attending your wedding, and yes, I'll be your maid of honor."

"That's wonderful. I can't believe it."

When I landed in Beirut two months later, Mira was hospitalized that morning. Diagnosed with mononucleosis, she was admitted to the medical center's infectious disease section, where visits were prohibited. Her parents had rescheduled the wedding.

Upon my arrival, feeling bad that she hadn't been able to forewarn me about her illness, she asked her older brother, Eddy, to take me out and make up for the lack of communication.

Eddy picked me up at my hotel the next day in a vintage silver-grey Mercedes 190 SL, his parents' college graduation gift. The car had a 45-rpm record player blasting top songs, such as The Contours' "Do You Love Me," while he made his car dance to the music—a highly seductive move for my seventeen years. The lively, quirky energy differed significantly from the grim mood I had experienced in Switzerland. It was a boost of adrenaline.

Beirut wasn't Cairo, but it was close enough. The language, food, and culture were similar. The weather was warm, and the people were welcoming, too. There, I reconnected with friends I hadn't seen in a while. I felt at home. The home I had just lost.

During the day, we drove along the Mediterranean seaside road (*corniche*). We admired the view with the sound of the waves caressing sandy shores and the dazzling sun shining on the horizon. We often had dinner in the evening at Al Ajami, the signature Lebanese cuisine restaurant. We met with mutual friends and danced the night away at Les Caves du Roi Club, the "in" dancing spot. I hadn't experienced such a busy social nightlife. Having felt estranged from my peers, I suddenly reconnected with them and had a blast.

One morning, Eddy stopped his car at a scenic spot by the corniche. We went down, took a few steps, then stopped. He looked at me, clutched my hand, and kissed me. I extended my arms behind his neck and kissed him back. As a seventeen-year-old on vacation from her gloomy new home environment that first kiss was the sunniest exchange in a long time.

My parents were strict about my outings in Cairo. They allowed me to spend time with friends they knew and whose parents they also knew. One parent drove me to and picked me up from their home. Going to a nightclub was forbidden, as was coming home past eleven, which my parents granted permission only when I turned seventeen. Without my parents' knowledge, I had gone twice with friends to a club, The Tree (*Al Shagara*, named for the tree in the middle of the partly roofless nightclub), but missed the fun time by leaving at 10 p.m. to go back to my friend's house where my ride home was waiting for me.

Dad called four days after my arrival in Beirut, saying, "I heard you're going out every night with this man five years older. Dating is not the reason I consented to your trip to Beirut."

"Dad, Mira got sick. I can't see her. Visits are not allowed. Eddy is her brother. He's just showing me around."

"You've been shown around enough. It's time you come back to Switzerland."

"But Dad…"

"No, but Dad. Tomorrow, you're on a plane back home."

I resented the command. Infatuation had started to bud between Eddy and me. Leaving too soon upset me. When I met him at seventeen, Eddy reconnected me with the energy and liveliness I left behind in my hometown. Life around him was colorful compared to my otherwise foreign, new, grey world.

I told Eddy about it. He said, "Don't worry. We'll see each other again in Lausanne, where you live, or Paris, where you often go. I enrolled in a business school outside of Paris in the fall."

"Great," I said, as my mood lit up.

Eddy emphasized, "I wanted to gain business experience before starting to work. The school's location outside of Paris will allow us to see and get to know each other."

The prospect restored a smile on my face.

The following morning, I was on the Middle East Airlines (MEA) flight back to Geneva, looking forward to seeing Eddy again and wondering what the future held for us.

A few days later, he wrote me to schedule our next reunion. We agreed he would visit me in Paris during the family trip around my October birthday.

9

PARIS, FRANCE, OCTOBER 1962

Mom, Dad, and I arrived in Paris on that drizzly day in mid-October. Dad had signed a major contract with a commodity company and decided to celebrate my eighteenth birthday at the Hotel Crillon, where we used to stay in Paris.

Eddy came to pick me up on time and handed me a gift-wrapped bottle of Nina Ricci's L'Air du Temps perfume in front of my father, who looked stern, peeked at the gift, and said, "I want you home by eleven."

We both shouted, "Yes," in unison before running out the door. We went dining and dancing at Chez Régine, a Parisian nightclub. We were expert twist dancers and leaped off our chairs upon hearing Chubby Checker's "Let's Twist Again."

Eleven turned out to be 3 a.m. I returned to our hotel suite to find my parents pacing in the living room. My mother's face was red, my father's white. Mom yelled. Dad lectured. He said, "No seventeen-year-old daughter of ours disrespects her curfew and returns at dawn. Where were you? You're not going out again with this man who's not up to his word."

Mom said, "Is this your thank you to us for bringing you to Paris for your birthday? Staying at Winston Churchill's May 8, 1945 hotel suite when Charles de Gaulle announced the end of WWII?"

What does Churchill's sleeping quarters have to do with my lateness coming home?

"It was your decision, not mine," was not well received. "I'll be eighteen years old in two days" was not well received either.

I took responsibility for the lateness. My parents were still not appeased.

Eddy asked me out again and again. Despite my parents' resistance, I begged them to change their minds and promised to respect my curfew. They agreed with daytime outings, only on weekends—business school and studying filled Eddy's weekdays.

My parents thought they had won the argument, and so did I.

October is generally a fabulous month in Paris. Eddy and I took long walks by the riverbanks in a cool fall breeze. Yellow, orange, and brown fallen leaves crackled under our footsteps on the sidewalks. New exhibits and shows made intellectual and social life exhilarating and our trip memorable.

Eddy liked to drive from Place de l'Etoile to Place de la Concorde at full speed, blasting The Platters' "Smoke Gets in Your Eyes." A couple of times, he drove too fast, and I had to ask him to slow down. Speed seemed to be his pace.

Agreeing to daytime outings did not fulfill my parents' aim. It led to flirting. We did not become intimate, but we grew to know each other. I was infatuated. He was persistent in reaching out to me. We enjoyed each other's company, and our developing relationship.

10

LAUSANNE, NOVEMBER 1962

Soon after the Paris trip, Eddy came for an overnight trip to Lausanne. He stayed at a nearby hotel as my parents would not consider having him sleep at our home. The first night we went out, he asked me to marry him.

For a fleeting moment, I thought, *This is premature, too fast*. We had met less than three months ago and seen each other only a few times, but I was recently eighteen and swept off my feet. I thought I knew it all.

"Yes!" I blurted out, paused, and continued, "You'll need to speak to my parents."

I told my parents about his visit and its purpose. Mom and Dad looked at each other. Mom sighed. Dad, for once, took his time to answer. He shook his head and said, "Marry you?"

"Yes, marry me."

My parents looked at each other again, nodded, and said in unison, "Don't you think you're too young?"

"I'm eighteen," I stated emphatically.

They sighed.

Dad said, "Your mother and I will meet with him."

Dressed in a suit and tie, Eddy was punctual for the meeting. We walked in together and sat down in the living room. Mom squeezed a tissue in her hand. Dad kept his lips tight. Eddy said, "I fell in love with your daughter and came today to ask your consent to marry her."

Silence filled the room. Mom bit her lower lip. Dad again took his time and said, "How old are you?"

"Twenty-three."

Dad nodded. "Do your parents know about the proposal?"

"Yes, I told my parents."

Dad nodded again. "And they agreed with it?"

"Yes. My parents agreed."

Dad continued nodding. He paused for a while and said, "This is what I would like you to do. Roam the world for the next twelve months, date all the women you want, and become intimate with those who agree. Should you feel the same in twelve months, I will consider your request then."

My parents looked at each other and sighed; they looked at me and sighed again. Eddy held his breath. He did not know what to say—a rare event for him. He mumbled a few words and excused himself.

The moment Eddy walked out the door, I lost it with my father for the first time. Outraged, I stomped my feet, shook my arms over my head, and screamed at him from the top of my lungs. "You told him to date other women, to have sex with other women. How could you do this to me? How could you?"

Only nodding his head, Dad took it all in calmly. When I stopped, Dad said quietly, and Mom screamed, "What is this premature marriage idea? Focus on your studies."

"I am. Both are not mutually exclusive." I pivoted on my two heels and ran out, slamming the door behind me. I rushed to my bedroom and sobbed with my head pressed on my pillow and yelled, "Leave me alone!" when I heard Mom's footsteps behind the door.

My eighteen-year-old self considered my parents' behavior to be the ultimate betrayal.

LAUSANNE, DECEMBER 1962

I had just left Egypt. Eddy represented the hyphen (*le trait d'union*) linking past to present. No one, except my peers, understood my identity, who I was. I had to introduce myself, spell my name, and explain myself at each step. All of this led me to feel deracinated, displaced, leaving my home, my social network.

Eddy reconnected me with my roots. He captured the world as I had known it. I was attracted to what he represented: my country of origin, my culture, my home, my food. I went to school in the same classroom as his sister. I knew his parents, his younger brother, his home. My story was our story, our group's story. The story of our country we had just lost.

I believed I had made a sound choice of a husband. I also thought marriage would lead me to self-determination, to break free from parental control. Marriage seemed the fastest way to get there—where I wanted to be and what I wanted to do next.

Eddy presented himself well. The prominence of his personality made up for his small stature. He matched my intellectual drive with his ambitious dreams. Likewise, I dreamed big. I wanted to complete my studies. I wanted to achieve and leave my mark behind me.

Smart and articulate, Eddy focused on himself during our conversations—not on me or us. My way to stop him from saying, "I will, or my plans are," was to kiss him. Then, I got his attention for as long as our embrace lasted. Then he resumed saying, "I have an idea."

Eddy's saving graces were his lively personality and quirky wit. Constantly swirling, he was also fun-loving and spunky like me (in close circles). His unpredictable personality seemed woven into the fabric of the politics and social context in which we met.

Eddy matched our familiar, yet unreliable, changing times.

12

LAUSANNE, 1962–1963

During the twelve-month hiatus, I reconnected with Bobby, a friend from Cairo. We met in a movie house, sitting at the two ends of our group of friends. At the intermission, he reached out and offered me a piece of chewing gum. I blushed and thought, "This guy looks cute and friendly." I asked a friend who he was, and they whispered his name. I recognized his surname as belonging to a notable Lebanese family—his parents and mine were friends.

Through them, Bobby and I saw each other again in Lausanne. I was thrilled to find someone I knew from back there. He soon became my best friend and daily companion. He visited me at home. Mom and Dad welcomed him with open arms.

Classy and elegant, Bobby looked like a movie star. He was kind and tender. Surprisingly, he was anxious and somewhat shy—though he had no apparent reason for self-doubt. Soon, my heart warmed up to Bobby. I cared the world about him and wondered, even hoped, that a commitment would pan out of our encounters. When I put my head on his shoulder, I felt secure. His eyes spoke volumes as he held my hand and listened to my woes. It was clear that he loved me but was nonverbal about his feelings. He wanted me to experience them rather than hear them. Over time, our friendship grew closer. A romantic, but not intimate, relationship developed between us. We hugged. We pecked. That was it.

Bobby was known for his strict, prim, and proper behavior. Public opinion and surrounding values guided his conduct and course of action, even if it meant going against his wishes and desires. Deep down, Bobby knew what he wanted, but his constant consideration of what he should or could do made him appear indecisive. Picking his eyebrows and looking straight toward a point on the horizon, he often stayed quiet instead of speaking up.

Despite his many remarkable qualities, I expected more from Bobby and wished he expressed his feelings verbally and explicitly. As I read nineteenth-century Russian literature, I had romance and passion in my mind. I wanted to wear my red shoes and go dancing. I wanted to spread my wings wide and fly high. Of course, I had every intention of pursuing my studies, expanding my knowledge, and obtaining an advanced degree. Yes, I was determined to do it all.

At times, I wondered if my personality was too expansive for Bobby. Was I too much to handle? Perhaps my behavior, energy made Bobby tentative. Maybe I wasn't upfront. I didn't share what I wanted, what I had in mind. It's possible that this was my perception and not his.

In any case, I made sure I stayed true to myself. Maintaining honesty in my interactions with Bobby was essential to me. Had Bobby expressed his feelings, I would have followed suit and waited until we completed our studies. But that would have been another life story, not mine.

Bobby and I were too young to make the right decisions. We were both eighteen (he is only five months older than I am). Shall I say I was young? Indeed, I was. And I indulged in my youth as much as I could.

Eddy, a colorful and outspoken business school graduate, five years older than me, offered me a definite, immediate way out of my dull adoptive environment.

I liked it. It seemed alluring.

13

LAUSANNE, EARLY AUGUST 1963

Eddy reappeared ten months after the initial proposal. We had kept in touch but didn't see each other. He asked to meet with my parents to propose again.

Eddy's assiduity paid off. It seduced me. I made a hasty choice carried by the frenzy of the moment. Eighteen-year-old infatuation and impatience misguided my judgment, costing me a critical decision.

I urged my parents to meet with him.

During his meeting with my parents, Eddy informed them that he had returned earlier than expected because he had enrolled in a prestigious MBA program near Boston, seeking to supplement the incomplete degree he had from his European experience.

My parents welcomed the information, harboring the wish I would change my mind while he was gone, a conflicting message.

As soon as we were alone, I asked Eddy with widened eyes. "How come you didn't say a word about the second business school?"

Without answering my question, he said, "It's a unique opportunity for me."

I felt left out. Eddy had not shared his decision. Perhaps he was too busy doing what he considered best for himself. My lips remained closed.

I missed my first opportunity to confront him—a mistake I lived to remember. Over time, my nonconfrontational behavior would negatively affect my marriage and life.

14

LAUSANNE, EARLY AUGUST 1963

My parents said they would speak with me and get back to Eddy. In private, they expressed their disapproval of my marriage choice in full detail. They stated their perspective, sparing no words, giving me warning signals.

I remember my father's mourning look and my mother's teary eyes telling me they objected to my marriage based on three main counts: my age (eighteen years old, not a marrying age in their recently updated European view, too young to know what I wanted and who was a good match for me); my studies (I had to complete them and follow in my family's academic footsteps); and my choice (from the few meetings my parents had with Eddy, they thought his money-oriented views came at the cost of his values). They also wondered about his choice of a teenager (five years younger) as a spouse rather than a young adult his age.

My parents reported that my cousin, Eliane, who knew Eddy socially, had met with them. Adding to their concerns, she told my parents, "I know Eddy. He's not the right man for Djenane." She then spoke with me privately, stressing he was a materialistic womanizer. "If you marry Eddy, happiness will not be in your forecast." I heard my cousin but did not heed her advice.

My parents liked Bobby a lot, perhaps too much. They considered him a gentleman, a son. His parents were close friends of theirs. They shared their conversation with Bobby's mother, emphasizing what they believed I needed to hear: "Bobby loves Djenane. He has been in love with her from the day he saw her in Lausanne."

I wish Bobby had told me this instead of his mother telling my parents.

Then they both looked at me and said, "He would be a great husband."

My parents were crystal clear about their concerns regarding Eddy. I heard them but did not listen to them. Mom talked to me. As she perceived me as unresponsive, she did not mince words or control her tone and went on a tirade, "Are you anesthetized? Can't you see what you're getting yourself into?

Eddy is going to rob your potential. Didn't you hear what your cousin said?"

Dad took me aside and explained each point he made. "You're making the wrong decision. Can't you see what a gentleman Bobby is?" Exasperated with me, he paced the living room, looked at me, and shook his head, saying, "You want to have your own experience? Go ahead. Do it! What will I do with your mother's objection to your chosen husband?"

From the tower of eighteen years of age, I stood up to my father and answered, "It's up to you."

After one more long conversation, Mom and Dad reluctantly agreed with my marital choice. Mom verbalized her fundamental disagreement, "You don't know what you're doing."

Dad repeated, "I'm letting you go through your experience."

My parents did their best, to no avail.

I was determined to follow through with my decision and stated in no uncertain terms, "I know what I'm doing. Eddy is the one."

15

BEIRUT, MID-AUGUST 1963

Eddy's parents and mine met in Beirut to formalize the proposal and seal the deal, as done in Middle Eastern families. Our parents decided on the date and location of the engagement. We felt we had accomplished our mission.

When my parents agreed, Eddy asked me out and said, "Let's elope."

"Are you serious? After all we've gone through, you want us to let my parents down and elope?"

"Why not?"

"I will not do it. We've defied my parents enough."

Eddy's suggestion was revealing. My excitement over getting married overshadowed a deeper consideration of who I was marrying.

Upon hearing about my upcoming engagement, Bobby nodded and said, "I wish you happiness."

I wished he had said more.

16

LAUSANNE, MID-AUGUST 1963

At the decisive junction, I passed up a reliable, honorable man and married an unreliable, bold man. And I stood by my choice and took responsibility for its aftermath. In the interim, I built my backbone and character and later flexed my psychological muscles.

My choice is emblematic of Robert Frost's "The Road Not Taken":

> Two roads diverged in a wood, and I—
> I took the one less traveled by,
> And that has made all the difference.

17

BEIRUT, LATE AUGUST 1963

Eddy and I were engaged in Aley, a city uphill from Beirut, at my paternal cousin Prim's home. A week later, my parents hosted a reception at Les Caves du Roy, with relatives and friends cheering us on.

Eddy started his first year of business school at the end of August. We kept in touch through letters and occasional phone calls until he finished the year in May 1964, except for a few days we saw each other over Christmas.

18

LAUSANNE, NOVEMBER 22, 1963

Claude, a friend, and I walked through the busy Place St. Francois on our way home that evening. Suddenly, the street was filled with frenzy. People accelerated their pace. Clamors were getting louder. The two of us stared at each other, confused about the upheaval in our surroundings.

"What's going on?" I asked a passerby.

"President Kennedy was shot."

"Is he still alive?"

"No."

Stunned, we started running home, feeling our world fall apart again. Uncertainty haunted us.

19

LAUSANNE, 1963–1964

While Eddy was in the US, I continued to study, see Bobby daily, and focus on the fun part of the wedding preparations. I can't remember what led me to seek counseling soon after Eddy flew to the US—not the norm at the time, neither in my country of origin nor in my place of residence. Inner doubts about my decision and my parents' influence must have triggered my need for guidance, leading my steps to counseling.

Searching for the right person, I came across Father Maurice Zundel, a Jesuit priest, theologist, and philosopher, at a crossroads between mysticism and ethics in Pierre Teilhard de Chardin's lineage. He also had the merit of knowing my Jesuit paternal uncle, a prolific linguist and writer, and the editor of the Arabic-French Dictionary, titled *Le Belot*.

Father Zundel agreed to meet with me weekly for spiritual counseling, the best I have ever had. He sharpened my sense of self and raised my attention to essential aspects of life.

Slim and somewhat hunchback, Father Zundel had been on a strict, self-imposed diet since he was eighteen years old, which only comprised tea, dairy, mashed potatoes, and beans. We met in his tiny, dim room with two-and-a-half walls filled top to bottom with theology and philosophy books.

With his faint tone of voice, he was an inspirational source of love and wisdom. I shared how I met Eddy, his eagerness to marry me, his tendency to keep things to himself, and his self-centered disposition. We had dynamic conversations covering issues I had at heart, especially education, mothering, and marriage, in essence my choice of a husband. Father Zundel listened attentively and gave me powerful insights in response to my essential questions. "Concerning your studies, you'll have to invest in your education to be independent, self-sufficient one day."

"Mothering is very clear. Let this consideration guide your behavior: 'Am I the mother my children would have chosen?'"

I also asked for his counsel regarding my marital choice. It took him a while to gather his thoughts. Leaning his head in his left hand, he gave me an insightful synthesis of Eddy's personality.

"You need to know your future husband's emotional-behavioral thermostat is dysfunctional. You must accept and live with that knowledge if you marry him."

Father Zundel had not met Eddy. His assessment, based on my sharing, was jarring to accept. While it wasn't what I wanted to hear, it didn't surprise me. Father Zundel's words carried much weight and remained etched in my mind. I heard and remembered what he told me—though I didn't listen to his third insight.

As time passed, I became acutely aware that Father Zundel had been right all along. My mind was set on a forever and ever commitment. My parents' marriage served as my role model. I chose a man who shared similarities with my father while lacking his care and commitment. In my view, at the time, Eddy was going to be my husband forever.

20

LAUSANNE, JUNE 1964

When Eddy returned to Lausanne for the summer break, he announced he had taken an academic gap year and was vague about the basis of his decision. Our marriage was the official reason, though the underlying one remained murky. In passing, he mentioned wanting to gain some applied business experience before moving on to the second year of business school.

The gap year decision slipped under our radar. The frenzy of wedding preparations monopolized everyone's attention, especially mine. I omitted—perhaps avoided—for the second time discussing Eddy's motivation to hold off business school for a year, reinforcing repression in my interaction with him.

Eddy also demanded a prenuptial agreement—at the time, a culturally atypical, if not odd, demand, which separated our pre- and post-marriage assets legally. Our conjugal expenses were his charges. Eddy had no assets or income; his father was in good health, and mine was too.

Eddy drafted the agreement. I read it but didn't make much of it. I wasn't there for present or future financial gain. Dad reviewed it, remained pensive, and made a few edits. I agreed with the change. A lawyer ratified the final document. After perusing it, Dad took me aside and said, "The prenuptial agreement may benefit you someday. Who knows?"

History proved my father right.

21

LAUSANNE, OCTOBER 1964

Eddy and I were married in Lausanne the day after I turned twenty, at the beginning of his gap year. My spiritual counselor and my paternal uncle officiated the wedding. Loulou, my maternal aunt, was my maid of honor. Bobby agreed to be my best man. Though they formed an odd couple, I had chosen the two people closest to me—one by blood, the other by heart.

We celebrated our wedding with 250 relatives and friends at the Beau-Rivage Hotel in Lausanne. Holding each other close, we danced our first dance to Edith Piaf's classic "La Vie en Rose." A French violinist, Roger Borieux, whom Dad liked, followed us on the dance floor.

What an unfit song title for the married life about to unfold!

22

BEIRUT, 1964–1965

Right after our wedding, the violin's music faded away.

We relocated to Beirut and settled in a one-bedroom flat by the seaside. Soon after, Eddy's peculiarities surfaced one by one. His behavior steadily tested the vows I made to be married forever and ever. I was shocked to find out that the man I fought my parents to marry behaved differently from the one he presented, and I expected.

In the initial months of our marriage, Eddy would whisper sweet nothings to me while I slept, which left me feeling incredibly happy when I woke up. However, when I asked him about it, he said he didn't say a word to me. Whenever I questioned him, saying, "Why would you deny expressing your feelings?" he either laughed or didn't answer, and the behavior continued for a few months. It stopped suddenly after I asked, "Are you brainwashing me?"

An odd behavior appeared next while visiting my parents for Easter. One afternoon, Mom noticed a small silver vase missing from the living room. We looked for it. After a while, Eddy said, "I took it. I gifted it to a business acquaintance."

"How come you didn't ask me? I would have bought you something," Dad said.

"You took it from the living room without asking?" I said.

"I want it back!" Mom burst out.

Eddy left the room without apologizing or showing any sign of shame or guilt. Dazed by his behavior, I rushed after him and said, "What business acquaintance? You don't know a single person in Lausanne."

He didn't answer.

"Are you nuts? How could you do such a thing?"

He opened the apartment door and left without explaining himself. Later that day, he returned the object to its assigned spot without uttering a word.

"Where was it?"

"I brought it back."

"Why did you do such a thing?"

"…"

I asked Eddy again and again about the missing piece. He continued to give me muted or unsatisfying responses. Not wanting to cause a rumble in my parents' home, I stopped arguing without getting an answer clarifying the deed.

Mom didn't get over the episode, reinforcing her initial perception of Eddy, but abstained from mentioning the subject with him or me, as she sometimes did with other topics. She said it all with her eyes and facial expressions and gave another earful to Dad, who told me, shaking his head, "I let you have your experience. Now your mother is giving me a hard time."

Eddy's behavior contrasted with the persona and assiduity he displayed when we met. I was stunned. My parents, Father Zundel, and Eliane warned me to be cautious before marrying him. I remembered their words. Were they right?

Two months later, money issues surfaced. One evening, at home, Eddy leaned forward, flaunting his right Oxford shoe on the coffee table in front of the couch where I was sitting and said without a preamble, "I won't take you with me to the US for my second business school year unless your father gives you money."

Seething, I scanned him from top to bottom, looked at his shoe, and flatly said, standing up, "I don't respond well to threats. I won't ask my father."

Eddy's offensive request contradicted the signed and sealed prenuptial agreement he had required and drafted, which stated he was responsible for our household and personal expenses. Despite the intimidation, I never asked Dad for money or shared Eddy's demand with him.

I decided that I would stay in Beirut during the first business school semester. I knew it was odd, though I wasn't unhappy about our decision and left it at that. It was time for a break, for some recovery space. We both needed to introspect and reflect.

Have I made a faulty decision? I lamented within myself. Eddy showed his character after our marriage. I considered my options. None were satisfying. It was probably the right time to call it quits.

I didn't.

I felt devastated and ashamed. After all the fuss and fighting, I couldn't bear to tell my parents they were right. I became hypervigilant and constantly on the lookout to tweak Eddy's behavior. I thought I could change him.

I had not yet turned twenty-one.

23

BEIRUT, SEPTEMBER 1965

Eddy started his second business school year without me. He told me he was coming back to Beirut for Christmas. My parents wondered why I didn't travel with Eddy. I told them I would be a distraction to his studying.

Did I miss Eddy or think much about him during that time? I'm not sure. I wanted to know if my still-young marriage would make it, despite the 8,713 kilometers between Beirut and Boston.

Bobby, also based in Beirut and starting a mutual fund, offered me a job as his assistant. This was my first paid job. I accepted. Work was rewarding. This new independence boosted my self-esteem. My mind was far from money-related contentions. For the first time, I felt autonomous. My responsibility was to myself. First and foremost, I experienced freedom. And it felt good.

Bobby and I enjoyed working together. Our relationship became even closer as time went on. Being around him made me feel secure. He resumed being my daily companion. I trusted him. His heartwarming energy comforted me. We slowly rekindled our close friendship from before I got married. I felt loved and experienced love. We became romantic again, but not intimate. It was a pleasure to put my head on his shoulder and have him be tender with me. We held hands, embraced, and kissed longer at that point but stopped the bliss there.

24

BEIRUT, DECEMBER 1965

When Eddy returned to Beirut for Christmas, he asked me to join him in the US for the second semester of his academic year. I agreed. I still wanted to save my marriage even though I wasn't sure where it was going. So far, the ride had been filled with twists and turns. My marital journey was too short for it to be over. I was committed to pursue it to the end.

Was my ego driving my behavior? Yes. I had been hasty to start my marriage and didn't want to show impatience to end it.

Bobby was the last person I wanted to implicate in my interpersonal tribulations. I wouldn't, couldn't do it to him. He was very dear to me. I didn't want to inadvertently take him on a bumpy road that wasn't part of his traditional lifestyle.

Upon learning of my travel plans, Dad gave me money to cover my trip and expenses abroad without my asking him.

Eddy's initial demand for money was put to rest.

25

CAMBRIDGE, MA, JANUARY 1966

My first days in Cambridge were exhilarating. I was married. I lived in the United States. That we drove an old, clunky Volkswagen and we lived on a shoestring budget didn't matter. The world was mine. I felt elated to discover the United States.

I planned to save the funds Dad gave me for a time of need and only withdrew twenty dollars every Friday to cover household and personal expenses combined. On the first bank withdrawal, I composed a short rhyme and recited it to Eddy who couldn't hide a smile:

> What day is today?
> Today is Friday.
> What day is Friday?
> Friday is bank day.

"You became a poet," Eddy said.

After balancing my budget for a while, I realized I could spend nineteen dollars a week and save one dollar to treat myself to a strawberry tart and endless cups of coffee at the Patisserie Française—on Friday afternoons, after the bank.

A dear friend from Lausanne, Munirah, who was in Cambridge with her husband and toddler son, joined me. We chatted to no end, savoring our delicious lunch, feeling energized by the abundant coffee we drank.

26

CAMBRIDGE, FEBRUARY 1966

A few weeks later, a neighbor informed me that a Cambridge school was looking for a French teacher to replace theirs who was about to go on maternity leave. I jumped upon hearing the information. The timing of this possibility came spot on to fuel my budget.

When I called, the school referred me to a top officer at the Cambridge Department of Education, who immediately scheduled an appointment to meet me. Dressed professionally, I walked into his office, where he asked me to introduce myself. I told him my age, student visa status, and native French proficiency.

The interview went well. The officer told me the position was temporary, teaching a twelfth-grade class for a glorious salary of $125 a week starting the following Monday. Elated, I counted my blessings for the weekly fortune I was about to earn. It was not only an earning position but a healing one as well. The frustrated student in me became a teacher.

On my first day, I arrived at school at 7:30 a.m. to meet with the school principal who would introduce me to my classroom. At 7:55 a.m., he stepped out of his office, introduced himself, and after social graces, we walked down the hallway to my classroom. He opened the door and walked in, with me following.

The students in the classroom were big. There were lots of them. Shaken, I cleared my throat and asked the principal to step out for a chat.

"I expected to see twelfth graders."

"These are twelfth graders."

"Twelfth graders are this big," gesturing with my hand below my waist. "Not in the US."

The confusion came from the disparity between the French and American education systems. In the French system, at the time, grades started from twelfth grade up to first. When the education officer told me I would teach that grade, I was pleased to be with little ones and never thought of big twelfth graders.

How am I going to handle a class of twenty-two students close to my own age?

I, a twenty-one-year-old, walked into the classroom with a pounding heart, sweaty forehead, and frozen smile. The seventeen- and eighteen-year-old students stared at me. The situation reminded me of the movie Blackboard Jungle and Bill Haley's song "Rock Around the Clock." The thought of Glenn Ford uplifted my spirits.

I took a deep breath and regained my composure.

Sitting at my desk, the teacher's desk, I introduced myself. That went well. I continued by reassuring them I would follow their teacher's curriculum. A few students mumbled. Wanting to assert my new authority, I grabbed something from the drawer and tapped on the desk without looking. It turned out to be a soundless eraser.

I blushed and walked to the back of the classroom and repeated in French, "Bonjour. Je suis votre institutrice de Francais qui remplace Mme Crystal qui est en congé maternité," asserting my authority and demonstrating my French mastery while regaining my breath and self-control.

After that, my voice tamed the classroom rumble. I began teaching. My first class worked well, as did the following ones. The students grew to appreciate a young, French-speaking teacher.

One day, I walked into the classroom and saw students throwing paper balls in the wastebasket. Rather than making a fuss, I joined the game, sealing my reputation. Students accepted me. Week by week, work and I became an excellent fit.

Six weeks later, I received my tax papers and planned on paying them. I was making a living. I felt proud. I looked at the address marked on the tax papers and rushed there to pay. A lengthy discussion ensued when the representative asked for my social security card. It started calmly but picked up in intensity when I ascertained I didn't have one. The representative then asked me to wait. She needed to make a phone call and kept me waiting until two men appeared soon after.

The two men introduced themselves as FBI agents. They led me to a private office, where they asked me to retell my story.

I did, adding, "If I had known I needed a social security number to work, I would not have taken the job and come here to pay my taxes."

Upon hearing my statement, one of the FBI agents stepped out of the office, possibly calling the person who hired me or checking with a superior. When he returned, he directed me to pay my taxes, pledge not to work again until I had a social security number and give the FBI my whereabouts for a year to ensure I was living up to my word.

That settled my first deportation threat.

Despite losing my job, my salary, and my income, the experience began soothing my wounded inner student, trusting she would thrive one day.

When Eddy heard the story, he shrugged his shoulders and said, shaking his head in disbelief, "You went running to pay your taxes?"

He had missed the healing point. The unfulfilled student had become a teacher.

27

NEW YORK AND BEIRUT, JUNE 1966

After completing his MBA in May, Eddy accepted a job offer in the investment banking division of a securities firm based on Wall Street. We returned to Beirut for the summer with the upcoming job in mind. Eddy wanted to establish contacts with potential clients and discuss his business plans with my father.

Loulou hosted a dinner at her apartment for my parents, who joined us from Switzerland, and my in-laws, who lived in Beirut. Following the initial social graces, the conversation centered on Eddy's career. He presented the investment bank to the group and outlined the contribution he thought he could make to the hiring company. Everyone nodded as they listened attentively.

Suddenly, out of nowhere, Eddy announced to his astonished audience, "I will need funds to do all this. I will need to be financially independent."

"I thought you were taking a job," Dad said.

"I am. I also need you to finance me."

"Finance you? Explain it to me."

"What are you talking about?" I said.

"I think it would be best if you let me manage your assets," Eddy said, sounding entitled.

"What?" I shouted.

"I am asking your father to run his estate."

With almost no business experience, my twenty-six-year-old husband, eager to jumpstart his career, asked my fifty-one-year-old father, an expert in commodities and finance, anxious to reboot his career, to give Eddy his assets to manage.

As soon as Eddy made his second demand for money, publicly this time, the conversation heated up.

"Are you serious? You're asking to manage my assets…" Dad said.

"I'll do an excellent job, better than anyone else," interrupted Eddy.

"What experience do you have?" Dad said.

"I just completed an MBA program. I have the knowledge and the know-how."

The more Eddy argued, the more indignant Dad became. He kept pacing the living room, raising his voice and repeating, "You want me to finance you? To give you my assets to manage?"

"Yes. I'll do it better than you," Eddy said on a high note.

That brought the discussion to a head. Beside himself, Dad drank a scotch too many.

Eddy's parents were tongue-tied as I tried to handle Eddy, my Mom, her husband, and Loulou, one person at a time.

"Enough. Let's go home," I told Eddy, who kept validating his demand.

"Your father would benefit from letting me invest his funds," Eddy claimed.

Then in front of everyone, Dad looked at Eddy straight in the eyes, stretched his arm, putting his right index over his thumb, forming a zero, and yelled, "This is what you are."

"Dad!" I screamed as I grabbed Eddy's arm to step out the door, trembling. Eddy, unflappable, disregarded my father's gesture and, to my surprise and dismay, continued arguing that he could appreciate my father's assets if he had total control.

"Why would my father give you control of his assets? Ask your Dad for his!" I shouted in the elevator.

The aftermath of that infamous evening was difficult to live. The men dug in their heels. Much effort and diplomacy on the part of my Mom and myself over time helped thaw Dad's and Eddy's frozen relationship. Mom played a crucial role in this. Maybe she sensed that I was becoming aware of Eddy's inappropriate behavior but was not yet ready to leave him.

28

NEW YORK, SEPTEMBER 1966

At the end of the summer, Eddy and I flew back to New York. He joined the investment bank right after Labor Day. He appeared eager to go to work in the morning and satisfied with his job at the end of the day. New York City's energy invigorated me. When I walked around midtown, I thought, *I love this city. I want to be here forever*. Views of the skyscrapers, the hustle and bustle of the sidewalks, and the friendly people hidden behind their rough exteriors blew me away. New York offered me job opportunities. I declined them all—even an offer at the United Nations. One experience in Cambridge was enough.

After working for a few weeks at the investment bank, Eddy told me, "I'd like to take the bank's Middle Eastern representation to Lebanon."

"Will the bank be interested?"

"I believe they will. I will provide them with new opportunities."

29

BEIRUT, FEBRUARY 1967

Less than six months later, Eddy and I were back in Lebanon. He was on a high from achieving his goal. I felt conflicted. I knew I would miss New York, but I was also happy to be closer to my family and childhood friends.

The day after we arrived in Beirut, a friend offered me a male white miniature poodle puppy from her litter. I was an ecstatic first-time dog owner. The puppy was a tiny white bundle of joy with an endearing, feisty personality. His name, *Youpi*, meaning happy excitement in French, came spontaneously. He followed me everywhere and jumped on my lap whenever possible. The bonding was heartwarming.

In contrast, the evening he met Eddy, Youpi ran to him, nipped his ankle for no reason, and wouldn't let go. "What is this dog? He's wild," Eddy said, jumping off his seat.

"He's a puppy."

"He's rough, out of control."

Youpi's behavior toward Eddy surprised me. Was he immediately jealous or disliked him?

30

BEIRUT, MARCH 1967

In October 1966, just before our move to Beirut, a prominent Lebanese financial organization faced liquidity distress and required financial assistance. It coincided with the launching of the Wall Street investment bank's representation. Eddy struck the idea of refinancing the Lebanese bank through the US bank—the deal turned out to be huge and complex.

Eddy was working tirelessly to identify potential structures for the refinancing. He was constantly on the phone, discussing plans and establishing as many contacts as possible. Eddy appeared enthusiastic and proactive in ensuring the success of the deal. He relied on Dad's expertise to finalize his contract, his first. Dad became an asset. He hoped that Eddy's success would discourage him from making empty claims about managing his estate.

Dad stayed in the background and shared his knowledge with Eddy. According to a business school professor, Dad played the role of Cyrano de Bergerac to Eddy's Christian, assisting Eddy in closing the deal.

When Eddy signed his landmark contract, he didn't acknowledge or compensate Dad for his contribution, but he no longer asked Dad to finance him or manage Dad's assets.

Eddy put his second demand for money to rest.

I brought up the issue of unpaid dues to Eddy. He shrugged it off saying, "I am young. Your father is established. It isn't a big deal."

"Nothing is a big deal for you."

When I related the exchange to Dad, he said, "Let it go. It's the cost of peace in the family."

31

BEIRUT, APRIL 1967

The deal sprung Eddy's meteoric career in the banking and refloating industries. Success propelled him into the illusion of invincibility, where the voice of reason is often inaudible or unpleasantly heard. As Eddy's success rose, my visibility increased but my voice decreased in its wake.

Eddy was fawned over by the business and social communities in Lebanon. He made it big and soon seemed to turn every deal into success. Obsequious yes-men and yes-women surrounded him, flattering him, further inflating his innately massive ego. Invitations flooded in, attention focused on him, on us. The brouhaha was intense.

I had lived the exhilarating fame of success with my parents in Egypt— the elegant parties with notable people, trendy music, sumptuous dinners, champagne popping, animated conversations with occasional chuckles. My memory is also forever imprinted by the sudden silence that followed political turmoil. The phone stopped ringing. People stopped calling.

Cynical about success as I experienced it and ambivalent about Eddy's success and some associates, pride and concern alternated in my mind. I told Eddy, "I don't trust a few people around you."

"They're fine."

"I worry things might slip."

"Everything is under control."

"Remember what happened to Dad overnight?"

"It was national politics—not the same."

"Human nature ..."

"Totally different."

Eddy's reassurances did not satisfy me. I brought up my concerns about some of Eddy's closest associates and advisors during a Sunday family lunch. Eddy's mother adored him and would not dissent with him in a social setting. Eddy's father, a dedicated family man and an extremely cautious businessman, agreed with me.

Our voices were drowned by the eager-to-please majority. We tried to raise our voices above the surrounding euphoria. Our points flew above everyone's heads. No one heard us. No amount of arguments, discussions, or loud voices could sway opinions. All we got were empty promises that all would be fine. At some point, Eddy's father looked at me, shaking his head with his eyes, saying, "No use."

Thrilled with the outcome of the conversation, Eddy kissed me in the elevator on our way home, saying, "You see, you have nothing to worry about."

"They said what they knew you wanted to hear. I said what I thought and felt, what I had to say."

32

BEIRUT, JUNE 1967

A few days after the family lunch, Eddy's mother pulled me aside and said, in a motherly tone: "Look what the CFO, Mike, a Harvard Business School graduate, is doing. He earned my son's ear and trust by flattering him for his accomplishments. Do the same. That's your security blanket. You will have your husband in the palm of your hand." (*Tu auras ton mari dans la paume de ta main*). French and Arabic expressions.

"Even if I don't believe what I'm saying?" I said.

Taken aback, she repeated, "Do what Mike does."

Flattering Eddy, boosting his ego, and bending to his wishes and whims might have been the road to marital success, but I wasn't a business associate. I was his wife. I wanted to tell him what I thought and felt. I spoke my mind out and wouldn't have behaved differently.

Eddy appreciated it as much as he wished my thoughts aligned with his. He knew I was the only one who told him things unaltered by the roaring environment. I wasn't part of the band.

BEIRUT, NOVEMBER 1967

As the months passed, I turned into a security guard watching over Eddy's entourage powerplay, anxious about what might happen. I was still not too fond of some of them, men and women alike.

Karl, Eddy's younger brother, shared my views on business players and dealings, but as the younger brother, he didn't challenge him. He kept his thoughts close to his chest.

Mike, Eddy's closest adviser, was hard to read. He was extremely smart with a sharp sense of humor. Eager to please Eddy, he tended to agree with him and provide feedback supporting Eddy's arguments. Eddy, in turn, seemed to listen to Mike, but with Eddy too it was hard to discern act from fact.

I would have preferred seeing individuals from the Lebanese business establishment around Eddy and shared it with him. He heard what I said and shifted from the reassuring tone to a more practical if not cynical one, "It's business. The others are competitors."

"Business doesn't have to be this way. I was born and bred in a business environment."

"You don't know what your father had to deal with."

"It's hard to hide when living under the same roof."

"These men know the ropes and have connections."

"Their connections must be similar to them."

"They are fine people. What's your problem?"

"I'm uneasy around them."

"Uneasiness is not a criterion."

Eddy questioned the validity of my impressions based on non-material evidence and tried to sway my perspective. I said what I thought and felt. I wanted to be true to myself. Eddy heard me without heeding what I was saying. He viewed me as his lucky charm, as Dad viewed Mom. He wanted me to stand by his side and agree, often saying, "Just be there next to me. Everything will be fine."

And business-related matters continued to be fine—while I was there.

34

BEIRUT, EARLY DECEMBER 1967

As soon as I got married, I wanted children. I wanted to create a family. Eddy was on board. I didn't take contraceptives to allow physiology to run its course. Knowing we were settling in Beirut firmed our decision.

Within that period, I experienced intense pain on my left side. Upon examination, my cousin Prim's husband Robert, my obstetrician and surgeon, recommended an emergency surgery. My left fallopian tube had to be removed due to a severe infection.

Robert attributed the infection to Eddy's extramarital sexual activities. He called him and raised his voice saying, "Stop your deceits. We need to talk. Come to my office. Now."

Eddy didn't contest accountability. He nodded without speaking.

"Respect your commitment to your wife, to your marriage."

"I am. I will."

"You owe Djenane a child."

"…"

The condition incensed me. At age twenty-three, my procreative ability had diminished by fifty percent after three years of marriage. Until that discovery, I had no idea Eddy had extramarital affairs. His behavior was questionable in many ways but did not raise suspicions in that domain. Intimacy was constant.

When I thought about who Eddy had revealed himself to be after our marriage, I saw the writing on the wall. It had sexual indiscretions written all over it. Eddy had the personality of a man leading a double life.

Infidelity, too, Eddy!

Concrete evidence and its impact on my reproductive potential were beyond my tolerance.

As soon as Eddy came home, I grabbed him by the collar and shook him, screaming, "How could you do this to me?"

To which he replied, "This is nonsense."

"You're lying, Eddy. Your constant lying is sickening. It makes it impossible for me to trust you."

"…"

I was beside myself, ready to slam the door and walk out, but held myself back.

I stayed.

My main goal was to have a child. I thought that being young and having a husband at home would increase my chances of getting pregnant, with only one fallopian tube. Instead of seeking another man and involving him in my journey, I decided to stick with the one I already had.

35

BEIRUT, MID-DECEMBER 1967

Soon after, once or twice a week, Eddy claimed, "I am going to an all-men business dinner. That's what they often do in the Middle East."

How convenient!

After one of those dinners, Eddy came back home reeking of Estée Lauder's Aliage, a fragrance that I did not wear.

"You smell like Aliage!"

"I met a business acquaintance who hugged me."

"What a hug!" I snapped.

"What was I supposed to do?"

A few days later, Eddy left under the same pretext. When he returned and was getting ready for bed, I noticed scratches on his back, running from his shoulder blades to his waist.

"You like it rough," I shouted.

"What are you talking about?"

"You have a long scratch on your back."

"I had an itch and scratched my back."

"Show me."

Despite my insistence, Eddy was unable to reach or follow the marks, which appeared to be caused by a woman's nails. The scratches reappeared a few times, each time followed by renewed arguments, before suddenly ceasing.

That night, I couldn't sleep well. My usually sound sleep was disturbed by nightmares of Eddy's infidelity. I felt even more ashamed of the mess I had gotten myself into and angry about the deception I experienced from my husband's behavior before and after our marriage.

In the weeks ahead, I searched our social circle for a woman wearing Aliage or with long nails, but none of the women we knew matched those descriptions.

Rumors circulated about Eddy's infidelity. Friends and family members claimed that they had heard or seen him being unfaithful. Most of my friends warned me to be mindful of my well-being. An acquaintance confirmed that their sister had seen Eddy with a woman who wasn't part of our circle, while another suggested I should consider hiring a private detective.

"Enough. I heard plenty. It's all rumors," I said aloud, feeling distraught while again thinking, *Is this the man I fought with my parents to marry?*

My public response was to appear incredulous and hide my feelings, keeping a straight face and frozen smile. Privately incensed, I vacillated between rushing to a secluded area and crying my heart out or confronting Eddy, who denied any wrongdoing or spun reports as he saw fit, often saying, "I won't talk about such stuff. You and I have sex all the time. Do you think I am Tarzan?"

It didn't take long for rumors to reach my parents. Outraged, Mom used her staple sentence, "I told you so. You didn't listen," to no end with me while Dad repeated, "I let you have your own experience," lifting his arms up.

36

BEIRUT, 1968

As much as I detested marital feuds, I loathed being married to a liar and cheater even more. Eddy's infidelity tainted my sexual drive. I engaged in mechanical sex and considered withholding intimacy. Abstinence would justify Eddy's sexual escapades and create a rift between us—one I was not prepared to handle just yet. Adultery on my part would sanctify Eddy's behavior—and I wouldn't drag someone into my murky conditions.

Not having identified a clear exit strategy, I felt ill-equipped to slam the door and face the world without a professional degree or a solid savings account. My funds and potential earnings were not enough to cover my living expenses. Surviving in the wild was not a viable option for me.

I didn't want to ask for alimony from my husband or financial support from my parents. Eddy would have probably tried to convince me to stay and argued that my reasons for leaving were unfounded. My parents would have welcomed me back with open hearts and arms. They would have been proud of me for making the difficult decision to leave.

My ego stopped me. Perhaps that was my biggest mistake. I did it anyway. I felt ashamed to return to my parents as a defeated woman, relying on them for support. I had fought so much to gain their approval for my marriage. And now what?

My dilemma left me feeling stuck—as if my wings had been clipped. I perceived myself through the skewed scope of Eddy's behavior. To comfort myself, I visualized asking Eddy to leave. I wanted to be ready for D-Day (Divorce Day). Farewell lines popped into my mind: We can no longer live together. We need to separate. Please leave.

Meanwhile, I withstood my impasse by being increasingly detached from Eddy, less implicated in his goings and less affected by his antics.

That's why I stayed—looking for a reliable way out while waiting patiently for the *where*, *when*, and *how* of my leaving, while standing on my two feet, still holding my head high, my chin up.

37

BEIRUT, SEPTEMBER 1968

Seeking support, I asked Father Zundel, who was leading a retreat in Beirut, to confide in him and asked Prim to join us. She and I were very close. I trusted her and confided in her that I was unhappy in my marriage.

Father Zundel and Prim listened patiently as I related what had happened since I had seen them last. In response, my spiritual advisor gently tilted his head and asked, "What do you want to accomplish in your life?"

"I want to pursue my studies."

"You can start your studies right now."

"I don't have the peace of mind I need to study."

"What else do you want to accomplish?"

"I want to have a child and get a divorce," I said.

Both stared at me in disbelief and chimed in, "How are you going to reconcile having a child and divorce?"

"I will have a child. Then I will divorce," I said.

"How about the child?"

"The child will be with me."

"Without a father?" Prim and Father Zundel said in unison.

My spiritual advisor continued, "Could your husband do or say anything to change your mind about the divorce?"

"He owes me a child. The divorce will come next."

Silence prevailed.

I had just granted my philandering husband an exemption and my marriage an unwarranted extension. While standing externally, wobbling internally, I bit my lower lip and stayed despite marital infidelity and differing values.

My youth led me to marry. My head would guide me out of marriage—at the right time and place.

38

LAUSANNE AND BEIRUT, 1972

My determination to have a child persisted. Five years of hope and hopelessness alternating every month stunted my expectations. Neither Robert's hormonal pill nor fertility treatments in France or England helped me conceive with only one tube.

After several attempts, I was finally able to schedule an appointment with a prominent obstetrician in Geneva, highly renowned for his innovative fertility procedures. At the initial June consultation, he recommended his latest experimental method.

Eddy said, "Do what you want."

Mom and Dad were hesitant about the treatment and recommendations. Mom said that she was going to pray for me to conceive. Dad nodded in agreement with her prayers.

I was gung-ho resolute to go through the procedure. No one was going to stop me. Confident about my decision, I flew back to Beirut for the summer, returning to Switzerland in September for my medical appointment.

Mom prayed to the Virgin Mary with ardent devotion and made novenas nonstop. She asked for help getting me pregnant and firmly believed her prayers would be answered.

One night at the end of August, I dreamed I was pregnant. Robert confirmed it the next day when I saw him. "You made it," he said.

"We all did, I feel it was a group effort," I said, and immediately canceled the Geneva appointment.

Mom and Dad were ecstatic when I called to share the good news. I thanked them, saying, "Your prayers are powerful. They worked."

Mom didn't seem surprised. I think she teared up as she remained silent and out of breath for a short while.

Thrilled did not fully describe the way I felt—I was ecstatic. Eddy seemed happy too. After years of hoping, persistence had finally ushered in success.

Protecting the pregnancy became my primary focus. Robert and I met regularly. The first ultrasound exam solidified reality for me when I heard the fetal heartbeats, chiming great joy.

Despite the attentive care, at about sixteen gestational weeks, I experienced mild sporadic contractions. "Don't worry," Robert said, "We will treat the tightening with ongoing hormonal therapy. You will also reduce daily activities. With this dual approach, you will be able to maintain your pregnancy to thirty-eight gestational weeks."

"I can do this."

"I will check you every other week and you'll let me know if anything comes up."

Reassured, I went home committed to follow the medical plan that seemed reasonable and comprehensive.

39

BEIRUT, APRIL 9, 1973

While my due date approached, political tensions between Israel and Lebanon increased. Israeli air forces targeted Palestinian camps located not too far from our seaside residential neighborhood on April 9, 1973. Beirut's energy remained unchanged despite the danger. Its inhabitants were used to political outbursts. Only when the air raid siren sounded did traffic significantly slow down and resume once the siren sounded again to indicate that the danger of airstrikes had passed.

A few days later, my contractions intensified. Robert said, "As you are at thirty-eight weeks of pregnancy, I will schedule an emergency Caesarean section for tomorrow morning to avoid complications, with a risk of miscarriage."

"Will the baby be OK ?"

"No worries. Everything will be fine. Why don't you come over to our place this evening. Ask Eddy to join us. I will walk you step by step through tomorrow's procedure."

"It's my decision based on your medical recommendation."

"You are both having a baby. I will call him," Robert said.

Robert and Prim did everything in their power to reassure me that the baby and I would be fine. Robert tracked Eddy down to inform him of my medical status. I was not as motivated to include him. I knew Eddy would defer the decision to me.

Indeed, Eddy said, "Let Djenane decide. Everything will be OK."

"Why don't you come over, so I can walk you through the procedure."

"It's her decision. No need for me to be included."

As he hung up the phone with Eddy, Robert was hyperventilating and mumbling four-letter words in Lebanese. "What kind of XYZ husband did you pick for yourself?"

I shrugged.

"He's totally off," Robert said, shaking his head and looking at me. "Eddy doesn't seem to get it."

"He's leaving it up to me. I'm having a Caesarean section."

Prim, who remained calm, said, "He may be having an off day."

The situation turned into a satirical comedy. I greatly appreciated Robert and Prim's support and effort reaching out to Eddy, but it was moot, given who Eddy was. That much I knew. I had learned it through experience.

I excused myself and returned home.

40

BEIRUT, APRIL 15, 1973

As I parked my car in front of the building where we lived, I bumped into Karl who was also a dear friend with an excellent sense of humor. I told him what was happening. He told me he would drive Eddy and me to the clinic first thing in the morning. I took it as an act of love. Karl was not known as an early riser.

As soon as I saw Eddy, I told him about his brother's offer. "Good! Let him take you. I'll see you later after the baby is born."

"You mean you're not coming with me? What kind of nonsense is this?"

"You know me. I don't like hospitals."

"Neither do I. It is a special, fortunate circumstance, plus it's a maternity ward, not a hospital."

Eddy was unwilling to come along, and given his behavior, I didn't want him to accompany me either. I ended the argument by saying, "I don't need you to come. I don't want you to come."

The wraparound terrace of our apartment overlooking the Mediterranean beckoned me in. I walked around it twice and lay down on a lounge chair facing the view. The sea was agitated, and so was I. Gigantic waves were slamming against small boulders at the nearby Eden Rock Bay. Each slam matched the internal tension and anger I harbored against Eddy for his lack of commitment. Dejected by Eddy's behavior, I was also frustrated with myself for expecting him to behave decently.

From the corner of an eye, I saw Youpi jumping on the lounge chair. He cuddled by my side and turned himself into a white ball of fur. Having him next to me and caressing his head calmed me down. His warmth, the softness of his coat, were soothing. I looked at him, stroked his neck, and saw him opening an endearing eye to check on me.

With focused effort, I shifted my mind to my in-utero baby and its well-being. A few minutes later, I was in a better frame of mind to call Mom, waking her up to announce the upcoming birth of her first grandchild.

Mom was ecstatic upon hearing the news. She told me that as soon as we hung up, she would eagerly contact the airline company to book the first flight to Beirut.

41

BEIRUT, APRIL 16, 1973

The night would not end. While tossing and turning in my bed, I felt frustrated with Eddy, who was fast asleep on the other side. At dawn, I got out of bed and jumped into the shower. As water was splashing over my head, I looked out the window to see a cloudless blue sky. I prayed to God for a baby girl and let my prayers soar.

Karl picked me up on time. "Is Eddy ready?"

"He's sleeping."

"Sleeping? He's not coming?"

"No."

"Are you kidding me?"

"No."

"Shall I shake him up?"

"Please don't. At this moment, I don't want him around."

Karl hugged me and continued saying, "I understand. We'll have more fun without him."

I hugged him tightly, saying "Yes!" And I meant it.

We arrived early at the clinic. The staff was bewildered to see me without Eddy and asked where he was.

Robert shouted in no uncertain terms that he would give him a piece of his mind, garnished with more Lebanese expletives, then yelled at Karl, "Where is your brother?"

"He's following us soon."

"What kind of brother do you have?"

"I stopped trying to figure that out."

The situation was turning again into a satirical comedy. I didn't want to partake in it. Karl continued by saying, "Djenane is having the baby, and my brother is having the contractions."

Everyone, including me, laughed.

Karl's humor saved face for all. I didn't participate in the interaction, wishing to distance myself from Eddy's behavior.

At that moment, my focus was on my soon-to-be-born baby.

When I woke up from anesthesia, I heard my obstetrician congratulating me saying, "You're the mother of a baby girl."

God answered my prayer.

Overjoyed, I asked to see her. The head nurse told me they were taking care of my newborn, and soon she would be ready to meet her Mom.

I couldn't wait to hold my daughter in my arms. I also couldn't wait to see my mother. She had left me a message with the nurse saying she was arriving in the mid-afternoon. We now shared an additional bond. We were both mothers of daughters.

As soon as my newborn was prepped and I could breathe easily, Prim and Robert challenged me by saying, "If you want to see your daughter, you have to get out of bed and walk to the nursery room."

"What a devious challenge," I said, "I just had surgery."

They meant what they said. Two hours after surgery, I ambled step by step to the nursery, which seemed to be across the globe from my room and stood behind the glass panel—a mother panting to meet her daughter.

I felt fatigued and out of breath. Fortunately, a clinic chair awaited me in front of the nursery. I quickly sat down, feeling relieved. It wasn't long before Robert and Prim asked me to recognize my daughter, a tricky request. I looked and looked and pointed to an infant with features like mine. A nurse lifted her and showed her to me. Tender feelings flowed toward her. Then I saw the head nurse gesturing with a worried facial expression. She stepped out of the nursery and said, "No, no, it's not your baby."

My consternation must have said it all.

The baby nurse rushed back inside and came back saying, "This is your baby!" lifting my red-haired, blue-eyed, beautiful daughter. Seeing her for the first time triggered an "Ah" of love and tenderness. When I held her in my arms, her name, Joelle, sounding like joy (joie), came to mind. That was what she was for me. The head nurse wheeled me back to my room with Joelle in my arms and joy in my heart.

When I returned to my room, Eddy and his parents were by my bedside (as is customary in Lebanon). Although I appreciated the caring attention, I felt somewhat overwhelmed by having so many people around me just a couple of hours after a Caesarean section. I shivered; my feet were frozen. I asked the nurse nearby to please get me additional covers, but Eddy had the first response. He removed his socks, put them on my feet, and seemed proud of his problem-solving efficiency.

Eddy's uncle, an affluent industrialist known for being outspoken, walked into my room a few minutes later and handed me a small package. He said, "I got you some sweets. I hope your daughter will be sweet. If it were a boy, I would have given you a more important gift, but for a girl, sweets will do."

"I'm thrilled to have a daughter," I replied, biting my lower lip realizing that his comment was in line with the region's cultural norms at the time.

Mom arrived midafternoon. The two of us were euphoric. We hugged, laughed. My daughter was as perfect in her grandmother's eyes as she was in mine. Mom had composed a song for me when I was born and sang it to Joelle the second she saw her.

When everyone left, Robert told me, "Unfortunately, you cannot breastfeed your daughter. I surgically removed a grapefruit-size fibroid from your uterus and transfused a liter of blood. The procedure requires an antibiotic regimen for two weeks."

"Is there any other way?"

"Regrettably not."

"Could we wait a few days for the antibiotics?"

"No way. You'll be at risk for a major league infection."

Disappointment poorly describes how I felt. I held onto Joelle tightly while the nurse injected me with a medication syringe to prevent milk surges.

My heart swelled with an unstoppable "Ah" when I walked home five days later. The bliss of holding Joelle in my arms superseded all else. I was a doting mother who peered at her newborn multiple times a day. When I didn't see her moving or breathing while she slept, I got anxious and dabbed a feather on her nose. Her wiggles made me breathe again. Eventually, I stopped using the feather after I became accustomed to watching Joelle sleep.

42

BEIRUT, APRIL 29, 1973

Less than two weeks post-delivery, the political situation escalated in Lebanon. Nearby artillery and deflagrations made everyday life hard to keep a newborn at home. Prim and Robert strongly recommended that Joelle and I return to their clinic, where I could wait out the political crisis. They were concerned about our safety and milk penury, challenging my ability to feed Joelle.

As soon as I accepted the recommendation, I told Eddy. He said he would stay in his office and visit us. Karl offered to drive us to the clinic. Was he filling in his brother's omissions?

On our way to the maternity ward, we avoided the sounds of military weaponry at a distance. It felt like a haven once we got there. I gave Karl a well-deserved hug.

Only Youpi posed a problem. His presence at the clinic was excluded. Prim offered to take care of him at her home.

The head nurse helped me settle Joelle down at the clinic in the room I had occupied for the delivery. The relocation and political turmoil of the last twenty-four hours got the best of me. I went to bed and fell asleep.

Half an hour later, a clinic nurse woke me up saying, "Prim called to inform me that Youpi ran away from her home when someone opened the apartment's main door."

"He must have gotten scared," I said.

"I'll call the police," the nurse said and spoke on the phone in her flawless Lebanese, "I'm reporting the loss of Youpi."

"Male or female?"

"Male."

"How old is Youpi?"

I gestured to the nurse two years.

"Two years old!" yelled the policeman.

"He ran out."

"Ran out!"

"What kind of family are you?"

"His description, please."

"White, small, furry."

"Furry!" the officer yelled over the phone. "You called about a dog while humans are dying!" he said, slamming the phone.

I swallowed my tears and held Joelle tightly before handing her back to the nurse.

The following morning Eddy's mother called, saying with a cheery voice, "I have good news for you. Youpi is safe. He is going to be returned to Prim."

"Wonderful!" I cheered back.

She continued to give me the step-by-step of Youpi's recovery journey. "He's such a smart dog. After he ran out from Prim's home, Youpi found his way to the lobby of a nearby hotel. He sat next to a lady, trying to get her attention by bumping his muzzle against her leg. She was astonished to see a well-kept small white poodle with no owner around. She found his identification and contact information in the collar around his neck and called you. When she was unable to reach you, she found my number."

43

BEIRUT, MAY 1973

Ten days later, ceasefires followed the violent eruptions. The political situation settled down, which is often the case in that part of the world. My infant daughter and I went back home with a three-month stock of baby formula.

Political events soon challenged our decision. The Israeli artillery, known for its precision bombing, again targeted the Palestinian camps, a few miles away from where we lived. Despite the Israeli shooting acumen, camps were close enough to raise concerns about marginal errors.

Much anxiety floated in the building and among our neighbors. I focused on Joelle. She was my number one concern. We stayed at home but sought refuge in the basement. The penthouse of a four-story family building was deemed unsafe for a less than five-week-old. Although the basement was spacious and clean, its living conditions were precarious. The architect hadn't pre-planned for seven families to cohabit there for a few hours, let alone a few days—though our first-floor neighbors kindly offered to let us use their restrooms and kitchens.

One daybreak, things seemed quieter. I left Joelle with Eddy and hurried upstairs to shower and bring along some necessities. Standing in my daughter's bedroom picking up a few diapers, ready to go back to the basement, I heard an airplane engine. I looked in front of me and saw a small Israeli fighter plane flying extremely low in the empty field at the back of the building.

The Israeli pilot's face struck me. His expression stood out. I gasped silently—my mouth wide open.

I ran down the staircase, rushing to the basement. Out of breath, it took me a couple of minutes to say, "I saw… an Israeli plane and pilot …" and then explain what I had just experienced to my disbelieving family members.

We remained sheltered in the basement for a few more days, spending fewer hours every day. After weighing war risks against the everyday challenges of living underground with a newborn, Eddy and I returned to our apartment. The windowless hallway in the middle of the apartment became our refuge. The minute I heard bombing or shooting, I would grab my daughter and hide there. Survival consisted of a pre-packed bag with my daughter's essentials, along with bottles of water, comforters, and pillows, kept in the hallway, refreshed and restocked daily. Knowing how frail life could be and how difficult and complex it was to establish a viable ceasefire, we learned to shelter when necessary and to enjoy every moment of the truce.

Before long, life in Beirut resumed its peaceful pace. People congregated and made light of the latest political happenings while preparing for the next ones. The weather, usually magnificent in May, helped. Some people ventured to the beach, dipping their frustration into the Mediterranean's still cool water.

44

BEIRUT, JUNE 1973

When quasi-normal life resumed, I checked American University of Beirut programs for possible enrollment. Academic reinstatement did not seem feasible. Luckily, Joelle grabbed my attention. I doted over her. I also learned how to play bridge and participated in local tournaments. My performance led me to become a sought-after partner and develop a solid group of friends.

Munirah, a longtime friend from Lausanne and Cambridge, now living in Beirut with her husband and two children, joined me on the terrace one late afternoon. Three-month-old Joelle was in my arms when Youpi jumped on her and slightly bit her wrist. Stunned, I thought he was jealous, acting the same way he did when he first saw Eddy.

From that day on, Youpi growled every time I carried Joelle. Weary, I took him to his veterinarian who confirmed Youpi saw my baby daughter as a rival he must defeat. Understandable, but not livable. Youpi was also angry with me. He showed it by peeing and soiling my bedside every day, sometimes multiple times. He proceeded to do the same everywhere in the apartment, including on our most precious carpet. The smell was horrific. Stunned and distraught, my tolerance reached its limit.

The veterinarian strongly recommended that I place Youpi for adoption. He knew an ideal home for him. When I hung up the phone, I felt saddened and guilty at the thought, but I was also overwhelmed by Youpi's behavior. I loved my daughter and wanted to protect her. I also loved my dog. He had been part of my life for close to six years. A dilemma between my daughter and my dog was the last thing I expected or wanted.

The following day I called the veterinarian and asked him again for a solution to my quandary. "Adoption is the best solution; otherwise, you and Youpi are going to live miserable lives."

I mulled over the hard decision. As I didn't come up with a better option, I gave the veterinarian consent to contact the adoptive lady and initiate the procedure. Crestfallen, I hugged Youpi tightly, apologized to him, and dropped him off with a basket of goodies at the veterinary clinic.

Anxious about Youpi's well-being, I called the veterinarian the next day and every day for a week until he politely asked me to stop querying. "Youpi is happy with his new owner, and the lady is delighted," the veterinarian said.

"Are you sure?"

"I am very sure."

Not having Youpi around was a heart-wrenching loss. Guilt followed me for a long time—even though I knew life would have been unbearable for Youpi and me. His memory shadowed me. I am forever grateful for his love and care, especially the night before delivery when he watched over me. Every time I think about it, I have a twist in my heart.

My growing daughter needed my attention. With an "Ah" chiming in my heart, I cherished each moment I held her. That profound joy intensified my desire for another child. As an only child, it became a deep desire of mine. I would try to have another child.

Was it fair to want a child knowing I wanted to divorce?

45

BEIRUT AND LAUSANNE, FEBRUARY 1975

"*Maman*," Dad said over the phone.

"Mom, what's the matter?" (*Maman, qu'est ce qu'elle a?*)

"Mom, cancer," he mumbled.

"No. Not Mom!" I screamed.

Mom, healthy up to age fifty-seven, had been diagnosed with lung cancer. As soon as I hung up the phone, I entrusted Joelle to my sister-in-law, booked the first flight from Beirut to Geneva, and drove from the airport to see Mom in Lausanne.

Life as I knew it, once again, had been disrupted.

The day after I arrived, Dad and I hugged Mom tightly before accompanying her to the first appointment with a highly recommended oncologist to discuss her upcoming treatment. We met him at his ebony-painted and carpeted office. Ivory accents throughout the room did not uplift our visit's gloomy mood and purpose.

The oncologist, a tall skinny man with a receding hairline, greeted us at a distance and motioned for us to sit down. He gestured for Mom to take the preferential seat closest to his desk—the one nobody wants.

He then looked at Mom and spoke in a monotone voice with a distinct German accent. "After reviewing your medical records, I recommend surgery as soon as possible, followed by radiation. Based on the treatment results, I may increase the radiation and add chemotherapy as needed."

Silence settled in.

Treatment decisions were up to Mom. Dad stared at me, frowning. I stared back. I knew he wanted to speak, but Mom had asked him to leave it up to her. He looked pale, rolling a tiny piece of paper between his thumb and index finger. I didn't know what to do with myself, clasping and unclasping my hands on my lap and crossing and uncrossing my legs too often, almost losing my high heels when Mom's stern stare caught my attention.

The oncologist can't be talking about Mom. Mom had been a devout

Catholic who dedicated her life to Dad and me and prayed for both of us. She was also an ascetic who didn't smoke or drink.

Mom seemed to have expected what she heard. She broke the silence by asking, "When can you schedule the surgery?"

The oncologist picked up his phone, checked with his assistant, and came up with a date. Remaining calm, Mom immediately queried about pre-op preparation, surgery, and chemotherapy side effects.

Silence prevailed one more time.

The oncologist interrupted it by saying, "I will see you the morning of the surgery." He stood up, indicating our time was up, and bowed down.

We left the oncologist's office without words.

46

BEIRUT, FEBRUARY 10, 1975

Upon receiving the prognosis, I immediately flew back to Beirut. My plan was to return to Lausanne with Joelle, now a two-year-old, as soon as possible and invite Loulou to join us. Having Joelle with me gave me the flexibility to stay longer if needed and the ability to boost my parents' spirits and energy levels.

Once in Beirut, I told Eddy, "I must fly back to Lausanne. Mom has cancer."

"Do what you have to do."

"I want to take Joelle with me and invite my aunt."

"Fine."

"We're leaving as soon as possible."

"Fine."

"It's going to be a tough time. I need your support."

"You have it. I have a meeting. Must run," Eddy said. And he was gone.

Eddy didn't give me the opportunity to say we would be intermittently apart for quite some time. It wasn't what marriage was supposed to be. I was worried that the distance would make our already unstable relationship worse. My mother's health was in danger, and given the situation and our respective roles, there wasn't much else we could do or say.

47

LAUSANNE, FEBRUARY 13, 1975

Less than forty-eight hours later, Loulou, Joelle, and I were ready to catch our flight to Geneva. As the car arrived to take us to the airport, Mom called me, saying, "Go to the bank. Withdraw everything you have there and bring it with you."

"Another time, Mom, the car is downstairs."

"Do as I say. I have a bad feeling about the political situation in Beirut," she said.

I acquiesced.

Mom's cancer had coincided with an escalation of the Lebanese civil war. Everyday life was unpredictable and unsafe. Ethnic factions subsidized by national, regional, and international militias were fighting each other, exacerbating sectarian divides. I pressed my foot on the gas on my way to the White Sands (*Ramlet el Baida*) neighborhood branch. I withdrew my meager funds, emptied the safe, and drove home at full speed, where a car was waiting to take us to the airport.

My heart was heavy once again as I boarded another plane to Geneva. Based on necessity and urgency, our departure mirrored our flight from Egypt. Exceptional circumstances prevailed. The political situation was unpredictable.

During the flight, I showed Loulou what I had in my bag. "What's all this?" she said.

"Everything I own."

"Are you nuts? What if someone steals your bag?"

"Mom had a hunch."

"She's not well. That's why," she said, exasperated, turning her head toward the porthole.

I shook my head, hugged my daughter, and kissed her forehead. With her big cerulean eyes and curly ginger hair, Joelle looked like a Renoir painting. I felt blessed to have her with me and held her even tighter as she curled in my arms.

When we arrived in Lausanne, Joelle rushed to her grandparents' front door and rang the doorbell. Dad opened, bending his head and torso, asking her, "Who's there?" Joelle answered, "Pupuce," the nickname he had given her. He opened the door with a big smile, and she jumped up and wrapped her arms around his neck, saying "Gedo!" the name she had for him.

Joelle ran into the apartment, hopped onto Mom's lap, saying, "Nona," and embraced her. Loulou and I followed her into the living room. Mom was sitting in the green armchair behind her desk. She looked pale and vulnerable in her off-white silk shirt, woolen skirt, and beige Hermes silk scarf. Her freshly styled hair and lightly applied makeup showed she had groomed herself to welcome us.

Mom smiled when she saw us. Her hazel eyes shone. She looked at me with the love I needed right then and there. I hugged her and got a whiff of Diorissimo, her favorite perfume, with its lily of the valley fragrance.

Mom excelled at controlling her verbal but not her facial expressions. I gazed at her, hoping to sense her mood. Dad stood behind me, holding the back of my chair. He was restless. Any reason he had for pacing in the living room or elsewhere in the apartment served as tension release. Loulou held my Mom's right hand while her eyes watered. Nine years younger than Mom, she took on the protective role that day. At a loss for words, my aunt kept repeating, "I'm glad to see you, glad to be with you."

Mom began singing the nursery song she had composed when I was born and reworded when I had Joelle. A spate of cough interrupted her tune. Dad immediately engaged Joelle in conversation while Mom drank some water and took a deep breath to regain her composure.

48

LAUSANNE, FEBRUARY 15, 1975

Loulou and I tried to create a soothing atmosphere at home for the next two days. Joelle's presence uplifted my parents' spirits. Dad boosted Mom's resilience in every way possible, often shouting *Wesh el Saad*, the nickname he gave her (meaning the face of happiness and prosperity, in Arabic). Hearing himself being optimistic about her procedure also comforted him—but not enough. I occasionally saw him heading to the den, and I could hear the bar door opening as he poured himself a drink. He came back holding his usual tumbler filled to the brim with scotch.

I called Eddy in the evening, seeking support during these dire circumstances. He failed to answer my call and only returned it the following day. His delayed response made me concerned and frustrated, as I still expected more from him.

49

LAUSANNE, FEBRUARY 20, 1975

Dad and I felt relieved when Mom returned home a few days after her successful surgery. Our initial feelings matched our unspoken concerns about what awaited us ahead.

Dad continued to visit the home bar, where he indulged in scotch. Mom was aware of his self-medicating behavior and confronted him about it, stating her thoughts in no uncertain terms. With each passing day, she grew more resolute in her arguments. "I have observed you going back and forth to the den, pouring yourself a drink. That's enough!" she exclaimed.

Dad remained silent.

I voiced my concerns privately as well. "Dad, you seem to visit the home bar more often than before."

"I worry about your mother. Both of you are the center of my universe."

"I too am worried about her, but I don't want to also worry about you."

"Don't."

"It's a slippery slope."

"I'm worried about your Mom for good reasons…"

We left it at that. I had Mom, my daughter, and my distant husband in mind.

As Mom was recovering from surgery, Loulou flew back to Beirut. Two days later, she called us. "Guess what?"

"What?" I asked.

"The bank where you had your funds and safe was bombed yesterday."

"Are you serious?"

"Very serious. It's a pile of rubble."

I ran to share the scoop with Mom, and tell her, "Thank you."

Mom shook her head but avoided saying her staple "I told you so," and did not bring up the subject again.

50

LAUSANNE, MARCH 1975

Six weeks after her surgery, Mom underwent radiation every other week. She endured her treatments without complaining and felt grateful when she experienced fewer side effects. Her disposition inspired Dad and me. We admired her resolve.

I sat beside Mom and held her hand, saying, "I love you. I'm proud of you."

"I love you too," she answered.

After three weeks of radiation, Mom's oncologist called to tell her the results were promising. Mom felt encouraged. Dad and I were holding our breath. We hoped and prayed Mom would recover.

Dad continued pacing the living room. A loud "Thank you, God," preceded "Wesh el Saad" as he stroked Mom's hair before visiting the bar, oblivious to her disapproving glance.

51

BEIRUT, APRIL 1975

Reassured by the positive medical outcome, I flew back to Beirut to speak with Eddy. Long-distance communication wasn't smooth between us.

"At the very least, I hoped you would support me verbally," I said.

"I am," Eddy said, and segued to his current deals.

"I have to balance my time between my family and my parents."

"Do what you have to do."

"I wish you would tell me more about how you feel about our circumstances."

"Fine. Hmm… I think I will pursue my deal with…" was one of Eddy's responses.

"I meant about our separation."

"It's fine. The separation won't make a difference between us."

And here too … we left it at that.

When I heard him make such statements over the phone, I felt like hanging up and instead said, "Mom is calling me." I had learned from experience that I wouldn't get more from him. Empathy was beyond him.

Eddy was in his world, unreachable, busy working on his deals and discussing them. My goals were to comfort Mom, ease Dad's sadness, and take care of Joelle while going through an emotional juggling act and wondering about my marriage, my future.

Eddy and I were speaking without connecting but also without colliding. We couldn't afford collision—Eddy for work disruption and me for dedication to my mother and daughter. He and I were two worlds, each revolving in its respective systems. We were also two Venn diagrams intersecting about our daughter, whether Joelle was with me (most of the time) or with him, along with Mazelle, as the nanny I had hired liked to be called.

52

LAUSANNE, EARLY MAY 1975

With the addition of chemotherapy, over time, Mom struggled with multiple complications and debilitating fatigue. Dad and I were terrified to see Mom in such pain.

"What else can we do?" Dad wondered.

"Continue to present her with a positive attitude."

"Yes, for sure."

God, please help Mom. She lives by your rules.

Mom called me one day to tell me her thick brown hair, which she maintained mid-length with attentive care, was falling out. I returned to Lausanne as soon as possible. When I saw Mom bald, I thought I would capsize. She looked devastated after removing her wig. Rather than cry, I hugged her, burying my head in her shoulder.

Mom grabbed her wig nearby and quickly put it on.

Several times at night, I tiptoed barefoot into Mom's room. Often awake, she tried to lift her head and with a raspy voice whispered, "I love you" between two coughing spams. If she was asleep, I watched her, feeling relieved that she had a brief respite from coughing.

Back in bed, I found it hard to fall asleep. Heartwarming memories of my parents' life on our terrace in Cairo came to mind, and it was strange to compare them to our current unsettling situation. In those memories, Mom was elegant, laughing, hosting guests, while Dad was at the center of conversations, loud and opinionated.

53

LAUSANNE, MID-MAY 1975

In moments of sadness and solitude, I wondered again, *Where is Eddy?* and called him. "What's going on?" he often started.

"We're trying to cope."

"I'm on this deal. I'm flying to London tomorrow, probably to New York next week. I have another call. I'll call you back."

Did he call me back? I don't remember. If he did, the exchange must have been the same. I felt he was letting everyone down, including myself, and shared my feelings with him.

"What do you want me to say?" he asked.

"How about 'I care'? Or 'I'm thinking of you.'" I said.

"You know that."

"It's not enough. I need to hear you say it."

"I'm working."

"That's no excuse. Express your feelings."

"I love you."

"You say it because I asked you," I said with tears welling in my eyes and feelings of doom in my heart, as Eddy seemed unaffected by our separation and unaware of my plight. His estrangement from my situation struck me as indifference. It was not the relationship I wanted for myself. His behavior made me feel deserted, and I resented it, and him.

Eddy didn't change. My feelings for him did.

LAUSANNE, EARLY JULY 1975

After five months of treatment, medical examinations and tests showed Mom's cancer was in remission. Her oncologist discontinued chemotherapy and monitored her medical status every month.

Mom was gleeful. She regained her pre-cancer self in spirit. Her contagious laughter made our day. Dad exuded joy. When he thought he was alone in the living room, he wiped his eyes and said loudly, "Thank you, God." I lit candles at church.

God, is Mom being rewarded for her righteous behavior?

Based on the encouraging medical results, I felt comfortable going to Paris with Joelle. Eddy was meeting us there. Upon leaving, Mom hugged me, held my hand, and said, "You have been so loving, Djenane. Have I expressed my gratitude enough?"

55

PARIS, MID-JULY 1975

Political volatility in Lebanon increased. Lives were at risk. The kidnapping of notables and assassinations of politicians in broad daylight occurred to public outrage but to no avail.

Eddy and I decided to stay in Paris, a city we both knew well. I had visited it frequently with my parents and later with Eddy, and he had been there for his studies and business meetings. We rented a furnished apartment near the lively neighborhood of Avenue George V, which is also close to the Champs Elysees. We enrolled Joelle in an excellent school where Bobby's daughter also studied.

Living in Paris would have been a pleasant experience if it hadn't been for our forced move due to political instability in Lebanon, which reminded us of our departure from Egypt. It was my seventh move across four continents after Mom and I left Cairo. The significant difference with this move was that it was initially supposed to be temporary, but it became permanent. Although I traveled back to Beirut, I never lived there again due to the highly insecure and often life-threatening political situation in the region.

Soon after we implemented our relocation our parallel lives resumed. Eddy flew to somewhere. The next day, Joelle and I were on a train heading back to Lausanne. I was eager to make sure Mom was doing well and Dad was keeping his distance from the home bar.

56

LAUSANNE, AUGUST 1975

om and Dad welcomed us in the bay-windowed den. Joelle pulled a doll from the nearby toybox. I sat on the floor next to her and engaged in her play. Dad read a financial publication. Mom reminisced about life in Cairo—the sunny days, the clear blue sky, and the glorious sunsets, saying, "Do you remember the view we had from our home?"

"I will never forget it."

"Me neither. It was so pretty."

"Our view of the Alps and Lake Geneva is pretty awesome," I said, not wanting to trigger a sensitive storyline.

"Had Nasser not taken power, we would still be home," she said, and continued, "I miss my parents and siblings," sharing anecdotes of life as days passed used to be (*ayam zaman*.)

"Yes, but you received outstanding medical treatment in Lausanne."

"I would have gotten a good one in Cairo, too," she said, nodding.

Dad shook his head, frowning, "Why are we still lamenting about a country that dispossessed us, that took everything I worked hard to earn? Dad also worked hard for what he bequeathed to Djenane. We need to be thankful to Switzerland for welcoming us."

I nodded my head with empathy—deep inside grateful that Mom was well enough to carry on and that Dad was patient enough to listen without saying a word.

Dad and I felt relieved.

Life seemed to settle into our new normal.

LAUSANNE, DECEMBER 24, 1976

ancer remission was short-lived.

In the fall of 1976, Mom resumed coughing and had difficulty breathing. A massive dosage of chemotherapy yielded no medical improvement—only acute side effects.

I hurried back to Lausanne from Paris.

Mom looked exhausted. In the morning, I suggested we sit in the den and helped her walk there from her bedroom. The stroll provided her with a change of scenery that she needed. Those ten steps took her ten minutes of strenuous physical labor, defying her breathing limitations. Her accomplishment made her smile as she sat down on the blue couch, panting.

Mom's cancer took a steep downturn in mid-December 1976. Mom became weaker by the day. Dad and I worked hard at maintaining a positive demeanor. Alarmed by the circumstances, I took three-year-old Joelle to celebrate Christmas Eve with my parents. Eddy was traveling somewhere and meeting us on December 25 in Gstaad, a nearby mountain resort.

Dad and I bought a Christmas tree together. While I decorated it, with Joelle assigned to the lower branches, we invited Mom to join us and participate in the ornamentation as she always had. The heirloom trimmings and twinkling white lights illuminating the tree infused light into the living room and made Joelle's eyes sparkle. The four of us gazed at each other, delighted and smiling when we finished the tree decoration.

Joelle was all over Mom at the Christmas Eve celebration. I tried to be my cheerful self. Dad had invited their best friends, two couples, for drinks and snacks. Santa Claus brought merriment to all, especially to my daughter.

Mom seemed to enjoy the evening, basking in Christmas Eve's loving and soothing effects, especially Joelle's presence. She rarely coughed. Seeing Mom having a "decent" evening comforted Dad—though he slumped his shoulders a few times with a sad look. So did their friends.

It was almost Christmas Eve, and I had no clue where Eddy was. At that moment, I lacked the motivation and mental strength to pursue him.

58

GSTAAD, SWITZERLAND, DECEMBER 25, 1976

Joelle and I drove up snowy mountain roads to Gstaad the following day. The view along the drive was spectacular. It coated some of my pain. I kept telling my daughter to fill her eyes with the beauty surrounding us. I needed to breathe. Midway, I stopped the car and opened the window. I bent my head backward and took deep breaths of mountain air, some for me, most for Mom. And we made it to Gstaad by midday on Christmas Day.

Eddy was already there.

Joelle celebrated Christmas again and saw Santa Claus once again. We took her out for an early dinner on Christmas night. To our amazement, Elizabeth Taylor was sitting at the table beside us with her husband and younger daughter. Soon after, she stood up and took the youngsters at her table to dance with her in a circle. During the dance, Elizabeth Taylor looked at Joelle with engaging eyes and extended an inviting arm toward her.

"Go ahead, sweetie," I said, encouraging Joelle to accept the invitation.

After a brief hesitation, Joelle took Elizabeth Taylor's hand and rounded with her on the dance floor. Although Joelle was too young to know the star's fame, she had a memorable experience. When the music stopped, she whispered, "That was fun."

I smiled at the star and embraced Joelle tightly, saying, "I'm so glad for you."

Joelle's experience that evening was significantly different from my family's, leading me to reflect on the diverse perspectives of life.

Eddy and I resumed our relationship without any mention on his part of what I was going through until I said, "Aren't you going to ask me how things are?"

"I know how they are—not great."

We both left it at that.

59

LAUSANNE, EARLY JANUARY 1977

Mom's cancer metastasized in early January 1977. Her pain was constant. Her breathing became labored, her cough excruciating. The oncologist raised the prospect of her imminent death. Denial overtook me. *There's no way he's talking about Mom.*

God, why is Mom suffering so much? Why?

In the evening, the thought sank deeper. I shivered under my covers, curled in a fetal position with my head buried in my pillow. Was there anyone I could turn to? Eddy? I wasn't interested in hearing his one-word opening line, followed by a list of his trips and deals. Dad was just as distraught as I was. His entire world revolved around Mom and me.

As I struggled with overwhelming feelings, paradoxically, I sought solace and succor from my mother. She was the one I turned to for support. I slipped into her room. She wasn't sleeping either. The moment she saw me, she knew something wasn't right. I knelt by her bedside, leaned my head on her right side, and wept silently while she stroked my hair, saying in a faint murmur, "Djenane…," attempting to soothe my fear of seeing her go.

Mom did so much more that night. As she was losing her life, I gained insight and awareness about how to regain mine. I had to restructure my life. Time was ticking. If this was the end, I couldn't continue on the same path. I didn't know *when, where,* or *how,* but I knew divorce would happen. I would make it happen. I wanted to end my marriage. I *had* to end it. That night, at that moment, I promised myself to leave my marriage and live by my own rules.

And I felt Mom heard and understood my experience beyond words.

Given the grim prognosis, I needed to be near Mom and have Joelle with me. Lausanne had to become my temporary relocation.

My parents' apartment was a spacious duplex with three bedrooms, each now occupied. Dad couldn't stand seeing his wife suffering. To recharge his batteries, he moved to the guest room downstairs. It became his cave. I no longer could share my room with my daughter. As Mom's health deteriorated, she coughed endlessly. I checked on her several times a night, gave her water, or propped her up. I was also concerned about Joelle should the worst happen. She was very attached to Mom. A thoughtful and sensitive toddler, she might become anxious and make undue mental associations with my demise.

I booked a room in a family hotel across the street for Joelle and her nanny, Mazelle. Joelle and I spent the mornings together at a close-by playground, and in the early afternoon, she came to the apartment if Mom was not in severe pain. I would take her to the hotel in the evening to put her to bed as often as I could.

Mom and Joelle were my primary concerns. Dad came next. I relegated Eddy, the absentee partner, silent responder, to the background. Had he made himself available, had he come to visit, had he called me regularly, he would have been with me at the forefront, but he didn't, and I didn't pursue him. Our exchanges were functional and less frequent.

I called him to share what I had organized for Joelle.

"Good idea. I don't think I'll make it to Paris this week or next."

"Mom is not well. I wouldn't have been able to leave Lausanne either."

Dad no longer had the emotional resilience to encourage Mom. Perhaps he felt it would be disingenuous on his part. Dad, a 5'10" stout eloquent man with an oversized personality, commanding voice, and loud laughter, couldn't bear to know Mom was terminally ill, hear her constant cough, and be unable to ease her pain. He avoided daily vital medical issues as much as he could and entrusted me with the caretaking decisions.

Dad's posture became more hunched over and his head tilted forward. Several times a day, he would walk up the stairs to Mom's bedroom door and ask, "Feeling, OK? Yes?" Or ask me, "How is she?" Then he would cross his arms on the staircase ramp, bury his head in his left arm, and sigh. Fearing Mom heard him, he would glance at me, turn his head without waiting for an answer, which usually consisted of a nod, and go downstairs to hide in his room under the pretext of skimming through his files.

When her cough allowed, Mom dozed in the afternoon. I took Joelle to the playground or sat in the living room downstairs, reflecting on the day. Soothing memories from the past overlapped with my apprehension about the immediate future.

Mom's cancer consumed my emotional tank. I was at a loss trying to identify means to ease her pain, to soothe her. I lay in bed night after night tossing and turning until dawn, terrified that Mom would die while I was alone with her, not knowing how to help her.

Mom wouldn't do such a thing to me, but who knows? It might be beyond her control. Dad would be an added concern—not help— in the impending final scenario.

To prevent my falling apart, toward the end of January, I hired a night nurse to stay with me next to Mom. Psychological energy is finite. I did what was the right thing to do, the best I could do, given the gloomy circumstances.

60

LAUSANNE, MID-JANUARY 1977

To clear my mind one afternoon, I opened a window door and stepped onto the balcony. I was suffocating emotionally and needed brightness to lighten up the dismal circumstances. As I gazed upon the stunning view of the Alps in the background, with Lake Geneva stretching out before me and Swiss cities, such as Nyon, visible on one side and French towns, such as Evian, on the other, I was left breathless. It reminded me of my Cairo bedroom view with a Swiss twist.

The Bise (a cold, dry wind) belied the radiant sun in Switzerland. Shivering, I walked into the living room and sat on the couch facing the bookcase. My parents' shelves were stacked with bound literature and history books. The sight reminded me of the dissertations of my grandfather and uncle. I wondered what had happened to them. I also wondered how I would resume my studies under the current circumstances.

Immersed in my thoughts, I hardly heard the doorbell ringing. I stretched my head to see who visited us on that chilly afternoon. Prim was at the door, surprising me with her visit.

"I'm so happy to see you. You came from Paris?" I said, jumping off the couch to hug her.

"Yes, I took the TGV (train). I understood things were tough as I haven't heard from you in a few days."

Prim knew about Mom's illness and Eddy's sexual escapades. She was the first and only one in whom I confided about both conditions. I also shared with her my attempts at having Eddy change his behavior. We brainstormed ways to address it. She had confronted me about my marital plans when I was still unwilling and unable to hear her.

"How are you managing?" Prim asked.

I lifted my arms and said, "One day at a time?"

Prim inquired further, "What about your studies?"

"I researched ways to resume studying. Life took over. I will do it. I owe it to myself."

"That's right. You owe it to yourself."

Prim and I chatted until dawn. I updated her on the latest household developments. It was an emotional exhale. We understood and empathized with each other.

61

LAUSANNE, MID-JANUARY 1977

The next day, before catching her train back to Paris, Prim looked at me and said, "Emotional pain elicits reflection and introspection. Whatever you want to do, take your time to do it right. No rush. One day you'll look back. You must feel comfortable with your decisions and actions, live with them, and face Joelle."

After Prim left, I pondered over what she had told me. I needed to focus on Mom and Joelle, and worried that tackling more would cause me to collapse.

Mom's shrilling cough pulled me out of my thoughts. I rushed upstairs. I could hardly see her as she blended with the beige headboard and bed cover, which once lightened up her space. Her energy matched the fading light of dusk. I rearranged her bed position and propped her up with pillows.

Mom looked frail. She had lost substantial weight. Deep lines on her forehead and around her mouth marked her emaciated oval face with black circles under her once sparkling hazel eyes. Her now short grayish hair fused with her ash complexion. She let out a grunt of pain. I gave her a glass of water to soothe her throat. She gazed down at my hand and up at my face. I saw love in her eyes when she said, "Thank you."

I pulled a chair nearby, sat close to Mom, and held her right hand. Hearing her rasping breath, I saw the end—the end of her life. If this was the end of a decent woman, I would not waste my life on an unworthy man.

Mom lifted her head up and said in a rough voice, "You will not be alone after I die. You have Joelle."

I wasn't surprised that she didn't name Eddy.

"I want to have you around, too," I said in a strangled voice, clenching my left fist and staring at the beige carpet.

She took a short breath and said, staring at me, "I want to die at home. Please don't let them take me to the hospital."

"Mom, what are you talking about?"

"You know what I'm talking about," she said in a low voice, looking at me.

"I will speak with your doctor."

I stepped out of Mom's room and bumped into her general practitioner down the stairs. Having become a family friend, he visited Mom every day at home.

"Mom asked me not to send her to the hospital. Do you think it will be possible?"

"It all depends on how her condition evolves."

"How do you think it is evolving?"

"Not the way we would like."

He explained two scenarios. As Mom's lung condition deteriorated further and further, she would be less and less able to breathe and would suffocate. A horrendous death. The more her condition declined, the more excruciating her pain would become, which could only be relieved by morphine. Morphine dependency takes hold fast, and higher dosages of the opioid are required, causing her death before her lungs collapse. A less painful death.

"No hope of recovery?"

"None I can see."

"I don't want Mom to become addicted to morphine."

"Do you want her to suffer more, to choke?"

I wept, hearing his words. "Of course not."

"Djenane, I must tell you: Four years ago, on August 15, Assumption Day, your mother made a vow to Holy Mary that she would give her life away for you to have a child."

"I did not know that," I said, out of breath.

"I know. I had to tell you to inform your decision in the upcoming days."

My body became numb from head to toe. How would I make the unthinkable decision? Tears ran down my face. I took a few steps to my room and collapsed on the bed.

After a while, I knelt at Mom's bedside, crying quietly with my head cupped in my hands. We looked at each other. I didn't have it in me to address the topic with her. She saw me choking back tears and gently caressed my head, saying, "Djenane."

62

LAUSANNE, EARLY FEBRUARY 1977

Mom was in acute pain a few days later, warranting the first morphine injection, which relieved her for almost twenty-four hours. The subsequent injections had a shorter effect, lasting only a few hours. When Mom waited to receive her "medication," she would moan about it and become distraught.

If a committed woman, wife, and mother like Mom suffers so much, what lies ahead for my imperfect self?

Every day, I witnessed Mom's increased craving for morphine. Mom, who didn't drink or smoke, had become dependent on an opioid.

In my sleepless nights, I went to my room, punched a cushion, buried my head in it, and wiped my cheeks.

God, how could you allow this to happen to my puritan mother?

Meanwhile, Eddy's whereabouts remained unknown. I was exasperated with him for remaining silent and absent, and with myself for expecting him to behave differently. I had to stop wishing that he was someone he was not.

My life was about to undergo a tremendous emotional upheaval with Mom's demise. It was my hope to avoid another Herculean task afterward. Most of all, I feared breaking down and being unable to handle what was to come.

63

LAUSANNE, FEBRUARY 10, 1977

A week later, Mom and I lay side-by-side on her bed with our shoulders hunched together. A glass night table lamp dimly lit the room. She leaned her head against my shoulder, grasped my hand, and looked down at it. She coughed and gasped for air. I filled her glass with water and added a pillow to her right side.

Mom whispered, "I'm dying."

"No one is dying," I said, while fearing the worst.

"I need some air. Please open the window."

"It's bitter cold. It's February."

"I know. I need to breathe."

A damp, icy draft billowed through the veiling and filled the air with a pine aroma, diluting the antiseptic scent and dropping the temperature in the room. I shivered. The cold was miserable, especially the piercing wind whipping my skin. To protect myself, I wrapped a shawl around my neck, covering my mouth and nose.

Mom took a deeper breath, tried to sit up, and fell on her right side, shaken by an apoplectic cough. I sat back down next to her and handed her some water. She held my arm to lift herself. Her hand felt weak. It had lost some grip and aged in weeks, with veins showing under her skin and her unpolished nails turning blue.

We remained silent for a while. I could hear Mom's husky breath.

"Mom … Let me close the window. I'm afraid you might catch a cold."

Mom looked through me with inanimate eyes. "My day is soon," she sighed.

"Mom. Have faith," I heard myself saying. "You're Catholic. Only God knows."

"You're talking about God. My day must be very close."

"Mom, I will tell your doctor to speak with you," I mumbled as I sat even closer to her and embraced her right arm.

Am I screening medical information from Mom?

"I love you," she managed to say in between coughs.

"Love you too, Mom," I said, holding her hand and repressing my tears, unsure she heard me through bouts of cough. I reached over to hand her another glass of water.

"Close the window," she said, "Your hand is cold."

I wrapped my arms around her right shoulder, tearing silently, sniffling. I lifted my head and saw her gazing at me.

"You need a tissue," she said, still mothering me.

The prognosis created a dilemma for me, haunting me until the morning. I didn't have it in me to tell Mom the dire truth. Dad didn't have it in him either. Mom felt her health failing and knew her demise was nearing. Her medical status had to be addressed by her general practitioner. I called him and asked him to speak with Mom.

"I have already done it. Your mom knows," he said.

The answer puzzled me but clarified Mom's most recent exchanges with me.

"What does she know?"

"The end is nearing."

"Oh my God."

I called Eddy and asked him to be ready to fly over.

LAUSANNE, FEBRUARY 14, 1977

Three days later, in the midafternoon, Mom seemed calm; her cough decreased; her breath became regular. She surprised me when she asked in a clear voice, "Please hand me my mirror, powder, and lipstick." She fixed herself up as best she could and said, "Ask everyone to come up one by one."

I rushed downstairs, puzzled.

The four or five intimate friends who used to drop by after work to keep Dad company were in the living room. Mom spoke to each person alone, then to Dad and me separately, and afterward jointly. I never knew what she shared with the others, except what she said in my presence. I never inquired.

When done, Mom asked for me. I came up to her bedroom and lay down in bed next to her. She held my hand, squeezed it softly three times (our nonverbal I love you) and whispered, "I'm ready. God is coming to get me." She turned her head, smiled, and mouthed: *I love you*. She then closed her eyes and lips and didn't open them again.

Mom died the following morning, February 15, 1977, at 9 a.m.

65

LAUSANNE, FEBRUARY 15, 1977

Mom's dead body was the first I ever saw. I sat nearby, keeping her company, but no longer dared to hold her hand. I couldn't bear that she wouldn't press my hand back three times. That would confirm that Mom was gone.

One of Mom's close friends interrupted my thoughts. She joined us and waited with me until the funeral company came. Dad could not handle the situation. He sobbed and took cover in his hideaway, until I checked in with him later to let him know Mom was leaving. Dad followed me to offer Mom our wet goodbyes without saying a word.

That day, Dad stopped drinking and never drank again for the rest of his life. That day I made the firm decision to end my marriage—though I still had no idea *when, where,* or *how* I would end it *legally*—I knew it had already ended emotionally.

LAUSANNE, FEBRUARY 17, 1977

I felt I had no one to turn to for support or comfort. Dad was as devastated as I was. None of my close friends had lost a mother. More than ever, I became determined to depend solely on myself. Nothing new for me. I had been deciding for myself since I was a teenager.

The feelings I repressed during Mom's illness came pouring out. I harbored so many, so intense, so deep. I sobbed about the loss of Mom, my derailing marriage, my incomplete education, my search for finding a decent way out. I sobbed, except in front of my daughter. My life needed reconfiguration, with no idea where to start, with no time to waste.

Dad and I reunited relatives and friends for the funeral. Loulou accepted Dad's invitation to attend the funeral. When she arrived, she shared she couldn't bear to see her sister dying and seemed shaken by her absence.

Eddy stood by my side throughout the funeral and condolences at home. His presence supported me that day. It patched the facade of our crumbling marriage. My head-to-toe black gear matched my bleak, teary demeanor. I was in a daze, looking around. Everyone was still present except Mom.

After the funeral, Eddy and I spent some time with Joelle; then he had to go to Geneva to catch a flight to somewhere.

As soon as Eddy left, Joelle and I walked back to my parents' home for the first time since Mom had passed away. Joelle looked for her grandmother and asked me about her. I told her she had gone on a trip. My then three-year-old daughter looked at me with a sad look in her eyes and told me, "Grandma wouldn't leave without saying goodbye and taking her glasses with her. I saw them on her dresser."

My face turned red. My three-year-old daughter caught me in a blatant lie. I who said I wasn't a liar didn't have the fortitude, at that moment, to tell my daughter that her grandmother had died. Telling Joelle would crystallize the loss I couldn't face and the need to console Joelle the deed I couldn't fulfill. I felt embarrassed and guilty.

Just then, Dad walked in, saying, "Pupuce!"

Joelle smiled and rushed to him. Taking her by the hand, they walked away, and I was off the hook.

67

LAUSANNE, FEBRUARY 18, 1977

Realizing I would never see Mom again was devastating. I had to let the thought sieve through me. The transition between a physical or material to an ethereal or spiritual relationship is long, unbearable.

Grief hit me hard when I went into Mom's bedroom to fix her belongings and opened her closet. Mom's Diorissimo, mixed with my grandmother's lavender sachets, took me back in time and space. Dad's reflection in the closet mirror, standing behind my own, in front of Mom's empty bed, jolted me. I didn't want him to see tears streaming down my cheeks.

"I will give Loulou everything she wants to take from Mom's clothes. I will come back to take care of the rest. Now, it's too soon." I said.

Dad nodded.

⛰

Loulou began planning her trip home, a perfect opportunity to share what was going on behind the scenes in my life. As she entered the den, I said, "I have something to tell you."

"Good timing," she said.

"My marriage is beyond repair. I tried my best. Eddy is a womanizer; his values don't match mine. I confronted him but haven't seen any improvement in his behavior."

Without allowing me to elaborate, Loulou shrugged her shoulders and burst out, "What's your problem? You're married. Your husband is successful. You have a child. What more do you want? So, what if Eddy has affairs? Most men do."

"What about my dignity? My belief system?"

"Who cares about your dignity? Your belief system?"

"I do!" I yelled, getting up. "And my feelings? How about my feelings?"

Loulou lit one of her extra-long cigarettes and puffed the smoke toward the ceiling. "This is the importance of your feelings," she said, shrugging again as I left the room.

After a moment, I caught sight of her walking into Mom's room and opening the closet. What I expected to be a sad moment for both of us turned into a fashion fest over Mom's wardrobe. She asked two friends to join her and advise her on what to choose. As they entered Mom's bedroom—a mausoleum forty-eight hours ago—they seemed to be having a boutique time. I heard them giggle unabashedly. An upgraded wardrobe overshadowed civility. I could not tolerate it.

Loulou's disregard for my feelings and Mom's memory offended me at a moment when my emotions were raw, and I felt vulnerable. I had just lost my mother, and my aunt was slipping away too. Loulou's own marital difficulties might have colored her response and distorted her perception of my sharing.

I had a hard time coping with Loulou's behavior and was about to have a brawl, but instead, I decided to engage in physical activity. I needed to move and clear my head. So, I ran down the stairs to the living room, grabbed my coat, rushed to the elevator, and dashed onto the street. I zipped around the block several times, then stopped at the drugstore and the newspaper stand, where I picked up some magazines out of breath.

68

LAUSANNE, EARLY MARCH 1977

I had to go back to Paris with no time and space to reflect on the loss I had just suffered. I had to pull myself together and keep my head up. Dad didn't need worries added to his sorrow. Joelle shouldn't have to worry about her mother. She needed a strong, inspirational mother, not a weeping willow. My marriage was in shambles. I was distraught and exhausted. Most of all, I was angry at God's design.

Yet, I heard: *Don't question God's plan. Human minds cannot comprehend it.*

Ten days after the funeral, I picked myself up and resumed my family life. I returned to Paris with Joelle—concerned about Dad living alone, missing Mom terribly. She was his cornerstone, his life compass. I was worried he would be unable to cope with her loss.

In keeping with his promise, Dad was abstinent. I told him, "I am proud of you. Mom sees you. She's proud of you too."

Dad seemed encouraged and further motivated by those words. Checking in with him twice a day was my meager attempt to ensure he was doing well. I invited him to visit us in Paris, see Joelle and chat with her. The two of them enjoyed their exchanges.

After twirling and twirling on my decision to end my marriage, life pushed me into action. My goal was to find the exit scenario that would be least disruptive to my daughter's life. Divorce first. Education next. The two nagging thoughts demanded attention and action. I didn't want to multitask. I wanted to excel at both tasks.

69

PARIS, MAY 1979

The doorbell rang at precisely 7:30 a.m.

We had just finished breakfast. The aroma of French coffee and croissants was still in the air. Joelle brushed her teeth and washed her hands, ready to start her kindergarten day, leaving home at 7:45 a.m. I left her with Mazelle and went for my second cup of coffee.

The early call surprised me. Wondering who it was, I omitted to look through the peephole and opened the door. The mother of one of my daughter's classmates stood ahead of a male trio. She forced herself into the apartment, pushed by her husband, the group leader, escorted by two muscular men.

"I came to soften things," she whispered in my ear while giving me a bear hug.

"If Eddy pays, if he does as he's told, everything will be fine; otherwise, my husband means business. Things could become nasty," she whispered, before swirling and rushing out of the main door and down the spiral staircase.

It stunned me to see her with that entourage (the couple were separated), in my home at that odd hour, with my daughter, a classmate of her daughter's, a few steps away. We knew each other socially but were not friends. Her ambiguous whisper lingered in my ear as I understood it bore an unsavory matter.

⛰

"Where is he?" asked the leader, walking uninvited into the apartment, catching Eddy on the phone in the living room.

"Hang up," the leader said with authority, "Or I will let them know, whoever they are, what kind of rotten guy you are."

Eddy hung up the phone and said, "What's going on?"

"You know what's going on. You owe me money. Pay now."

"Please lower your voice. My daughter is in her room on her way to school," I said to the leader, concerned she might get scared.

"No one is leaving this apartment," he said.

"My daughter has to go to school," I said.

"No one is leaving," the leader repeated, raising his voice.

"Please, let's be calm," I said, using my softest tone.

"Your wife is a lady," the man said. "What is she doing with a scoundrel (*magouille*) like you?"

Thinking the situation was getting heated and wishing things would calm down, I asked if anyone wanted coffee or tea.

"Coffee," they said in unison.

"You're lucky she sticks with you," the leader said.

Eddy's glazed look and caved chest signaled trouble. Joelle needed to be spared the situation unfolding in the living room. I clasped my hands together and gazed around the room. Twisting my wedding ring around my finger, I said to the men, "I will order the coffee and check in with my daughter while you sort things out."

I went to the kitchen and told in Arabic to the Egyptian butler, Mahmood, who had been working with us since Eddy and I got married fourteen years ago, to run to the office and let them know what was going on at home. He had one foot out of the delivery entrance when one of the muscular men came in. He stopped him, saying, "Not so fast," and stood with his back against the kitchen door.

"We don't have sugar," I said.

"Madam, do you think we're fools? No one goes out means no one goes out," he said.

Concerned that things were slipping out of control, I asked Mahmood to make coffee for everyone. Then I went to my daughter's room to ensure she was still unaware of the rumble unfolding in the living room. She had just completed her daily morning routine and was ready to go to school. I told her she had to leave home later that day and told Mazelle to stay in the room with her until I told them otherwise.

I returned to the kitchen to ensure Mahmood presented the coffee without sugar. Avoiding losing face with the gang seemed ridiculously important on that day.

Stepping into the living room, Eddy was curled on the couch with his head bent forward. The group leader ordered him to pay—to pay in full, at once.

"Please lower your voice. My daughter is at home," I said to the leader.

"Tell him to pay," he responded.

Eddy was a shrewd businessman, but I had no idea how bold he had become, or what the present money argument was about. I moved closer to him. While bending a knee on the couch, I held his shoulders with my hands and stared at him, saying in a staccato tone, "If you owe them money, pay it. If my daughter finds out what is happening here, you will be in big trouble with me."

I dropped his shoulders, stood up, turned around, and leaned against the door. Eddy looked dejected but didn't move. The group leader went close to him as if he were about to shake him. The two muscular men circled over him. I noticed bulges on their middle-left chest sides.

My forehead sweated. I stepped again closer to Eddy. Using a monotone voice, I said, "You heard what I told you."

"You must pay," the leader yelled.

Eddy sat upright on the couch, attempting to negotiate with the leader. He appeared overwhelmed by the leader's arguments when he said, "Allow me to explain…"

"Nothing to explain. Pay," the leader cut him off.

The muscular men made a chorus, using loud voices, recriminations, and expletives to create tension and perhaps cover the disputed payment details.

"How about if we show you what we mean?" the leader said.

The two men came closer. They surrounded Eddy, lifted him, and threw him on the couch. I think I heard him screeching. I stopped myself from screaming. The leader's eyes glared at me. "Stop, men! We have a lady amongst us. Madam, please step out. Let us talk to this *magouille*. Your husband doesn't seem to get it. He must pay."

I refused to leave.

"Madam, please leave," the leader said in a firm, low voice.

One man walked toward me.

"Leave my wife out of this," Eddy yelled for the first time.

"I trust you will agree on a solution," I said to all before walking out of the living room, trembling inside, hoping things would cool down.

Just then, I saw Mahmood standing at the door with coffee cups on a tray. I nodded and told him to serve the coffee and went to check in with Joelle. She seemed unaware of the unfolding wrangle. I breathed. She wanted me to read to her. I stayed for a while, but I could not concentrate on the reading. I asked Mazelle to do it and went back to the living room.

Eddy was still sitting on the couch, receiving the same warnings as when I left, but now looking down. He seemed to have exhausted his arguments. He heard me come in, stood up, raised his eyes, looked at me with a frozen smile, and walked to the phone. He called and gave instructions to pay the demanded, undisclosed, amount. The leader verified the execution of the instructions and came back to the living room.

"My daughter goes to school now," I told the leader.

He nodded.

I leaped to Joelle's bedroom and asked Mazelle to take her to school, scribbling an excuse note for the lateness, and rushed back to the living room.

The men were drinking coffee. Conversations had become civil with a normal tone. Upon seeing me, the men stood up to say goodbye while excusing themselves for the intrusion and discussions.

The group leader asked to speak with me privately. We went to Joelle's now-vacated bedroom and sat face-to-face—I on her bed and he in an armchair.

"Madam, what does a lady like you do with a *magouille* like this?" he asked again.

"How come you forced yourself into a family home at an ungodly hour of the day with a child around?" I said, surprised by the smooth tone of my voice.

"He didn't give me another option. He would not pay," the leader said in a courteous tone.

"How come you took the law in your hands?"

The group leader gave me a thin, roundabout explanation. He was engaged in a business agreement, a word of honor, with Eddy, who owed him money and disregarded multiple requests for payment until this morning. He, too, loved his daughter and made sure nothing would happen to mine. He apologized for the intrusion and took my hand to kiss it, the formal European manner. I pulled my hand away.

"I would like to host a dinner at home in your honor. You are such a lady."

"No thank you. Please don't."

"I would like to. You can invite anyone you like, as many as you like."

"No thank you."

Eddy, intrigued by the duration of the chat, walked into the room. The leader told him about the invitation. "It's for your wife, not for you," he said, taunting Eddy.

"I declined the invitation," I said.

Eddy overruled my decision, saying, "We will attend with pleasure. Very nice of you."

The group leader excused himself, saying, "See you tomorrow," before leaving.

"Have you lost your mind, along with your honor?" I shouted at Eddy.

"My mind not yet," he said.

"How come you're working with this fellow?"

Eddy didn't answer.

"Give me an answer."

Still no answer.

"What's going on?"

"No big deal. We need to move on. Forget about it."

"Forget about it? Are you kidding me?"

Eddy's behavior was as shocking as the morning intrusion. I couldn't believe what I had seen and heard. Arguing with him about not going to the reception was moot. Eddy said, "Please accompany me. Show the upper hand."

"How come my going is so important?"

"We need to show a unified front."

"A unified front with a man who labeled you *magouille*?"

Eddy's arguments made no sense to me. He pleaded. I was exhausted. In the end, I consented to attend the dinner, despite not believing it was the right thing to do.

Kafka's *The Metamorphosis* came to mind. I didn't think I would witness a transformation unfold in my living room.

Was Eddy's thinking contaminating me? Was I falling into a Groupthink pattern? What made me agree with the decision that suited Eddy? I wondered whether I was putting who I was, who I aimed to be, in peril by agreeing with him, by going to that dinner.

I thought of Alfred de Vigny's *Eloa* for the first time since I had left high school. The poem focuses on an angel, Eloa, who falls in love with an evil male (the devil) who is chasing her and whom she tries to save—putting her essence at risk. Was I doing the same? Then I humored myself by thinking, *I'm no angel. Is he a devil?*

My questions remained unanswered. Nothing new. I knew Eddy's business headlines, but he didn't share the details with me, and I didn't insist on knowing them. I disagreed with his style in many ways, so I avoided having another topic of contention. Now I knew something was seriously wrong. My speculation ended there. On that day, I had heard and seen enough, more than enough.

The phone's ring brought me back to the present. Dad was calling me. Since Mom had died a little over two years ago, Dad and I had drawn even closer. I told him the personal information I used to share with her. We were coping in unison with Mom's interrupted life.

"How are you?" Dad asked.

"Fine," I said, skipping the early morning intrusion.

"What is going on?" Dad asked again, perhaps hearing some strain in my voice.

"I have the beginning of a sniffle," I told him.

I don't think he believed me but took my words at face value.

Hearing Dad's voice, chatting with him, knowing that he was there, was comforting. In passing, I told him who invited us for dinner the following evening. He acknowledged knowing the host. Neither of us elaborated on the topic.

Feeling soiled by the morning event, I took another shower and got dressed to pick up Joelle for lunch from her Ecole. She ran to me when she saw me. I hugged her and held her hand. By the time we got to my car, I could breathe fully again.

70

PARIS, MAY 1979

The next evening, I pampered myself for dinner and was pleased with the results. Eddy came to pick me up and gave me an approving look and loads of compliments, which I took as his way of thanking me for attending the reception. I didn't answer. I felt very much at a distance from him.

We arrived on time at the leader's apartment on Avenue Raphael, one of Paris's most exclusive addresses. It surprised me to see the leader's wife opening the door and wondered about her role in this unfolding episode. She greeted me with much effusion.

"Welcome to our home!" she said empathically. "My husband asked me to greet you because he knew you're a friend of mine. I'm thrilled to see you."

A friend! I would have been thrilled to see you, too, if you hadn't intruded into my apartment yesterday morning.

"Thank you," I said as she dashed to find her husband.

"I thought they were separated," I whispered to Eddy, who shrugged his shoulders.

Our host came to welcome us and led us to the living room. He was euphoric, greeting me and walking me into a large, beautiful living room. A magnificent Chagall painting dominated the space above an off-white couch with sky blue throw pillows. Blue hydrangeas (which I later found out symbolize apology) in large planters and crystal objects adorned the side and coffee tables surrounding the couch. Beethoven's "Moonlight Sonata" was playing in the background. Waiters, in black tuxedos, served Dom Perignon in Baccarat champagne coupes presented with a lace napkin on a silver tray.

I turned around and raised my coupe, complimenting the host on the breathtaking Chagall.

"It took me a long time to find it," he said, his face lighting up as he described the long process to find and acquire the masterpiece. We admired the artwork for a few minutes until he invited me to sit in an armchair facing it. The host and his guests toasted me, saying kind words. I hardly heard what they said.

I had an out-of-body experience. That is, I observed myself and everything around me as if it were happening from a location outside my physical body and as if events weren't real. The discrepancy between the previous day's forced intrusion and today's festive celebration was staggering. I held tightly to the arms of the chair to come back to the present and then planted my feet firmly on the floor to focus my attention on my surroundings, forcing myself to be in the moment and chat with other guests.

After a while, the host asked me to enter the dining room before him and sit to his right as the esteemed guest. The table was stunning with a pristine off-white tablecloth, two tall silver candlesticks, and sky-blue candles. I complimented the host on the splendid decoration.

"I have chosen the dinner menu for you, a selection of Egyptian specialties and bastilla, the Moroccan national dish. My cook is from Morocco."

Before he finished his sentence, waiters brought out a wide variety of Egyptian appetizers, including fattoush, baba ganoush, and kibbeh, followed by an appetizing bastilla, much to the guests' delight.

My mind experienced double screens during dinner. I was again shocked by the contrast between yesterday's home invasion and tonight's sophisticated dinner party.

Yesterday, I felt strained, and today, I am stained.

I wanted to go home. I wanted to be with Joelle. I wanted to speak with Dad. I wished Mom were alive—though I doubt I would have shared the experience with her. I hadn't with Dad. That night I thought about Mom's initial reticence toward Eddy. I tried to push the thought away but couldn't. Her prescience was spot on.

On our way home, Eddy attempted to engage me in conversation. I only said, "I wish they had extended elegance when they visited us at home." Then I remained silent, pondering over the crumbling internal structure of our marriage. I kept thinking about that early, odd morning when one woman and three men uncovered Eddy's underhanded ways of being and dealing.

I couldn't wait to hug and kiss Joelle. I wanted to take her, slam the door, and leave. *Then what? Where would I go?* I needed a plan before I could say, "I'm leaving you."

My education was incomplete. My identity was associated with Eddy's. My inner voice guided me to be patient, to wait some more—even though I made my decision and the evidence piled up.

I was going to leave Eddy one day—but not today, not yet.

71

PARIS, JULY 17, 1979

I visited Dad in the early evening before flying to New York the next day. The efficient yet discreet concierge of the Hotel Meurice must have informed Dad I was on my way up. I had waved at him from a distance. The door of Dad's hotel suite was ajar when I reached his floor.

Dad stretched his head, standing behind the door, smiling to greet me. I was puzzled to see him, an active sixty-four-year-old investor already wearing his night gear, off-white silk pajamas and black leather slippers. I had to stand on the tip of my toes to hug him.

"How are you feeling?"

"I wanted to relax. I've had a long day. Come in. We'll sit in the living room."

I followed him.

We sat face-to-face in two comfortable yellow velvet armchairs, with a rectangular coffee table in the middle. The living room's temperature was cool. The air conditioning's soft rumbling and shades half-closed decreased the July heat. I stretched my legs on the table and saw Dad raising his eyebrows behind his dark brown rimmed glasses.

"I'm tired too," I said, keeping my legs on the table.

Dad did not answer but continued to frown at my legs while asking me about my recent trip to Lebanon.

"I went to see my apartment," I said.

"Are you serious?" interrupted Dad. "What made you do that?"

"The car passed by the building on our way back from the airport, and I asked the driver to slow down. Men wearing fatigues carrying machine guns stopped us. I told them I used to live there and wanted to see my apartment. They invited me to go to the building. I accepted."

"You said you wouldn't."

"It was too tempting."

"I understand."

"Militiamen were everywhere."

"How do you know they were part of a militia?"

"They were not wearing Lebanese military uniforms."

Dad nodded, highly interested.

"They were in the entrance staircase. The building has become a barrack—my apartment, the headquarters, and the leader's residence."

"Who's the leader?"

"Who knows?"

"The apartment was plundered. None of our belongings remained. Everything vanished. The men occupying it might have done it—though I have no proof."

"You saw the leader?"

"Yes, he came to greet me. I asked him about our belongings. He said he did not know and insisted on offering me a cup of tea or coffee. I thanked him but didn't take his offer."

Dad nodded, incredulous.

"I couldn't believe that was where I used to live. It was Cairo revisited. I got to see what happened to our apartment after we left."

"True."

"We lost yet another piece of ourselves, of our past, a piece that makes up our jigsaw puzzle. Only memories remain, reminding us to build our future on solid ground."

Frowning, looking sad, Dad changed the subject asking about Joelle. He also asked me how I was feeling. Not wanting to add to his concerns, I gave him a brief response without mentioning the unsavory early-morning intrusion at home last May or my mental decision about my marriage. We were both still grieving the loss of Mom. Dad and I shared open heartfelt conversations but not so open as to worry him.

I stood up, got a bottle of Evian and two glasses, and poured some water. I sat down, drank it, and directed the conversation to his summer schedule and my upcoming trip to New York.

"Did I tell you that I saw Salvador Dali at the hotel, and we meet regularly for coffee?"

"That's fantastic, Dad! It must be fascinating to converse with such a renowned artist."

"I enjoy hearing him talk about his life and art."

"I'm thrilled for you, Dad."

He nodded.

Soon we were reminiscing about Mom and bantering about family, friends, the future.

"Your Mom was my rampart. I knew she was there."

"I know Dad."

"I'm still not drinking."

"I'm so proud of you."

"I'm happy you're going to New York. You love being in New York."

"I do."

"Please call me when you get there."

"I will."

Dad asked me a few times if I wanted to have dinner.

Parents in Middle Eastern cultures like to feed their kids. It's one of the many ways they show their love and care. I declined dinner. The conversation flow felt good. We chatted until sunset, which was close to 10 p.m. at that time of the year in Paris.

"Time to go home," I said, realizing it was getting late.

Dad didn't utter a word. He stood up, hugged me, and put on his dark brown brocade robe to walk me to the elevator. We took a few steps down the hallway and stood on the opposite sides of a tiny, old iron Parisian elevator door. He gazed at me lovingly and said, "Go have fun in New York. You love it. Leave the worries to me." (*Vas, amuses-toi bien à New York. Laisses-moi les soucis.*)

His statement jolted me. How come he said that? I gave him a bear hug and said, "Dad! I love you."

My voice broke as I contained sobs. Dad had touched a vulnerable chord, one I was repressing, and I didn't want him to see me break down. I wanted him to see I could keep my chin up. I stepped into the elevator and, in my anxiety, pressed the down button before saying another word.

72

PARIS AND NEW YORK, JULY 18, 1979

Eddy, Joelle, and I took a Concorde flight, leaving Paris CDG airport at 11 a.m. and landing at New York's JFK airport at 8:35 a.m., gaining six hours on the outbound.

Upon arriving in New York, Eddy and I bypassed our usual residence in the city.

"Where are we going?" I asked him.

"To visit a friend of mine."

"Now? Visit who?"

"You'll see."

The driver parked the car in front of a recently built midtown Manhattan skyscraper. We took an elevator to the 39th floor and walked down a long narrow hallway with green wall-to-wall carpet and beige walls. I pulled Eddy's sleeve asking, "Where are we going?"

"…"

We rang the doorbell. A building representative opened the door and handed us keys. I looked around, bewildered, and pulled on Eddy's jacket sleeve, demanding an answer. He turned his head, stared at me, but remained silent.

We walked into a bright and spacious living room with a stunning view of the New York City skyline. As I was about to ask him another question, Eddy handed me the phone receiver, saying, "Your father is on the phone."

"My father? How did he know we're here?" I said, as I took the receiver. "Dad?"

"I couldn't wait for you to call," he said.

"No worries."

"How do you like it?"

"Like what?"

"The apartment."

"Which apartment?"

"The apartment where you are. Eddy did not tell you?"

"No. I don't understand."

While listening to the conversation, Eddy glanced at me and said, "So what? He bought you this apartment!"

I put my hand over the transmitter and asked Eddy, "What are you saying?"

"Nothing…"

I gestured with my hand, questioning him, but he turned his back and looked out the window.

"I bought this apartment for you and paid the initial deposit," Dad was saying as I put the receiver back against my ear.

"Dad … Thank you! I can't believe it. You didn't say a word yesterday."

"I wanted to surprise you. You love being in the United States. You love New York. You'll live in New York City one day, I'm sure. The apartment will make it a done deal."

I was dumbfounded and mumbled again, "Thank you, Dad."

"Do you like it?"

"I do. It's beautiful. The view is amazing."

"I knew you would like it."

"I haven't seen all of it. We just stepped in."

"Call me back."

"I'll call you as soon as I discover all the nooks and crannies in the apartment."

"That would be nice." He paused and repeated, "Have fun in New York. You love it. Leave the worries to me."

"How come you didn't say a word when we walked in?" I asked Eddy in a frustrated tone and spun around to explore my new apartment.

Dad had not visited New York and bought the apartment without seeing it. Step by step, I went over it inch by inch and made myself and my family comfortable in our new home in the city.

When I was ready to call Dad and give him a detailed report, it was too late. I thought, *with the six-hour time difference between New York and Paris and his bedtime schedule, he must be asleep. I'll call him first thing in the morning.*

I never spoke with Dad again. I never told him how much I appreciated the generous, meaningful gift he had given me. Did I tell him loud and clear, "Thank you, Dad?"

73

NEW YORK, JULY 19, 1979

The phone rang early the next morning. Eddy picked up, turned his back, uttering only single words, "When? Where? How?" and hung up the phone.

"What's going on?" I said.

"Your Dad is not feeling well."

"Dad! What happened? Hand me the phone."

"Your Dad is sick," Eddy told me.

"Sick? What's wrong?" I asked.

"He's in a coma."

"In a coma? What are you hiding?"

An eerie moment. I remembered what I told my daughter when my mother died. Incredulous, I asked Eddy to tell me the truth.

He did.

Dad had died.

Dad had a stroke and passed away, probably soon after we hung up, in the hotel suite where I had left him thirty-six hours earlier. Dad told me he had a long day, but he didn't seem tired the last time I saw him. His demeanor was typical of someone who worked hard. Should I have asked him more about his physical condition? He was not ill. He had no chronic health condition. He had stopped drinking.

My mind churned over our last face-to-face and phone conversations. His last message kept replaying in my head. The first few hours, I felt numb, dissociating myself from reality. The shock was too horrendous.

Have fun in New York. You love it. Leave the worries to me.

Dad exhibited acute foresight and generosity. He knew New York had been my city of choice. I fell in love with it the first time I stepped out of an airplane in January 1966. He had just given me the *where* to go when I will walk out of my marriage. Gratitude and love filled my heart for what he had done, for how he had done it. "Dad," I cried out loud in shock, choking, digging my head in my pillow to cry louder.

Eddy and I took the first flight back to Paris that same day. We considered the travels and upcoming events inappropriate for six-year-old Joelle. Our daughter stayed in the apartment in New York with Mazelle, who had flown to the US a week earlier to visit family in Connecticut.

Virginia Woolf wrote, "A woman must have money and a room of her own if she is to write fiction."

I don't think it will be fiction; but one day, I will write nonfiction.

74

PARIS, JULY 20, 1979

*N*o one has my back now.

We were silent for most of the flight, apart from my sobbing and nose blowing. Not only was I mourning the loss of my father, but his death had also revived and amplified repressed sadness about the loss of my mother.

Mom died just two years ago. Now, Dad.

I slumped into my seat, caving my chest, shaking my head, keeping my eyes closed. How would I handle their loss?

All I wanted to do was lie down and cry. Yet so much was ahead of me. I was an only daughter, mourning my father's loss, making the death announcement, planning the religious services and my parents' funeral, and completing the legal paperwork.

God! Please give me the strength to be up to the task, up to my parents' memory and legacy.

Dad died in Paris, France, and would be transported to Lausanne, Switzerland, his city and country of residence. My mother's body was in a coffin, in a private funerary room in Lausanne. Dad had refused to bury her after she died. Switzerland allowed residents to keep their next of kin in that status at a dedicated cemetery area. Dad visited Mom every day and had a bouquet of red roses delivered to her funerary room twice a week, on Mondays and Thursdays.

"We will be buried together on the same day," Dad told me. His wish was about to be fulfilled. And I would be burying both my parents—on the same day, at the same time.

Dad survived Mom by only two years. He felt mortified about losing her. He loved her, held her on a pedestal all her life, and was always sentimental, effusive with her, taking each opportunity to tell her sweet nothings. He treated her with care and respect. Dad never raised his voice at Mom, let alone ever used derogatory language toward her. In an argument, he eventually acquiesced and agreed with her perspective.

My thoughts and feelings were bouncing against each other. Family duties took precedence over mourning and constrained my need to grieve my parents. After an overbearing silence, I lifted my head and said, "I have a lot to plan. I will deal with the funeral and burial. I will host a reception at my parents' home after the burial. My parents would like it. You'll take care of the travel arrangements?"

"Fine."

"I prefer to stay in a hotel in Lausanne. I'm not up to sleeping at the apartment."

"Which hotel?"

"Lausanne Palace? Closer to the house, familiar…"

"Fine."

We remained silent for a while, then Eddy asked me, "What are you going to miss the most about your parents?"

His question surprised me. "That no matter what I do, they'll have my back."

Eddy held my hand and said, "I'll have your back. Don't worry."

His response surprised me even more. On that day, at that hour, I needed comfort beyond all else. I held onto Eddy's hand, laid my head on his shoulder, and slept for a while.

Upon arrival to Paris, I was shocked to find out I had to identify my father's body at the Parisian morgue the following day. This mandated procedure enabled a French coroner to issue the death certificate for any non-French citizen dying in France without a next of kin present.

The identification was scheduled for the following morning at 6 a.m.

When I mentioned it to Eddy, he said, "Not for me. Go with Jacques (Eddy's driver)."

"How about what you told me on the plane?"

"…"

Eddy looked at me as if he didn't understand. Taking a quick step to the door, he turned around and said, "I have to go," and added "I'll book the flights," before slamming the door.

That's Eddy.

Where is the husband who said he had my back?

What he said on the plane was short-lived. I should have known better. I wanted him to be someone caring and compassionate, someone he was not. He wanted me to be dedicated to him and be his rampart against the tribulations of life. Someone I was no longer willing to be.

I didn't have the energy to fight him. I didn't want to break down.

Family duty prevailed and geared me to organize and schedule the two days ahead. It kept me busy for the few remaining hours before the identification.

75

PARIS, JULY 21, 1979

Jacques came to pick me up at 5:30 a.m. on that dreary, drizzly July morning to drive me to the Parisian morgue Place Mazas, along the Seine River by the Quai de la Rapée. Jacques was driving my electric blue Pacer, while I sat in the passenger seat. As he was about to speak, I gestured for silence. He had been working with us for over ten years and understood my nonverbal communication.

I turned my head and looked out at the bank of the Seine on my right. For a moment, I thought *Paris is a beautiful city*. Its iconic bridges connecting both banks were an amazing sight. An occasional passerby, cyclist, or runner accentuated the day's early hour.

My internal dialogue eclipsed the surrounding beauty.

Two days ago, I was speaking with Dad on the phone. He sounded glad to tell me about the apartment. And here I am—not even forty-eight hours later—on my way to the morgue to identify his body. Dad, a collector who liked beauty, aesthetics, the arts—at the morgue! God, I hope he can't see where he is.

We arrived at the morgue 5:55 a.m. A dark, damp, vaulted building built with rough, gray stones, the morgue was emblematic of its sinister purpose. A place one would only go to if mandated.

"Madame, I will accompany you to the identification," Jacques said.

"Thank you. I will do it."

"You're not going to go by yourself?"

"Merci, Jacques … I appreciate it."

"Madame …"

Jacques gave me the empathy my husband lacked. If Eddy didn't have it in him to come with me, I would go on my own to pay my homage to my father, to my parents.

At 6 a.m. sharp, I stood in front of Dad's mortuary, lifted my eyes, and saw his name printed on the right side of the door. I stared at the letters, having trouble registering they referred to him.

The iron doors of dimly lit individual rooms bobbled. Cold air smelling of disinfectant—an amplified smell of Mom's room the week she died—caught my throat. I sidestepped, stretched my head, and stopped.

The coffin stood in the middle of the room. I glanced at it from the right angle. Dad's body faced the room's front wall with a white sheet covering his head and upper chest. The coffin covered the rest of his body. I closed my eyes.

It can't be Dad … here … I'm having a nightmare, it can't be real, I'm again having an out of body experience.

Hesitant footfalls made me open my eyes. A morgue representative stood two steps behind me, gesturing to move forward to perform the identification and notarize my signature.

As I was about to step into the room, I heard a woman's voice saying, "The little lady is all by herself. The poor thing." (*Oh, la la… La petite dame est là toute seule. La pauvre!*)

Out of the adjoining mortuary room—out of nowhere—came a lady dressed in black who took my arm and said, "Let's go. We will go in together." (*Allons-y. On va y aller ensemble.*) I was so startled I'm not sure I even said thank you. The lady and I took two steps into my father's room and stood at the right side of his coffin. Just then, the morgue representative lifted the sheet, and I recognized my father's ashen face with his eyes closed, with a semblance of a smile on the right side of his lips. I felt dizzy, about to faint.

I nodded to the representative and signed the identification. He mentioned my father's body would be driven to the Centre Funeraire de Montoie (the burial place) in Lausanne within the next hour. I nodded again.

I clung to the arm of the lady, who took a few steps with me to the communal area of the morgue and whispered, *"Courage,"* before hugging me and joining her family.

By then, I was broken, unable to say thank you. The nameless, faceless lady gave me the empathy I needed that macabre day when I was at a breaking point, weak enough to receive it.

Images of what I just had experienced floated on my mind as I looked for Jacques. He was standing behind me, looking pale and pitiful. His first morgue experience, too. He took my arm and helped me walk to the car. I started shaking, my teeth shattering, and tears trailed down my cheeks. I felt I would throw up and faint. Jacques, tearing up himself, said, "I am sorry, Madame, really sorry. My condolences."

Jacques helped me lie down in the back of the car. As soon as he closed the door, I started wailing and stomping my feet against it and did not stop until we reached home. He then checked no one stood in the lobby, helped me out of the car, and rode the elevator with me. He rang the apartment doorbell and left me in the care of Mahmood, who was expecting me. I think I reached out for his hand and mumbled, "Merci ..."

I dragged my feet to my bedroom, managed to climb into bed, crawled under my bedcovers, and curled in a fetal position without removing my clothes. Mahmood sat on the floor at the foot of the bed. We both bawled—I out of disarray, he out of empathy, I think.

Exhausted, I dozed off for a while, was semiconscious for the rest of the day, and at some point, fell asleep for the night.

76

PARIS AND LAUSANNE, JULY 22, 1979

I didn't see or hear from Eddy until the following day. He was lying in bed next to me when I woke up. With a broken spirit and a groggy mind, still wearing my previous day's clothes, I got out of bed and started getting ready for the dreadful day ahead.

Eddy did not ask me about my experience at the morgue, and I didn't volunteer any information. He didn't comfort me or express solace, either. I was devastated and wanted to scream out my anger, but I needed to conserve my energy. I hadn't eaten in thirty-six hours and had no extra energy to waste on a useless argument or a fight with him.

How would he feel if the situation and roles were reversed?

A moot point, I sighed.

We have a functional, transactional relationship.

I asked Eddy to do some things, and he asked the same of me. As reluctant as I was to follow his business approach, he was to deal with my family and emotional issues.

As soon as I had gotten myself ready, I found the travel schedule on my nightstand. We were flying to Geneva at noon and then driving to Lausanne. The funeral and the burial were scheduled for the next day.

The flight to Geneva and the drive to Lausanne melted together in a mournful blur. I only remember disconnected flashbacks with gaps that seem lost forever in my black box.

In the first flashback, I am standing heartbroken, tears rolling down my cheeks, viewing my parents' identical coffins through the window of their private funerary room at the cemetery in Lausanne. A vase of withered red roses, the last ones Dad had sent to Mom, was in front of the coffins. *And here they are to be buried together on the same day, as Dad wanted.*

I found myself meditating and praying. *Is it Mom's intercession from wherever she is?* The thought startled me. When I lifted my head, dusk had set. Time to leave.

I was unaware of Eddy's whereabouts.

Nearing the Lausanne Palace hotel, I felt relieved we were staying there. I bumped into a dozen relatives and friends who had come for the funeral when I walked into the hotel lobby. I started sobbing but was comforted by their loving hugs and agreed to spend some time with them. Before 10 p.m., my two closest friends walked me to the elevator and then to my room and helped me get into bed, where I collapsed, half asleep.

The other side of the bed was empty.

77

LAUSANNE, JULY 23, 1979

In the next flashback, a day later, I'm dressed in black with opaque dark tights to attend my parents' funeral at the Roman Catholic Church of the Sacred Heart in Ouchy—the church where Eddy and I were married fourteen years ago on a rainy day. *I challenge those who say that rain on a wedding day is a good omen.*

I'm standing outside the church; Eddy is next to me. Each guest shakes hands with us before being ushered into the church. I control my composure until I see the grocery owner who referred to himself as *Laitier*, delivering groceries to my parents' home since they had moved to Lausanne. He used to open the front door my parents kept unlocked and walk in, yelling at the top of his lungs, "Milkman!" (*Laitier*).

Seeing him shook me up. It brought back a whole era, a now-obsolete way of being. I looked at him and, once more, wailed. His eyes and face became red. He turned his head and walked into the church without shaking hands with me. I was in a daze, looking around. Everyone, including Eddy, was still present. Mom and Dad were gone.

No recollection remains from the funeral, except for glimpses of the mass. Flowers decorating the church abounded. The choir sang Schubert's "Ave Maria" (my parents' favorite hymn) accompanied by an organist, giving the solemn mass an ethereal quality.

After the mass, we went to the Montoie Cemetery for the burial. Eddy was standing to my right. Wreaths of flowers with ribbons carrying the senders' names and messages surrounded us. I focused on a gorgeous one on a stand, just in front of me. The sympathy note on the ribbon expressed gratitude and appreciation for my father's business contributions to Eddy's holding company.

Who sent this? *That's a kindhearted gesture, a mark of appreciation!*

Right then, I saw Eddy looking surprised, turning around, and rolling his eyes at Ahmes, the firm's CEO and Munirah's husband. Unbeknownst to Eddy, Ahmes, a quintessential gentleman, had ordered the wreath and written the note. He bent over, gave me a huge hug, and whispered, "I'm so sorry."

I didn't know whether Ahmes was sorry for my loss or Eddy's behavior, or both. This gentleman's innate decency filled my heart with gratitude. Tears ran down my face.

In the last flashback, I am walking into my parents' apartment. It has turned into a ghost town, bearing the memories of those now gone—the apartment where I left parts of myself next to my mother in agony. I saw it anew but knew it was the last time I would host a function there, and one of the last times I would be there.

I scheduled an early dinner for relatives and friends who attended the funeral. In marked contrast to the sinister events that turned me upside down for these few days, nothing had changed in my parents' apartment. It still looked elegant and pristine with its breathtaking view.

Josephina, my parents' housekeeper for seventeen years and considered an extended family member, maintained the apartment to the level my parents would have liked for a formal reception. Everything down to the finest detail had been prepared according to their preferences. The lighting was subdued, not to interfere with the view of the outdoors. Flowers were arranged and placed in the designated spaces in the living room and den. At the selected spots, rose-scented candles were lit to enhance the scent of the real roses. My mother thought she had patented the idea and wouldn't divulge it unless pressed by a relative or close friend. Beautiful peach roses stood in the middle of the dining room table, covered with a delicate lace tablecloth, as well as crystal, silverware, and china.

Looking for Josephina to thank her and hug her, I found her wearing her formal black uniform. She wiped her tears when she saw me. We fell in each other's arms and sobbed. She then looked at me and said in a low, yet commanding tone I knew came out of care, "Enough tears for today! Your parents can see you. You're hosting this reception in their honor. They wouldn't like to see you this way."

I went up to my room, glanced at myself in the mirror, and got scared. My puffy eyes revealed my emotions of the last few days. In my black gear, I looked like a ghost. I dragged myself into the shower and freshened up. I glanced again in the mirror, brushed my hair, powdered my nose, and put on some lip gloss—the most I could and would do.

Afterward, I sat in the most comfortable armchair in the den and decided not to move from there. I needed to preserve my scant energy. The guests would have to find me.

Once more, Eddy wasn't there.

As I waited for the guests, I looked at the still beautiful and pristine apartment and recalled what Mom used to say, "We will die, and things will remain."

I stopped counting the times Mom was spot on.

Mom and Dad were no longer among us, yet the things they collected over the years were still around. Her approach to life was nonmaterialistic. She was all substance, no fluff—though she enjoyed art and elegance.

My gaze stopped at Dad's desk, a sizable Louis XV antique piece. The Maison Jansen in Paris had certified it as authentic when my parents bought it close to three decades ago. Since then, the desk's history had followed ours. It traveled from Paris to my parents' apartment in Cairo, which Jansen decorated and also helped my parents select signature pieces to furnish. The desk was in the den, where Dad worked over the weekends.

When President Nasser sequestrated Egyptians' personal properties, no furniture was allowed to leave residences. In the building where we lived, the government had in the lobby a division of the General Intelligence Service who were responsible for providing secret police to monitor sequestrated families' goings and comings and their belongings.

Considering these constrictions, Mom had devised a furniture exit strategy. It required the household help's agreement and silence to have pieces leave our apartment during the holy month of Ramadan just before religious Muslims would break their fast.

The surveillance parameters prohibited furniture from leaving the front lobby. The delivery elevator was the only option. Unlike previous pieces, the desk did not fit into it. After trying different approaches, the desk ended up in the kitchen without a way out of the apartment. Time ran short. As Mom was about to have a fit, an idea dawned on sixteen-year-old me. "Let's rope the desk and slide it down from my balcony."

Mom hyperventilated at the idea. "The antique desk going down roped from your bedroom's balcony!"

"Any other solution? The government agents are on the front side of the building. They're starting with the break of the fast (*iftar*) at this hour," I argued with pride.

"Let's rush. Our people need to eat," Mom conceded with a strangled voice.

Two minutes later, we roped the desk, and off it went down my bedroom's balcony. Not only was it an iconic view, but it also became a historic secret escape for Dad's desk. I rushed to the front elevator, went down to the lobby, trying to look as calm and collected as I could while wishing "Bon appétit" (*Saheteen*) to the government agents who were starting to eat.

Out of the main door, I ran as fast as I could to help the driver and the butler fit the desk in the station wagon to my mother's gesticulations from the balcony. The desk did not fit in or on top of the station wagon despite the twists and turns.

We were stuck again. I could see Mom losing her patience and temper. The desk stood on the sidewalk with no way or where to go. We couldn't bring it back through the main or service entrance.

We were ready to rope it back up.

Just then, a man driving a mule cart (*arabiya hantour*) rode in front of the building, an uncommon event in our neighborhood at this fast-breaking hour. I stopped the driver. "I would like to put the desk on your cart to transport it to my grandmother. Would you take me there?" I asked while sharing the address.

The mule's driver agreed. He stated his fee. I nodded. The help lifted the desk on the cart and waved goodbye, looking relieved. So was I, and waved goodbye to Mom who was bending over my balcony's railing, still gesturing and shouting. I couldn't hear her.

During the ride, I swayed back and forth while holding onto the backless wooden bench and almost fell off when the mule started to trot. Sitting next to the driver, with an antique desk at the back of the cart, I had a unique ride through the busiest streets of Cairo and wished I had a camera to capture the unforgettable event.

After a safe one-hour drive, the driver dropped me off at my grandmother's building in the Giza neighborhood of Cairo. I paid and thanked him, as he said goodbye with a bow and a big smile.

My grandmother stored the desk with the other pieces of furniture already there until they were shipped in the cargo of our non-Egyptian friends who were moving to Geneva, an undercover approach used by sequestrated Egyptians.

The doorbell shook me out of my reminiscences.

The first caller to arrive was Eddy's corporate lawyer, with whom Dad had also collaborated. I was surprised to see him first, so punctual, and thought it was Swiss precision. As soon as he expressed his sympathy, he said, "I came a few minutes early."

"No worries."

"Your Dad died prematurely."

I nodded.

"Is Eddy here?"

"Not yet."

The lawyer seemed relieved. "I wanted you to know that Eddy would not have concluded his last deal, the most lucrative deal of his career, if it were not for your Dad."

I became interested. "Really? How come?"

He highlighted that Dad devised financial strategies allowing the deal to go through and said, "Your father didn't get paid for his significant contribution. Eddy should pay you your father's consultation fee."

Stunned, I mumbled, "Sounds good. Thank you."

Other guests arriving interrupted our conversation. They knew the apartment well and found me easily to express their sympathy and support.

At some point, I looked toward the dining room and saw Josephina raising a bottle of Dom Perignon, looking at me. I nodded, stood up, and managed to say a few words celebrating Mom's and Dad's lives with relative self-control.

From then onward, I went on autopilot and had no memory of how the evening was or how it ended. I had asked my two closest friends to take me back to the hotel and walk me to my room at the end of the evening.

78

LAUSANNE AND PARIS, JULY 24, 1979

We had a midday flight back to Paris. I knew Eddy would emerge at some point and, as usual, be in a rush. I walked to my parents' apartment to meet with Josephina and thank her for all she had done the previous day and through the years.

The apartment was still and silent. All that remained were memories of those who once lived there. I told Josephina I would return at the end of the summer to clear the space and decide what to do with its contents. It didn't feel right to think about those things at that time. I gave her a hug and walked back to the hotel.

Eddy showed up in the hotel lobby a few minutes later, busy speaking with people, eager to drive to Geneva to catch our flight back to Paris.

As soon as we arrived at the Paris apartment, the weight of the past three days hit me. I was wiped out, beyond exhausted. I went to the living room, sat on the couch, and stretched my legs on the coffee table, sighing, remembering my father's facial expression when I crossed my legs on the coffee table in his hotel suite the last time I saw him.

Mom… Dad… I miss you so much. I can't believe I just attended your funerals and burials, both on the same day.

I slumped on the back of the couch, turning my head left and right. Tears were streaming down my face as I mourned the loss of my parents and their warning about my ill-advised marriage. Their passing made me fully aware of the fragility of life and the importance of making the best of every moment.

"I have a business dinner. Going out," I heard Eddy saying as he slammed the door of the apartment without coming to see me.

Nothing new. Still hurtful.

I leaned my head on the back of the couch and let the tears roll down my face and neck. Suddenly, I felt a quiet presence. Unable to lift my head, I opened my eyes and saw Mahmood staring at me. "Please give me a scotch on the rocks."

He continued staring at me and said, "But you don't drink."

"I didn't. Now I do."

"But Madame."

"There is no but Madame. Do as I say. Please."

He left and came back with the tiniest scotch I had ever seen.

"What is this?"

"Scotch on the rocks as you asked."

"This is a sample," I said, lifting the glass against the light, but didn't argue further and drank the scotch.

"Another one … Please."

"But …"

"No buts … Another one. Please."

Mahmood looked at me, sighed, went to the kitchen, and came back with a drink as meager as the first one. He handed it to me and sighed again.

Was I numbing my pain as Dad did when Mom got sick? Or connecting with him through his former drink of choice? Was I taking over?

The emotional load of the last few days and the two drinks, albeit small, gulped on an empty stomach, weighed on me. I almost fell asleep on the couch but pulled myself up to the bed and sank into a deep sleep.

I woke up the following day feeling like Atlas, carrying the entire world on my shoulders. How did I get myself in this tight spot? What enticed me to marry Eddy?

As I struggled to keep myself composed, I felt thankful to my parents for providing me a place to go after I left Eddy and started a new life. My aim was to choose the *when* and *how* of leaving him—the man I had defied my parents to marry—and build a life of my own.

Introspection and decision-making were not possible that evening. All I wanted was to catch a flight to New York, be with Joelle, and bring her back to Paris.

79

PARIS, 1980-1981

Life had diverted my attention from Eddy. I felt relieved not to think or know about his behavior. It was temporary. Updates came to me.

One evening, one of Eddy's male friends, a physician, called to apologize for himself and Eddy, saying he had just left a cheap nightclub where they spent a couple of hours talking to women with whom he would be embarrassed to be seen in daylight. Eddy's friend was appalled by the company Eddy chose. "As soon as we walked in, I asked him to leave and go home. He refused. I ended up leaving," he said.

"It is possible he is choosing company and a place that reflects his inner self. I am his public self, the one that he presents to the world," I said.

The following morning, I said to Eddy, "You like it rough and cheap too."

"What do you mean?" he said.

"…"

It was my turn to remain silent. I didn't disclose what his friend told me. I wanted to protect the information source.

A month later, on another late evening, things came to a head. A woman called requesting to speak with Eddy. I asked for her name. She gave me her first name and told me she was in New York, meeting him the next day in Paris. In mid-sentence, she stopped herself, possibly realizing that she hadn't reached the office with the time difference between New York and Paris, and asked, "To whom am I talking?"

"His wife!"

"I'm sorry. I'm so sorry. I didn't know he was married," the caller mumbled without attempting to cover up the scenario.

"He is and we have a daughter."

She hung up.

As soon as Eddy walked in, I blasted him about his sexual betrayals and told him, "Enough."

He said, "Probably a drunk. You're going to believe her?"

"She didn't sound drunk," I stormed. "And you gave her our home number."

"Exactly–because there is nothing going on."

"Enough! You've got to stop. I've had it."

"You're fussing over peccadillos," he said with entitlement.

He continued and said more than once, staring at me into my eyes, wanting to convey his intended message, "These are bimbos. You are my wife."

"I don't want to be the wife of a husband who has bimbos. How come you hang out with them as with men who call you *magouille*?"

"I'm a slut."

"..."

80

PARIS, 1981

Evidence cracking the foundation of my marriage was piling up. After each discovery, I bawled inward and became an expert at soundless shrieking so no one would hear my pain. I wanted to save face, to preserve my energy.

Most of all, I wanted two children who would be full siblings and so I would stay with Eddy until I claimed my second "I owe you"—another child. After the birth of my second child, I would divorce him. Then I would leave and take my two children with me.

Divorce would remain a mental decision until then.

All I could do for now was hold my breath and be patient for a bit longer.

81

NEW YORK, SUMMER 1981

In the summer of 1981, I moved my medical consultations from Europe to the United States. A friend of ours recommended an obstetrics group in New York City. I followed their treatment.

During a family vacation to Bermuda a few weeks later, I became aware that I might be pregnant.

Back in New York, my obstetrician confirmed it, "You are pregnant."

"Are you sure?" I said, with tears rolling down my cheeks.

"I am," he said, nodding.

My first thought was to give him a hug, but I shied away. I felt pure joy when I found out that I was expecting another child. It was exactly what I wanted.

My uterus had roared, but it pounded an unbridled beat. Within a few days, I started having mild contractions. My obstetrician classified my pregnancy as high-risk and determined that traveling was medically contraindicated. I had to remain at my home in New York for an unspecified duration.

Given the circumstances, my eight-year-old Joelle would return to Paris with Eddy and Mazelle to continue her schooling and daily routine. I would join them as soon as possible.

On the day they left, with sadness in my heart seeing Joelle leave, I called Marie, my mother's best friend, seeking solace. She had moved to Montreal, Canada, to live with her daughter and her family after her husband had passed away. When she heard the latest news, she exclaimed, "You're pregnant and alone in New York? I'm coming."

Marie arrived in New York two days later. Exuding positive energy, she was a delight to be around. I felt lucky to have someone to share my early pregnancy journey with.

Was I seeking a substitute for Mom? Was I organizing myself without Eddy? Most likely both.

The evening Marie arrived, she poured herself a drink, sat on the living room floor, leaned against the couch, stretched her legs under the glass coffee table, and started munching some pistachios.

I stood by the floor-to-ceiling window and looked at the glittering New York evening lights, with my back to her, and said, "I'm planning to leave Eddy."

"What? What is this then?" she said, pointing at my belly.

"I wanted to have two children—full siblings—from the same father before asking for a divorce."

"How come you want to divorce him?"

"His divergent moral values and sexual promiscuity."

"What would your parents have said if they were alive?"

The question surprised me, though not entirely from an Egyptian traditional perspective. "My parents would ensure that I thought through my decision and then they would applaud me."

Marie laughed out loud.

"My mother would refrain from saying, 'I told you so.' But her facial expression would say, 'What took you so long?'"

"And your father?" she asked.

"Dad would say, 'I let you have your own experience.'"

Marie chuckled.

I sighed and answered, "I represent a complex minority: female, only child, Copt Catholic, moved from Egypt to Switzerland with my parents, then from Switzerland to Lebanon after my marriage, then from Lebanon to the United States, back to Lebanon, then France, and finally to the United States from France, where I want to divorce my successful, affluent husband during pregnancy while planning to go to college and live with my daughter on my own in New York."

Marie chuckled some more, taking a sip of her drink, with a loud, "Cheers."

"Such a situation would make most people rattle," I said.

"Yes! It would," she said, jiggling her drink, forgetting the seriousness of the topic and lifting her glass with an even louder, roaring, "Cheers!"

82

NEW YORK, END OF OCTOBER 1981

At the follow-up visit, my obstetricians recommended I stay at home and exert no effort or risk a miscarriage. Medical visits were my only outings. I read or listened to music the rest of the time and maintained daily calls with Joelle in Paris. Eddy and I planned she would visit me on every vacation. Luckily the French school calendar was filled with breaks.

Joelle came to New York for the mid-semester break. The afternoon she arrived, she whispered to me, "Mom, I have something to tell you."

"Yes, sweetie."

"I went for lunch with Dad, at the restaurant where you often went together."

"Yes."

"There was someone with him. A woman, loud. I didn't like the way she spoke to Dad. She made me feel uncomfortable. I told Dad I wanted to go home."

"Sweetie, sorry, it happened. You can control your behavior, not that of others."

I figured out who the woman was, and I told Eddy, "Be mindful of who you take for lunch with Joelle. No need to make her feel uncomfortable."

There was no need to elaborate further. I could visualize the outing. Her report was informative. It gave me both insight and guidelines.

Marie and I did our best to entertain Joelle. I read to her. We played board games. Joelle and Marie went out in the afternoons and returned home with many tales. Joelle and I were very close. I was twenty-eight when I had her and could do cartwheels when I took her to the park.

I felt deeply saddened to see Joelle return to Paris, feeling circumstances were taxing her too much. I hugged her and said, "Sweetie. I will do my best to join you in a few weeks. If doctors require me to stay in New York, in the interim, I promise your Dad will fly you to New York at every break to be with me."

"Are you sure, Mom?"

"I'm positive," I said, hugging her tightly and trying to refrain from crying.

83

NEW YORK, NOVEMBER 1981

The week Joelle returned to Paris, I went for my scheduled amniocentesis, a prenatal test for women over thirty-five to assess the genetic and chromosomal development of the fetus at sixteen to twenty gestational weeks. The doctor explained the procedure for extracting a sample of amniotic fluid under ultrasound guidance. When I saw the giant needle the doctor held in her right hand, ready to jab my belly, I gripped the sides of the bed, trying not to scream.

The sonogram was the day's crowning event. Seeing my in-utero baby moving and hearing the heartbeats for the first time highlighted my unforgettable experience. At the end of the procedures, the doctor asked me if I wanted to know the gender of my baby. I said, "Yes."

"We will call you as soon as we have the results in about two weeks."

God, please, may the baby be a girl, so that the sisters can bond despite the age difference.

Two weeks later, the doctor called me, "All the results are within the normal range. Do you still wish to know the gender of your baby?"

"Yes!"

"It's a girl."

"I'm so happy. Thank you."

I was thrilled to have a daughter. Two sisters would be closer given the age difference.

God, thank you. You heard my prayer.

When she heard me hang up, Marie peered behind my bedroom door with a beaming smile. "*Hein?*"

"It's a girl."

"A girl ... it's a girl," she repeated with an air of consternation replacing her smile.

"Yes."

"You're going to have a collection of girls (*banat*)!"

"What do you mean? "

"St. Anthony let me down for the first time."

"St. Anthony has nothing to do with this. Men have the XY gender deter-mining factor," I said and swiveled myself out of the room.

84

NEW YORK, DECEMBER 1981

Week after week, my pregnancy became more complex. Mild contractions during the day increased in the evening, stressing me out. My medical team mandated home bed rest as much as possible.

Joelle came back to New York for Thanksgiving. We celebrated *en famille*, happy to be together for that holiday. I had a pinch in my heart seeing her fly back to Paris with her father—though we both knew she would return to New York three weeks later for the Christmas vacation.

The contractions increased to moderate by early December and the home rest prescription to total bed rest. Despite my staying in bed, except for showering and restroom breaks, the contractions intensified as the days went by. Hospitalization loomed on the horizon. I prepared for it mentally.

Despite my medical condition, I was concerned about my physical appearance. "Are you sure you want to cut your hair?" Jacqueline, my hairdresser, asked.

"I must cut it. Long hair would be challenging to maintain in a hospital," I said, twirling my hair with my fingers."

"You wore it long all your life," she said.

"Please go ahead," I said, closing my eyes not to see my long, light brown highlighted hair become short and medium brown, my natural color.

"Done," she said.

I took a quick look at my reflection in the mirror she handed me and said, "Thank you."

The moment I laid my head on the pillow that night, I began to weep, combing my short hair with my fingers. Anxiety-provoking thoughts about my tenuous pregnancy and my distance from Joelle brought tears to my eyes.

85

NEW YORK, CHRISTMAS 1981

By Winter Break 1981, mild contractions had escalated to intense, putting me at risk of miscarriage. I spent my mornings with Joelle. Marie, who had kindly extended her stay, took her out in the afternoons. Marie had the talent of infusing our everyday life with humor and lightness, dissipating the anxiety I was experiencing,

Christmas Day was family-oriented. Every now and then, Eddy joined us and went back to his calls and news. One late afternoon, he took a few minutes from business to tell me, "This apartment is too small with the upcoming baby. We need to check if the neighbor is willing to sell. I'll get in touch with him."

"Sounds good," I said, somewhat surprised, as he turned around and went back to his calls.

Joelle, Marie, and I spent New Year's Eve at home. Eddy left us at 11 p.m. to attend a party hosted by a business acquaintance who lived in the same building.

Contractions persisted at an intense level. Hospitalization was mandated on January 3, 1982. I declined taking an ambulance, concerned that Joelle would be alarmed. As I stepped out of the apartment with Marie, I hugged Joelle and told her, "I must go to the hospital overnight to check how your sister is doing. You stay with Dad. I'll see you soon, very soon. I love you."

Against medical advice, I walked to the elevator and out of the building with Marie. A yellow cab took us to the medical center where my attending physician had already called in my admission. As soon as I arrived, I was taken to a private room on a stretcher. A nurse and a resident greeted me on the obstetrics floor. The nurse handed me a drab hospital gown, saying, "Please put this on." Both immediately hooked an intravenous to my left arm (the one with the salient vein), dispensing ritodrine hydrochloride to diminish premature contractions, and told me, "Call us if you need anything."

I nodded, holding my breath. My questions would have to wait until the next day's meeting with the attending physician. During the night, I prayed for the well-being of my in-utero baby and kept faith.

In the morning, Joelle came to see me with Marie. "I'll see you in Paris as soon as they discharge me. I hope soon, very soon," I told her as we exchanged prolonged hugs.

Eddy and Joelle flew back to Paris later that day.

From that moment onward, Eddy made himself scarce. He became more hushed and absent than ever. Joelle headed back to her French lycée. My pregnancy became complicated. Hospitalization, initially intended to be short-term, requiring no family relocation, was extended. Marie stayed with me. And I met Alan.

86

NEW YORK, JANUARY 1982

As I lay in my inpatient hospital bed with an IV drip, praying and hoping my twenty-four-gestational-week daughter would make it to full-term, little did I know my life was about to pivot 180 degrees. Time and place escorted a passionate encounter to my bedside.

He appeared in my room, seemingly out of nowhere, with bursting energy and a radiant smile spread across his face. Suddenly, my world turned upside down. He dazzled me.

What a smile! I am attracted to his smile.

"Hi, I'm Dr. Alan. I reviewed your chart and would like to ask you a few questions."

Dr. Alan's interest in my medical condition prompted us to speak. "I am currently researching women who have difficulty conceiving and carrying a pregnancy to term," he said.

"Please sit down," I said.

"Thank you."

Dr. Alan explained my pregnancy's difficulties in a clear, detailed manner. I listened attentively, thinking *theory is one thing, and experience is another.* What he said was insightful. It helped me understand what was happening in my growing uterus and what I could do to support it.

Despite the understanding I gained, once I was on my own, intense premature contractions raised my concerns. Twenty-four hours bedridden in a hospital room were long. My mind churned anxiety-provoking thoughts.

I hope I'll make it. I will make it. Will I make it?

Shortly after, Dr. Alan became my primary medical source of information and encouragement. His kindness and investment in my labor of love touched my heart. I felt comforted when I saw him and encouraged when he said, "Stay positive. Follow the medical regimen." The medical team is doing everything possible to protect your pregnancy to full term."

"I know," I said with a sigh of relief.

"We will do everything possible for you to leave the hospital with a new-born in your arms," Alan said.

"Thank you. That's all I want, along with being reunited with Joelle."

In addition to the outstanding medical care I received, I also created a natural preventative approach that I hoped would diminish contractions and ensure the success of my pregnancy. The process empowered me. My stance shifted from passive and bedridden to active, devising solutions and fighting for my in-utero daughter's survival.

Whenever I felt contractions coming on, I visualized myself holding my infant daughter and singing lullabies to her. I listened to pre-selected upbeat songs while humming along and following the beat—sometimes swaying in my bed or wiggling my feet, which transported me to a different place and time. Positive thinking and deep breathing helped me feel energy coursing through my body, allowing me to relax and trust that I would carry my unborn daughter to term.

On calmer days, in between contractions, I reread Jean-Paul Sartre's *L'être et le Néant*, Pirandello's *Six Characters in Search of an Author*, and Beckett's *Waiting for Godot*. Reading allowed me to focus on other scenarios.

The medical staff nodded to my natural approach. No one questioned it. As an inpatient, I had exceptional medical attention. They did their utmost to ensure that I reached full term. Residents and interns visited my room several times a day to make sure that my soon-to-be-born daughter didn't need a preventative upward push to circumvent a contraction or, worse, a miscarriage.

Despite the attentive medical care and natural approach, my pregnancy required six emergency room (ER) visits, where I had to fast if I needed to be rushed to the operating room (OR). The ER tested my resilience and hunger as I sat with an IV in one arm, wired to monitors measuring vital signs, and hearing my in-utero daughter's heartbeat (over 150 beats per minute) while fasting.

When I found myself in these situations, I relied on a dear friend, Bob, who shared my love of contemporary music. We devised a plan. I'd call him, he'd come to the ER pretending to be my husband (Eddy had not been there) and hug me while slipping a sesame bagel (a favorite comfort food) under the bed sheet. I can still see his beaming smile the first time he came in. "They believed me," he said with roaring laughter. "He really has never been here?"

"Never," I said.

"Are you kidding me?" he said.

"No."

"He's sick. How are you handling it?"

"He won't be my husband for long."

"What?" he shouted, getting the medical staff's attention.

"Let's discuss this another time."

I managed to keep my composure while a nurse checked the monitors connected to me and a resident examined me.

As soon as they were done, I snatched a piece of bagel, pretended to yawn, and put it in my mouth. I gulped it down without moving my mouth or choking on it (I hadn't had any water either), or worse, being seen by the hovering medical staff. Each step was punctuated by loud, hard laughter—not advisable for someone lying in an ER bed hooked up to a bunch of monitors.

When Bob whispered, "How is the bagel?" I burst out laughing and almost choked.

"You're keeping your spirits high. That's great," said a nurse on duty.

Appreciative of the medical staff's diligent and dedicated care, and not wanting to complicate my pregnancy further, I handed the rest of the bagel to Bob who nodded in agreement.

Years later, a doctor told me, "If you were pregnant today, you would have had a miscarriage. In 1982, health insurance was humane. Authorization for medical services did not require complex administrative red tape from generally non-medical personnel. Since then, it has drastically restricted coverage and diminished services, while significantly increasing enrollment cost."

87

NEW YORK, FEBRUARY 1982

My universe in the hospital consisted of four people, one of whom was not yet fully formed. I was mainly focused on my daughter in Paris and my in-utero daughter. Marie and Dr. Alan formed my support group.

Every feasible school break, Joelle came to New York and then returned to Paris when school resumed. We spoke daily, often more than once. Maintaining close contact with her was essential. It wasn't enough, but it was the least disruptive thing I could do.

"I miss you," I said constantly.

Joelle would say, "I miss you too, Mom. I wish I were with you."

"Soon, sweetie, soon."

Multiple times a day, I caressed and held my belly and whispered to my unborn child, "I love you. Please be patient, wait for thirty-eight weeks."

During the February break, Joelle went with her father to Gstaad, instead of coming to New York. Winter skiing seemed an appealing option for the week vacation. Still, I accepted it reluctantly.

Most of all, I trusted my relationship with my unborn daughter and spoke with her openly. "Baby, be patient. Wait for the right time."

Marie was invaluable. She gave me the care and mothering I felt I needed then. Her smile and energy made my days brighter, lighter. Her uplifting support helped me carry my in-utero daughter to the predetermined Caesarean section date, the beaming light on my horizon.

As time went by, Dr. Alan's visits became the highlights of my days. He stuck his gleeful head in in the late afternoons or early evenings to say hello, and one day told me, "Please drop the 'Dr.' … call me Alan."

"Yes," I said, with some warmth in my heart. It seemed fine to me. We were in New York, much less formal than Paris. We also seemed to be the same age and saw each other every day, often more than once a day. Alan's intonation revealed a foreign heritage. Perhaps British? Not sure. I had my

French accent. Our respective accents created a communality.

"I am well impressed by your ability to cope while being hospitalized. Is your husband also here in New York with you?" asked Alan.

"No, he's currently in Paris with our daughter Joelle and brings her over as much as possible."

"And what about Marie?"

"She is my Mom's best friend."

"I see. And what about your parents?"

"They have passed away."

"I'm so sorry. It must be tough, especially now."

Marie witnessed how much I cherished Dr. Alan's attention and said more than once, "Be careful."

"I am," was my answer.

88

NEW YORK, MARCH 1982

My room had become a haven where my pregnancy and relationship with Alan evolved. Energy sparked the minute he came in. We were both aware of the warmth between the two of us. It was hard to miss. Those were timeless hours—time outside of time. Our conversations became more intimate. We laughed. We shared our upbringing and stories.

Regretfully, my memory of our heartfelt conversations has faded away. Probably it has something to do with my circumstances exacerbating the emotions I felt each time we talked and shared our background histories. I only recall that Alan started calling me by my surname, as it is sometimes done in medical school. He also introjected a sentence here and there: "Nakhle, you need to learn to deal."

Deal with what? I was dealing with a lot.

Glimpses of early conversations stayed in mind.

"Have you been to Australia?" he asked.

"Not yet."

"It's paradise."

"Egypt is the same. Did you visit?"

Alan shook his head.

When I was alone, I gazed out my window overlooking Central Park and mapped out my future from that perspective. My two essential goals were to be able to live with Joelle in New York and to reach the minimum of twenty-six gestational weeks and one kilogram of weight that a preemie needs to survive. Every day, I prayed to God to help me achieve these goals.

I also hoped that Alan and I could continue our relationship beyond the hospital. Keeping these goals in mind kept me motivated and energized. I trusted I would handle everything—even though I hadn't figured out the details.

Positive thinking filled my heart with joy. It had been a long time since I had felt this way. For the first time, I believed I could create my own life, away from the chaos I had known for so long and wanted to flee. While I didn't know yet what I had "to deal with," I was willing to give Alan a chance.

Family and friends became aware of my condition within a few days of being hospitalized. They called me, came to see me. My room turned into a lively social salon in the afternoon. People walking down the hallway overheard our conversations and waves of laughter.

Marco, a childhood friend from Cairo who was living near the hospital, became a regular visitor. He knew my parents, my home, my friends. Having met during our early teens, we maintained a friendship over the years, which was solidified when I started visiting New York regularly.

A talented raconteur, Marco enjoyed reminiscing about episodes from our teenage years. His favorite story was my sweet sixteen, my last birthday party in Cairo. Even though my parents were not supposed to attend, Dad became the center of attention by offering one drink to those who would shake hands with him and chat for a bit (in Egypt, the adults handled alcohol with teenagers at their discretion). Marco recalled, "I got myself to walk to your father. We chatted and sipped a drink together."

Bobby came to see me at the hospital. Seeing each other was magnetic. My heart pounded. His eyes said it all. Our marital status prevented us from expressing ourselves, though this time he said, "In the heart, nothing has changed."

"No, nothing has changed," I heard myself echoing, smiling and hugging him tighter.

He protruded his belly to lighten the situation—gourmet food had affected his once-athletic stature—and we took a picture comparing our bellies and laughing.

Business brought Eddy to New York from time to time. He stopped by with Joelle or chatted about her when school or a short trip prevented her from traveling with him. The first time he visited me, I handed him my passport, saying, "My US visa is about to expire. I have the letter from my physician stating that my medical condition warrants hospitalization till the baby is born. I don't want to become an alien."

"Don't worry. Visa extension for medical reasons is a routine matter. I will do it."

A couple of weeks later, when Eddy came to see me, he said "We're renting the apartment next door. We'll buy it later."

"Are you serious?"

"Yes."

"Isn't it going to hike the price, if we want to buy it?"

"We'll deal with it then."

"Ok," I said, thinking that there were no available funds to buy it.

Then I reminded him, "What's happening with my visa?"

Eddy said, "Don't worry. It is being done. Everything is OK," and continued by making jokes about the IV, the hospital gown, or how many weeks until my due date (he wouldn't remember from one visit to the next).

89

NEW YORK, MID-APRIL 1982

The number of inpatient days added up to ninety. Delivery was finally on the horizon. A Caesarean section date had been set for the thirty-eighth gestation week. Joelle and Eddy arrived in New York on the Friday before the surgery. Easter break was nearing in France. Upon her arrival, Joelle came to see me at the hospital with Marie. During her visit, we discussed various plans for my return home. I don't remember if Eddy came to see me on that day.

As usual, Alan came to spend time with me the night before the Caesarean section. He comforted me, telling me, "Everything will be fine. Next, I will see you with your daughter in your arms."

Throughout the night, medical and nursing staff visited my room, encouraging me. The goodbyes, the jokes, the hugs, and the cheers were both heartwarming and wrenching. I was looking forward to going home but was somewhat apprehensive about leaving my room, my cocoon, a womb of sorts. The medical and nursing staff were about to be severed from my life after playing a vital role in helping me carry my pregnancy to full-term. I had formed a positive connection with them over the course of my ultimately one-hundred-day hospital stay. I expressed my gratitude and thanked them for their exceptional care.

A historic blizzard in New York marked Sabrina's birth. Snow battered the city all night, covering it in a white coat like that of the hospital's staff. Snow fell until dawn.

Before the Caesarean section, the surgeon checked in with me early in the morning. A nurse wheeled me to the operating room after he left. An anesthesiologist greeted me and explained the procedure. I lost consciousness within seconds.

Upon regaining awareness, I heard the pediatrician telling me that my baby girl was fine, ready to meet her mother. My head turned toward his voice. It was 10:40 a.m. on the wall clock. The pediatrician handed me my newborn daughter wrapped in a cloth bundle. Sabrina seemed like the obvious first name for her. I liked the name. It was joyful and its starting phoneme, *Sabr* (patience in Arabic), was fitting given the one hundred days spent in the hospital.

God, what an unforgettable bliss when I saw her for the first time. She was part of me for nine months. Now she was her own person. The IV was removed. I could hold Sabrina with both arms, one behind her head, one behind her back, and hug her tenderly. I looked at her and whispered, "Sabrina, I love you. It's you, in a hurry to be born. We made it." I whispered again, this time behind her ears, "We made it. I love you. I'm blessed."

When the attending surgeon came to see me after the Caesarean section, I asked to breastfeed my daughter and heard the same answer my obstetrician in Lebanon had given me nine years earlier. In short, he said, "No way." He also added, "After what you have gone through, you also want to breastfeed her? Enough trouble for you. No breastfeeding."

Soon after, Alan came by to see me in the recovery room and told me, "You made it. Congratulations!"

"I think we all did. It took the entire floor with the three shifts, the emergency room, Joelle, Marie, and you. I wouldn't have done it without you."

"You did it all. It would be best if you relax and sleep now. You just had surgery."

"See you tomorrow."

Where is her father?

In the afternoon, I savored the joy of holding Sabrina in my arms. Ecstatic, I rocked her softly. My heart swelled with gratitude. I had Sabrina against all odds after nine years.

Joelle came with Marie and welcomed her sister with an open heart. I sometimes wondered if she felt relieved at no longer being the only daughter.

Eddy came into my room with Marco. He offered us big smiles and pleasantries. Seeing Sabrina, he expressed gratitude for her well-being and left for another meeting. Afterward, Marco shook his head, saying, "Eddy asked me to accompany him to a preliminary business meeting instead of heading to the hospital as agreed. He followed me when I said I am going to see Djenane and meet Sabrina."

"That's Eddy," I said.

I was not surprised. It was déjà vu all over again. Eddy replicated the scenario he used when Joelle was born. His loss. I was grateful for his contribution to the procreation of my two daughters, the way I wanted them to be full sisters. My decision. My wish.

90

NEW YORK, LATE APRIL 1982

Five days later, I was ready to go home. My hospital discharge couldn't come soon enough. Marie and Joelle came to pick me up. With teary eyes, but chin up, I was wheeled out of my room by a nurse to the hospital lobby. Holding my newborn daughter's head against my heart with my left arm and clasping my older daughter's left hand tightly with my right arm, I exited, my legs slightly wobbly, the hospital's main entrance for the first time in one hundred days.

The street noise and traffic were louder than I remembered. It felt disquieting. I had experienced calm in my 240-square-foot hospital room and felt anxious on a New York City avenue.

My daughters and I were on a whole new path. Location, language, culture, and background were all different. Life as we knew it had changed. The months of confinement and immobility had paradoxically freed me of marital ties, business constraints, and social obligations. Motherhood was accomplished. Mothering was beginning. A thrilling romance was also brightening the horizon.

My two daughters were with me. Life was good. New York, here we come.

Being discharged from the hospital was unsettling. So much had happened outward and inward in the last one hundred days. I was a different woman—a woman who overcame physical and psychological change.

I was the ecstatic mother of two daughters. Joy filled my heart and mind. Administrative chores and flickering images of Alan kept me busy until both girls fell asleep. Then anxiety-provoking thoughts popped up: *I won't see him tonight.*

Alan and I wanted to deepen our relationship, but we hadn't scheduled a date to see each other outside of the hospital. I called him right away, bursting with "I miss you."

"I miss you too."

"When can we see each other?"

"When would you like?"

"This evening, right now, but I will defer my wish to a week from today, dinner, my place. I want the girls and myself to adjust to the new family setting."

With a sigh of relief, I plopped on the living room couch and rested my head on the back cushion to think and plan. I felt confident that I could balance mothering, return to school, and start a relationship. Everything would be done at my own time and pace. The key was to do it right, one step at a time. Priority number one was to ensure my daughters' needs were met.

Eddy came home late that night. "We'll have the key to the apartment next door at the beginning of June."

"Sounds good. But how will it work?'

"It's only five steps away. No big deal. The day we buy it we will decide."

"Not the same apartment."

"Five steps away."

Two days later Eddy was off to somewhere.

91

NEW YORK, END OF APRIL 1982

I had many important things to deal with, starting with finding a school for Joelle in New York. I wanted her to be next to me and had no intention of sending her back to Paris. A friend of mine introduced me to a bilingual English-French school in New York City that was like her Parisian lycée. Joelle was interviewed and accepted right away during spring break. She worked diligently and achieved excellent scores in every subject. A few days after school resumed, she told me smiling, "I like my teachers and classmates."

"That's wonderful," I said.

Sabrina, an engaging newborn with big brown eyes and dark brown hair, followed her feeding and sleeping schedule like a pro. Cuddling her and kissing her shoulder, I basked in her heartwarming grin with immense joy in my heart. She emanated Johnson's baby lotion freshness. I often asked her, "How come you were in such a rush to be born?" while tickling her back and making her giggle.

I decided to undergo the expense of employing a nanny, allowing me to focus on my work and complete my studies twenty years behind. I hired Letty, a nice Filipina woman, and trusted her to be there for Joelle and Sabrina. With time, they developed a deep fondness for her. Letty also took on the role of the trusted keyholder of the household. She knew our schedules, whereabouts, the day-to-day expenses.

Marie offered to stay with us for a bit longer. She knew of my infatuation with Alan but was wise enough not to impose her opinions on me. She would say again, "Be careful."

I wanted to show my gratitude, so I invited every hospital staff member who took care of me during the three shifts (day, evening, and night) to have lunch or dinner at my home. I dedicated a plaque in their honor, and each name was inscribed. The Medical Center hung the plaque between the elevators on the obstetrics floor.

In my first post-delivery appointment with my primary care physician, he recommended a healthy diet and physical activity. After receiving gallons of IV fluid over ninety-four days, my body gained forty pounds, making me look like the Michelin inflated balloon character. Within a few weeks, however, I began to shed the excess fluid weight and feel like myself again. Day by day, I evolved from a procreating mother to a romancing woman—a welcome change.

I researched college programs that would allow me to resume my studies. Few offered that possibility. New York University was the closest and the most appealing to me. I intended to go check it out in person to know it better.

92

NEW YORK, EARLY MAY 1982

Alan's first visit a week later felt awkward. We were both adjusting our interaction to the new circumstances and conditions. I was a married mother of two daughters. My status did not stop us from having a wonderful time together. I was delighted to see his radiant smile, the first characteristic I noticed about him.

From then on, Alan visited my home at least once a week. We were getting used to knowing each other at home. We spoke but were more reserved than at the hospital because of my personal circumstances. He was interested in knowing everything about me from the day I was born to the day we met. He continued calling me by my last name and started whispering, "my darling."

I felt visible. Alan looked at me with genuine interest when I spoke. We discovered facets of each other's personalities. His sense of humor was excellent. "Your accent imitations are hilarious," I said, laughing out loud.

"I am happy to see you giggling," he said.

Joelle noticed it. As I put her to bed, she asked me, "You look happy, Mom?" reminding me of Dad's verbal style.

"Yes, sweetie. I am happy and grateful that you and your sister are with me here in New York." The best part was that I truly felt that way.

That evening Alan shared, "I was interested in researching medical conditions like yours, but most of all, I wanted to know this woman—You—who intrigued me and fascinated me, a woman who managed so well on her own."

Our personal exchange led him to address our future, a topic still premature for me. I needed to pause in between life battles. I wanted to know Alan, to be happy, to enjoy being with him—without having the pressure of making a decision, another rushed decision.

Alan had a different pace. He was determined. He sent me not-so-subtle hints through famous philosophers, such as Socrates. "The unexamined life is not worth living," he quoted. Then he asked, "When did you examine yours last?"

"I'm not sure. Was it this morning or yesterday?" I responded.

Soon enough, Alan weaved in our conversation, "I have a serious, committed, long-term relationship in mind that would include your two daughters." Keen to know my intention regarding our relationship, Alan repeated, "I am committed to our relationship."

A life-changing decision and a serious commitment were too soon, way too soon for me. I paused, took a deep breath, and said, "My daughters are my top priorities. While I want to be with you, my marriage will not end today or because of you."

"Understood," he said. "It's your marriage that is in the way, not your daughters."

"Can I give you something to drink?" I asked, wanting to shift topics.

Alan shook his head and said, "I'll help you. What would you like to drink?"

"Diet Coke."

"Diet Coke?"

"Yes. Help yourself. You'll find everything we have on the kitchen counter."

Alan came back with my soda and a large tumbler full to the brim with two ice cubes. I didn't give a second thought to what he was drinking. Our togetherness mattered more than the content of his glass on that evening.

While my relationship with Alan was heading in the right direction, I was concerned about its unexpected speed. Had I met another rushed man when I wasn't ready to be rushed?

Our conversation triggered some anxiety, rekindling my old smoking habit. Smoking had given me the illusion of puffing my worries away during my baccalaureate year at age fifteen, before giving it up twice after finding out I was pregnant.

The following week, my daughters and I celebrated our first Mother's Day. Together, we formed a loving trio. Life had taken on a smooth rhythm since I left the hospital. I savored the early phase of my romance, enjoying in some ways, and tiptoeing in other ways, into my unfolding New York life.

NEW YORK, LATE MAY 1982

Week by week, Alan and I felt closer to each other. One evening, he sang Jennifer Holliday's hit song "And I Am Telling You I'm Not Going," and, looking at me in the eyes, he added, "And I am telling you, I love you."

I melted and said, "I love you too," and got startled. Being ready to have my first romantic relationship was unnerving.

I am still married, I kept repeating.

For the past eighteen years, I had been faithful to Eddy despite his sexual indiscretions, committed to my marriage, and respected it. My dear Bobby courted me, and I found it hard to resist him. I held myself back. Mirroring Eddy's behavior was not my style. Meeting someone and falling in love unexpectedly was another story—my story.

I was a woman in love. That I was.

Who wouldn't fall head over heels in love with such a man? Every second we spent together brought us joy. I only wished not to wake up from such a dream reality. We hugged and kissed (when my daughters were asleep). It stopped there. We didn't become intimate yet. My body was still recovering from the seismic shocks of the complicated pregnancy and surgery. As a physician and medical researcher, Alan understood my condition.

My marriage had fallen apart. Meeting Alan brought it to a point of no return. Still, I wouldn't end my marriage and affect my daughters' lives because I met Alan. I would end my marriage because I no longer wanted to be married to Eddy.

Alan showed me what a meaningful relationship could be. Despite my intensifying feelings for Alan, I wasn't ready for a serious commitment. I had gotten engaged at eighteen and married at twenty. And I was still married! A marriage proposal would not sweep me off my feet. I was in the "I'm trying to get out of marriage" mode—not in the "I want to remarry" one. I wanted to have a relationship that could lead to a commitment—but not tie the knot—not that soon. Again!

I needed to prepare myself and my daughters for a life-changing decision before jumping into one and dragging them on a bumpy road. Joelle enjoyed an intact family up to the age of nine. Sabrina needed a father in reality—not in fantasy. I didn't want to be a mother who deprived her daughters of growing up with their father. As my spiritual counselor planted in my head, I wanted to be the mother they would have chosen.

Was I feeling guilty about Eddy? Not an iota. Is it possible that I empathized with Eddy's sexual indiscretions? Not an iota either. His random quickies with *demimondaine*s, as they say in French, differed greatly from developing a loving relationship.

I wanted to be responsible toward my daughters. Do the very best I could and tell them so—meaning it, feeling it.

Where was Eddy? I don't remember if he even returned to New York during those first three months. When he reappeared one day at home, we discussed logistics. He wanted the girls and me to go back to Paris. "Paris is your home," he said.

"Was. I'm starting a new life in New York."

"Ok, you just had a baby. Let's see. It must be a postpartum mood or something."

"Nothing would make me go back to live in Paris," I said, knowing I was building a life in New York.

94

NEW YORK, JUNE 1982

Where is my passport?

Clapping my hands over my mouth, I jumped off my seat and ran through the apartment, searching for it. After a brief blank, I remembered I had given it to Eddy for my US visa extension. Since then, Eddy had given me elusive responses to my visa status questions. I had stopped asking about it close to my upcoming Caesarean section, my primary preoccupation.

How would I stay in the United States if I don't have a visa?

Searching everywhere for my passport, I finally found it in the living room's desk drawer and the unopened letter from my medical team supporting my visa extension request. I flipped through it page by page and discovered my visa had expired. My status has changed from legal to illegal visitor! My passport still had a valid US visa when I handed it to Eddy at the hospital.

Furious, I called Eddy. "There is no limit to your irresponsibility."

"What are you talking about?"

"I gave you my passport on time. I had a solid, irrefutable argument and a legal status. All it needed was an extension. Now it's a mess."

"Don't worry. You make a huge deal out of molehills. I will have it fixed. I will get an immigration lawyer. He will fix it."

"You better … I can't trust you even with my visa."

"I have a million things on my mind. It escaped me. It will be done."

"Escaped you?"

The carefree tone of his voice ignited my tirade. "My passport wasn't a priority for you," I started, and only stopped when I found myself out of breath. "You better fix it!" I yelled from the top of my lungs.

Procrastination was Eddy's way of handling non-business-related issues. He would label them "for later" and then forget about them. When reminded, he would find costly solutions rather than address issues efficiently.

"Can you imagine?" I said to Marie.

Seeing me so upset, she suggested an exercise class and added, "Don't worry. Everything will be OK."

The next day Eddy called me. "We got the keys to the apartment next door. No need to be squeezed all together."

"Great. But we may never use it, if I can't renew my visa."

"I also found an immigration lawyer. He'll be in touch soon."

As soon as we hung up, a lawyer contacted me to meet with me prior to setting up an appointment with the US immigration authorities, if the attending physician provided an updated letter and the hospital gave copies of my records substantiating my extended stay.

I walked through a lengthy hallway with white walls and light beige wall-to-wall carpeting to meet the lawyer. He welcomed me at the door of his office overlooking the river and motioned for me to sit in an armchair across from his sizeable desk.

The lawyer and I went over the critical issues of my application for visa renewal. Based on his review of my file, the lawyer forewarned me, "The US immigration will probably deport you. It would be better not to argue with them or contest their decision. It would reduce your chances of ever returning to the United States."

I abstained from retorting, "I know better than to jeopardize my status." Instead, I stressed a few points. "I did not plan to extend my stay; my medical condition demanded it. Presently, US Immigration grants citizenship to a child born in the United States; the mother of a US citizen is unlikely to be deported but likely to be considered for a green card."

The lawyer restated the deportation line using his usual glum tone, probably trying to justify his exorbitant retainer fee, and told me before parting, "Please bring your older daughter with you to the appointment with Immigration."

The word deportation struck a deep chord with me. Sixteen years later, I faced a similar circumstance for trusting and relying on someone else for a matter important to me.

95

NEW YORK, MID-JUNE 1982

Joelle and I met the lawyer at the Federal Plaza in downtown Manhattan. We entered a busy building and walked into an office buzzing with activity. My daughter knew not to speak even when spoken to without looking at me and first getting verbal or nonverbal approval.

A clerk led us to the cubicle of a tall, skinny immigration officer. Wearing a white shirt billowing over his belt and rimless spectacles at the tip of his nose, he stood halfway up and gestured for us to sit down. His name was not on his office door nor on his desk. He asked for a few minutes to review the last letter in the file.

I froze.

Are we going to be on the first plane back to Paris?

My heart pounded faster; my face must have turned white. I clenched my hands over my crossed knee to give myself some countenance. I exerted all effort not to clasp and unclasp my hands on my lap and cross and uncross my legs way too often.

I hope I'm not grimacing. I'm trying to smile.

Right then, I looked up and saw the picture of President Reagan hanging on the wall. His benevolent smile comforted me.

The officer raised his head, looked at me, and said, "I have reviewed your file," pointing at it and then running his index finger through the five-inch-thick document (perhaps showing how much work my file had taken from him). Without pausing, he said, "Lift your right hand and swear to say the truth and nothing but the truth."

I said, "I do."

Silence prevailed.

Joelle looked at me; I smiled at her to comfort her and make her feel we were OK. The lawyer gazed at me with a warning in his eyes. I looked at my medical file and then at the officer.

The officer looked back and said with a firm voice, "Have you ever been a communist?"

In total disbelief, I said, "No."

Then he turned his head toward my nine-year-old daughter and said, "Have you ever been married?"

She looked at me, puzzled. I nodded for her to answer. She said, "No."

Then the officer looked at both of us, smiled, and said, "Welcome to the United States. We will mail you your green cards." He stood up and shook our hands goodbye.

I was elated. What I just heard was amazing. I think I mumbled, "Thank you." The immigration officer had just approved us for a green card. The outcome of the meeting met my highest expectations.

This officer and the lady at the morgue in Paris are two nameless, faceless, yet unforgettable individuals for whom I harbor everlasting gratitude. Both have had a profound impact on my life. As with the lady at that crucial moment, I regretted not thanking the immigration officer effusively or giving him a hug. I consoled myself by thinking it might have been inappropriate.

I didn't hold myself back with the lawyer. "Deportation, you said?" I smirked. Then I swiveled my heels, took my daughter by the hand, and walked away with a skip in my step. I didn't see the lawyer again.

On our way to her school, Joelle and I chatted about the landmark event we had just experienced. Soon we found ourselves in front of her school door. I hugged her in the lobby and headed back home.

The thought that I could live in New York invigorated me. Holding on to that positive energy, I knew I had an important phone call to make and needed to hurry back home. I dashed, lifting my head to look at the skyscrapers.

Thank you, God!

For the last few blocks, I sprinted in the streets, singing Jennifer Holliday's song, and adapting the lyrics to New York: *And I am telling you, New York, I'm not going. You're the best city I'll ever know. New York, I'm here to stay.*

"Hey lady, watch where you're walking," a taxicab driver yelled at me.

"I'm a New Yorker!" I yelled back from the top of my lungs.

I finally got home, exhausted, out of breath, rushed to the phone, misdialed, and redialed. After two rings, I shivered when I heard, "Hello."

96

NEW YORK, MID-JUNE 1982

A frisson ran through my spinal cord when I heard Alan's voice. "I have wonderful news. When can I see you?"

"I'm off this afternoon. I'll pick you up."

"I'll hop in a cab."

"Are you sure?"

"Joelle and I have been granted green cards."

"That's awesome. Let's celebrate."

"I'm rushing to the door."

Instead, I dashed into the shower. After giving my back to the powerful water flow, I let it run from head to toe, releasing scattered, residual energy from the morning. With my eyes closed, I drew hearts on the misty door and sang Jennifer Holliday's song again. I felt grateful for the morning outcome and, without skipping a beat, I sprayed shower gel all over my body, rinsed it, grabbed a towel, and dried myself as best I could. My feet were still wet. I dried them, one at a time, on the bath rug, then on the wall-to-wall carpet, and stared at myself in the mirror.

Glee shined all over my face. I wrapped myself in Jean Charles Brosseau's Ombre Rose, my perfume of choice, but didn't put any makeup on. Alan had seen me barefaced for one hundred days in the hospital and the last three months at home—no need to be made up at this point. What a relief!

I will be late.

I panted with impatience, sprinting down the hallway, and pressed the elevator button out of breath. It took forever to come and take me down. I stood with my back against the wall, which I often did, and bent my knees to do a core exercise. I heard inside my head Mom's voice saying, "Is this the time to exercise?"

Yes. The physical action displaced my attention from the impending one I was visualizing in my mind's eye. I walked into the elevator, the lobby, ran down the street, hailed a cab in the right direction of the traffic, and barely had the time to sit down while gasping the address to the driver as the taxi moved ahead.

Traffic was back-to-back. I was hyperventilating, drumming my fingers on the open window, tapping my feet on the floor.

"New York's traffic can feel so slow, when you're rushing," I said, unwinding.

"Oh yeah. It can," the driver said with emphasis.

We finally arrived. The taxi stopped in front of a modern building on the East Side of Manhattan. I paid the driver and hopped on the sidewalk without waiting for change, then sped into the building; I gave the doorman my name and told him where I was going. He ushered me to the elevator. I walked inside, pressed the floor button, and took a deep breath to regain composure, still panting on my way up.

Right away, my attention veered off to what would happen next.

Alan waited for me at the door of the elevator. I jumped at his neck. Without thinking further, I kissed him. We were in each other's arms, kissing and kissing and kissing again. He carried me to his apartment, still entwined and kissing, and lay me down on the couch.

"Would you like a cushion?" Alan whispered.

"No, I want you," I whispered back.

Alan smiled and kissed me again. In the curve of his shoulder, I cuddled my head and kissed him. Through my messed-up hair, I saw a glowing smile in the mirror on the side of the couch. I looked ecstatic, holding Alan in my arms. I wanted that image etched forever in my mind and retrievable on demand.

With my eyes closed I put my head back in the curve of Alan's shoulder and kissed him again as he carried me to his bedroom.

I visited a place I hadn't been to before and understood what the big deal was. It was as if Alan tuned into my vibration. There was a deep emotional connection between us, filled with longing and love.

When I came back to myself sometime later, Alan was in bed lying by my side, looking at me, his right arm bent with the elbow planted in a pillow and his head resting on the palm of his hand. I ran my fingers through my hair to fix myself up.

"You're beautiful," he said as a matter of fact.

"Thank you. I need to fix my hair."

"You look great. Let's enjoy this moment."

We clung to each other.

"I've been waiting for this from the first day I saw you," Alan said, flashing a soulful smile.

"So have I."

<hr>

Was I dreaming? Was Alan going to disappear?

He didn't. He was still there when I opened my eyes.

"Would you like a drink? I only have Stoli and water."

"Water will do."

"Water?"

Alan came back with a tall glass of water for me, and a sizable tumbler filled to the rim with only two ice cubes like the one he poured for himself at home. Tilting his head and lifting his elbow, Alan took a long swallow of the drink.

I stared in disbelief. "You have your vodka with water?"

"Rocks only. I'm off today."

"At this hour." *Is it the exception or the norm?*

"Let me show you around." Alan walked me through the one-bedroom apartment, wishing to familiarize me with his home, sipping his drink with gusto.

The layout and design of the apartment appealed to me. "Steel is an elegant color for a bachelor pad," I said.

"Thanks."

"Your apartment is sparse. It's making me consider lightening up the gazillion memory-filled knick-knacks displayed everywhere in mine."

Alan smiled and wrapped his arms around my waist, hugging me, and lifted me to embrace me with both arms. By the time we finished the five-minute tour, he had poured himself another drink.

97

NEW YORK, EARLY AUGUST 1982

Alan and I saw each other almost every day during the weeks ahead. Our relationship was steady. We frequently had brief meetings over a meal or coffee at midday when I visited him near the hospital between his weekly dinners at home.

We talked and talked. Alan shared his life story with me. He told me about Australia, his country of origin, and about completing medical school in Sydney. He married and divorced while studying before coming to the US for his residency and fellowship. A medical training center recruited him early based on his outstanding research in neonatal and complicated pregnancies and he became well-known and highly respected in his field.

Our interactions were always filled with high energy. I loved Alan's zest, his spunkiness. My daughters liked him too. Well, my older daughter did. My younger one was an infant.

Despite the intense attraction, Stoli gradually, but clearly, came between us. It was less intrusive when Alan came to see me or worked the next day. It had the upper hand when I visited Alan. On his days off, its presence was unmistakable. Alan sang along to the aria from Leoncavallo's *Pagliacci*, "Vesti La Giubba," often inebriated.

While Alan's condition differed from Eddy's, I was faced with another man who had a significant issue. Did life want me to learn to say, "No" and move on before I got pulled in and the issue became mine?

When I addressed his drinking, Alan gave me the same line Eddy had given me about his sexual escapades, the same line my father had given my mother about his extra drinking.

Alan said, "You're making a big deal out of a no big deal."

My response was, "I'm not. I need to feel secure you are in control of Stoli."

98

NEW YORK, MID-AUGUST 1982

Embarking on a relationship with a man who had an issue was not in my future—even if that man was Alan. My previous experience had immunized me against such a venture. Once was enough.

What did the alcohol reveal or blur?

"Are you sad?" I asked.

"I'm happy. I'm happy to be with you."

"How come you can't limit drinking to social drinking like I do?"

"What are you talking about? My drinking is social." As evidence, Alan showed me his hands. "Look. Solid as rocks."

"How about your brain? How is vodka affecting it?"

Alan's responses about excessive vodka consumption were unhelpful and emphasized the habit. I wanted him to be aware of his drinking instead of being in denial. Most of all, I needed to protect myself. As much as I loved and appreciated Alan, I knew I couldn't and wouldn't live with someone who overused alcohol, especially with my daughters around.

Alan must have been more aware of his drinking than he let on. When I least expected it, he said, "Please give me time. I need you to give me more time, I will control my drinking. I want to control it," and hugged me tightly.

Insight dawned in the following weeks. As I became more attentive to what needed to be done, I was determined to act. I would give Alan a year to manage Stoli, and then decide about our relationship.

Alan was surprisingly receptive to the idea and confident of his ability to control vodka. "Let's do it," he said.

"Let's," I said, captivated by his contagious self-confidence.

99

NEW YORK, LATE AUGUST 1982

While we were getting to know each other, it was time to think of Sabrina's baptism, since she was now nearly four months old. De facto, Alan was the godfather, and Joelle the godmother. As with my marriage, I chose the people closest to me. Eddy was flying somewhere around the globe. I might have told him in passing about the event.

I told the priest that Alan was a friend who had been near me while I was pregnant. In response to his question, "Is he Catholic?" I chose not to answer, "He is Jewish," and secured his acceptance as godfather, just lowering my lids.

The baptism took place at St. Patrick's Cathedral with the priest, godparents, Marie, Marco, and, of course, Sabrina and me. Afterward, we went home for hot chocolate and snacks, a low-key, intimate, heartfelt family celebration.

Life had settled into a comforting routine. It was time to address a pressing issue on my mind. I held the phone receiver and dialed the number scribbled on a piece of paper. "New York University? Please connect me with the undergraduate admission department."

It was time to pay back what I owed myself. What I promised my parents.

100

NEW YORK, END OF AUGUST 1982

I entered the Undergraduate Admissions Department at New York University, inspired by Marcel Proust, determined to make up for lost time. A representative greeted me and directed me to the Re-Entry Program at the School of Continuing Education at Shimkin Hall, a block away from Bobst Library.

The lounge of the Re-Entry Program was bustling with energy and activity. I presented myself and perused the brochures while waiting for the appointment. Each course seemed like an intellectual blast. I already knew the subjects I wanted to take the first semester: writing, logic, statistics. As I was daydreaming about my first day in class, someone called my name. I stood up. A smiling lady stood in front of her office and walked toward me.

The Re-Entry Program Director was courteous, soft-spoken. She welcomed me and made me feel comfortable. We chatted for a while. She was the first to boost my academic ego by saying, "You could earn credits for your life experience. The Re-Entry committee will likely recognize and validate it as expertise, provided each event is documented in a paper."

That was fantastic news. No wonder I love New York and the US. Only in the United States was I able to achieve my goals. I didn't have that opportunity anywhere else in the world. I tried at every major stop along my way.

The Director asked me to fill in the New York University Re-Entry Program application. The formal admission process required me to enroll in a seminar for students who had been away from school for some time and complete coursework, substituting for my BAC. I agreed with both. She then walked me to an assistant who gave me temporary student and library cards.

On this positive note, we scheduled a follow-up meeting three weeks after the beginning of the seminar. The Director shook my hand and said, "Welcome to New York University."

I left Shimkin Hall leaping in the street, humming a song from *Grease 2*, "Back to School Again," which popped into my mind.

At age thirty-seven, I felt young and exuberant going back to school, while at age eighteen and twenty, I thought I was too old. I shook my head. The time for self-judgment had passed. I looked at the sky, smiled, and said out loud, *Mom, Dad, I promised myself and you—I will complete my college education.*

"Girls, Mom is happy," I said to my daughters when I got home.

"What's making you happy, Mom?" Joelle asked.

"You and your sister."

"How did it go?" interrupted Marie, who had been visiting us for a few days.

As soon as I told her, she said, "Let's celebrate."

"I'm not sure I'm ready to celebrate. I need to start the program."

"Invite Alan first, of course, and the friends who have been there for you during your pregnancy," she said with a look of double entendre.

"Let's do it," I said.

I called Alan to let him know about my admission to NYU and find an evening where he was not on call to schedule the dinner.

"Excellent news," he said. "I have a surprise for you."

"What is it?"

"Did you hear me? I said, surprise."

"When will you tell me?"

"At the end of the party."

A few phone calls later, I had organized the party and decided the dinner menu with Marie, an efficient five-star chef. I hugged her and thanked her for her thoughtful suggestions.

"We are all set," she said.

"Great. Let's rejoice."

As I climbed into bed that night, thoughts crossed my mind. Had Eddy behaved differently, would I have started a relationship with Alan? Would I have enrolled at NYU?

Eddy's behavior gave me the comfort to organize a party with the man I loved, even though I was legally married. The thought humbled me. I was almost grateful for his behavior.

Did I need loud wake-up calls to take care of myself? My thinking and my life were changing. I would ask for separation first—my way out of a doomed marriage, a marriage only in appearance, but also in law—*I must remember.*

NEW YORK, SEPTEMBER 1982

Every time I think of Alan, of that evening, I smile.

"New York, New York," by Frank Sinatra—one of my favorite songs—was blasting in my Manhattan apartment, where I had gathered my chosen New York family for dinner. I hummed along while hearing parts of conversations and occasional laughter.

My eyes kept on veering toward the door, dreading a medical emergency would detain Alan.

"You look good. You seem to have overcome the last few years," said Marco, jiggling his drink.

Had I overcome them? That evening, I thought I had.

"Is it the doctor's effect?" he asked, triggering the silent interest of those sitting close to him on the couch.

"Let's say it's the New York effect," I said.

"Will Alan be able to make it this evening?" he continued asking.

I didn't answer and went to open a window.

The warm breeze made the white curtains flutter, candle lights flicker. The lovely late summer evening reminded me of my childhood in Cairo, where lively family and friends' reunions were customary.

A fleeting thought, *Where was I not so long ago?*

A cascade of memories flashed through my mind—five years altogether: my mother's deathbed, Dad's final words and parting gift, hospitalization and Sabrina's birth, living with Joelle and Sabrina in New York, and enrolling at New York University. And New York gave me Alan.

Manhattan's skyline, the buzzing sounds of Fifth Avenue, and the languorous tune of Hayno, the saxophone player two blocks away, my comforting props, made me feel at home with my two young daughters nearby.

Marco wrapping an arm around my waist brought me back to the present.

"I didn't mean to put you on the spot," he said.

"You didn't," I said.

A magnetic pull made me turn my head toward the door. There he was, smiling, gazing at me with his very black eyes with dark circles underneath. Alan's charisma filled the room, amazing me. I rushed, eager to greet him, elated to see him, oblivious to the journey landing me in his arms and to what the future might hold.

Alan hugged me. We held each other's gaze. I wrapped my arms around his neck and whispered in his ear, "I'm happy to see you."

"And me."

The room quietened; the music stopped. A loud silence demanded attention. My friends, who knew about or suspected our relationship, kept inconspicuous facial expressions.

I put my head on Alan's shoulder, held his arm, and we walked in together, hand in hand, to enjoy the gathering—formalizing our relationship. And the evening went on like a charm.

Alan walked with me to the next-door apartment. He hugged me, saying, "Let's go on vacation together."

"Vacation? What a wonderful idea."

"Where would you like to go?"

"I like the beach. How about you?"

"Love it. Have you ever been to Jamaica?"

"No."

"Let's go then."

"Yes. Sounds wonderful."

Our relationship was moving fast forward. The trip to Jamaica would be my first romantic escapade. I mused about my journey, my meanderings, culminating with going to Jamaica with the man I loved. I wanted to have fun, to enjoy, to love.

I felt euphoric about the positive turn my life was taking. I was beginning to think of Alan as "My Other" (*Mon Autre*).

Marie agreed to come to New York and stay with the girls while I was in Jamaica. Besides that, I don't remember any other preparations. We scheduled our vacation date close to my October birthday. Alan booked the airfares and hotel. I remember climbing the airplane ladder, looking for our seats, and giggling, holding each other's arms. I put my head on Alan's shoulder and counted my blessings, dazed, thinking about Jamaica.

102

JAMAICA, OCTOBER 1982

The tropical island atmosphere enchanted us with its aqua blue sea and golden beach shores—a drastic change from Manhattan. Bob Marley singing, "Red Red Wine," made me sway in my seat during the taxi ride from the airport to our hotel. An abrupt slam on the brake, matching our driver's speed, contrasted with Marley's melodious reggae music. Shaken, we arrived at the hotel.

The reception had a direct, breathtaking view of the beach. Plants with flowers, rich with fragrance, decorated the terrace. The receptionist greeted us and drove us in a golf cart to our private quarters by a crystal-clear creek. The two-story bungalow welcomed us with a basket of exotic fruits on the table and the soft rumbling of the window air conditioner.

I stood on the tip of my toes to hug Alan and thank him. I loved the setting and the accommodations. He looked at me with a radiant smile, pleased with his tour de force, and lifted me to hug me tighter.

"Shall we look at the bedroom?"

Alan and I took more than a look. We waltzed together in bed. In each other's arms, we snuggled and lost track of time. We lifted our heads by midafternoon. I blew my hair off my face, kissed Alan, and jumped out of bed saying, "Let's go swimming."

We raced each other to put our bathing suits on and ran to dive in the creek. The lukewarm seawater cooled off the burning heat. We laughed and frolicked in the water. We both reminisced about earlier experiences in our lives. Alan remembered swimming in Kirra Beach, Australia, on the South Pacific Ocean. Marsa Matruh, Egypt, a resort city by the Mediterranean, known for its white sand and limpid turquoise waters, came into my mind's eye. I used to walk up to my chin in water and still be able to see my feet.

After swimming, we sunbathed for a short while and then walked back to our bungalow, ready to shower, and gave our bedroom another round.

That evening we ordered room service and stayed in, getting to know each other better.

Alan and I spent four days and three nights together in Kingston. We rented a small motorboat to explore the surrounding bays. We wore masks and attempted some clumsy underwater swimming. We choked and quickly resurfaced.

We got along well with each other. Our interactions were filled with high energy. We danced to reggae music while the stars scintillated above us. Being close to each other was easy. Both the silence and chats were comfortable. Alan's zest and spunkiness made me smile.

The night before our departure, we took a long walk by the beach, hand in hand, my head leaning on Alan's upper arm, listening, and measuring our footsteps to the sound of the waves. After a long while, he said, "Let's have a drink."

"Hmm," I hesitated, holding Alan's arm tighter. He had only had an occasional drink during the vacation.

We sat down in two comfortable armchairs facing the beach. The moon, a silver-grey circle, lightened the Caribbean Sea. The whoosh of the waves rocked us.

"Two Stoli on the rocks, one single and one double, both with olives," Alan said to the waiter who stood near us. Alan waited for the server to return with our drinks and some nibbles and said, "I need to know where we're going."

"Your commitment means the world to me, but we agreed to a year. It has barely been a month," I said.

"I hardly drank the past few days," he said, and without taking a breath, Alan told me about his financial status: his salary, bank account, the value of his apartment. He offered to share my expenses as well as my daughters'.

"You're so loving. You want to be responsible for my daughters and me. Please understand. I need to stand sturdy on my two feet—without leaning on anyone. I'm in for a partnership—not for dependency. And there is Stoli. I need to—"

"It's not an issue. How many times do I need to tell you?"

"I hope you're right."

The waiter came back to ask us if we wanted another drink. I said, "No, thank you."

And I heard Alan say, "No, thanks."

The departure day came way too soon. The Manhattan buzz would replace the tropical island's smooth mood. We took a cab to the airport, knowing that reality would hit us hard. We hugged each other and remained in an embrace while listening to Lionel Richie's, "I Just Called to Say I Love You" until the taxi stopped at the terminal. We held each other's hands during the flight home. We had a lot on our minds, and both expected much from the other.

As he dropped me off at home, Alan leaned to kiss me on the neck and whispered, "I'm waiting for your decision."

I looked at Alan, hugged him, and whispered back, "We made a joint decision."

The time had come for me to speak with Eddy—regardless of my decision about Alan.

NEW YORK, END OF OCTOBER 1982

Afterr Jamaica, I spent even more time with my daughters. Joelle was a sharp observer and Sabrina a bundle of tenderness. The fall schedule kept me busy. A college degree crystalized my longstanding wish. Each class stimulated my intellect in particular ways.

Determined to help us succeed at our delayed college enrollment, the re-entry professor commended our classroom contribution and offered her full support. My classmates represented quintessential New York diversity across demographics. Soon I felt at home in our group of ten, engaging in discussions, asking questions. My academic self, feeling stifled for too long, was thriving. My brain thought it was about time.

Exercise became a priority. It helped me expend scattered energy. The treadmill I had bought one restless evening while working on a paper made up fitness hour around midnight. To achieve my goals, I had to exercise and stay in shape.

I was nearing forty—an adult with no time to waste. I wanted to develop myself, know myself, and let my true self grow and blossom. And I savored every step of the way.

Freedom was what I sought. Breathing what I needed. Lightness what I wanted.

NEW YORK, NOVEMBER 1, 1982

Stoli needed continued observation and discussion, although Alan had controlled it in Jamaica. The one-year probation was also needed to breach Alan's denial.

Meanwhile Alan was determined to move our relationship forward. One evening he offered me the key to his apartment. I said, "Thank you—so nice, but I can't take it." I was unable and unwilling to give him a key to mine.

Alan bolted off the couch and, for the first time, raised his voice, confronting me about my decision regarding our relationship, and asked again, "Where are we going?"

"I need more time."

"How much more?"

"We agreed. Stoli must be under control for a year—not days!"

"It's so long!"

"We agreed. I want to pursue my studies beyond a BA. I need to secure my material independence. Dad's fund to subsidize my budget is not bottomless."

"My plan includes you and the girls. I will share your and your daughters' financial responsibilities."

"That's what you said—not necessarily what I want."

"I will be by your side when you study and raise the girls. You need someone next to you."

"I want to be self-reliant, financially independent, counting solely on myself—without leaning on someone else financially."

"I am giving you my best, everything I have."

Moved, I hugged Alan, saying, "I know and deeply appreciate it."

"And?"

"We have known each other only nine months, one hundred days in the hospital, and six months since I came back home. We'll know once we complete a year."

Alan was hyperventilating, upset. For the first time, he stood up and slammed my apartment door leaving. I felt forsaken after he left yet determined to do what was right for the girls and me.

Soon after, Alan called. "We need to talk."
"Didn't we talk tonight?"
"Tomorrow evening after work."
"Fine." I closed my eyes and took a deep breath. I was spent.

105

NEW YORK, NOVEMBER 2, 1982

Alan's dark suit, favorite shirt, and necktie hinted at a crucial conversation. Looking somber, he gave me a bear hug and asked, "How are the girls?"

"Sleeping."

"Good." Alan said, sitting upright on the living room couch. "Early on, I told you I wanted a serious, committed relationship," he continued.

"That's what I want too. We agreed to wait for a year to make sure I am well anchored in my new life and you're in control of your drinking."

"Drinking is not an issue."

"It is for me. It is for my daughters. The last thing I want to do is expose them to heavy drinking and have them think I'm condoning it. I'm not."

"Is this an excuse? Are you still in love with your husband?"

"No."

"Then how come you're not divorcing him?"

"I'm not ready. I have my timetable."

"I need to know when you are leaving your husband and committing to me."

"I'm not leaving Eddy for you. I'm leaving him for me."

"What else is going on?"

"My life."

"What do you mean?"

"Over the past decade, I have faced a cavalcade of challenges and crises. I have two daughters. I need more time before I uproot their lives and mine. I have been uprooted more than once. I know how it feels."

"I understand."

"Let's see how you handle Stoli over time. The one-year tryout period will allow us to get to know each other better and decide what we want to do next. Meanwhile, I will implement what I told you about my finances and daughters."

"It's a long haul."

"My daughters come first. I am in an adoptive country. I need to reconfigure my course of action. It is my time, my time to build myself up."

"How about us?" Alan asked in a frenzy.

"Us is in the making. We're getting closer and closer."

"I love you."

"I love you too. Love is not the issue."

"I want to marry you. It can't happen if you're still married. Got it?"

"You proposed?" I said, hugging Alan lovingly.

"You got that right."

"Marriage is not an issue for me. I'm looking for a lasting, committed relationship."

"Marriage is not an issue for me either. Your husband is."

"I heard you."

"I want an answer," Alan enunciated one syllable at a time, standing up and walking to the kitchen, looking at me with droopy eyes. I heard him pour himself a drink. When he walked back, I glanced at him without uttering a word.

"One year is not that long. We will be together," I said, hugging Alan again.

"Twelve months," Alan sighed. A faint smile appeared on his face as he murmured, "Fine."

I hugged him again and said, "That makes me happy."

Alan held me in his arms. I rested my head on his shoulder, feeling relieved after successfully resolving the issue.

I lit a cigarette and flopped on the couch, resting my head on the cushion. It was my first drag in Alan's presence. Feeling the illusory tension relief from the cigarette, I wondered whether a drink had the same effect on him.

Alan's facial expression was funny. He seemed surprised, saying, "You smoke?"

I tipped my head back and chuckled. "Tobacco, I resumed smoking a few days ago," I said, puffing away the tension from the conversation as much as I could. "You see you don't know me as much as you think."

"When did you start?"

"When I was a teenager. I didn't smoke when I was pregnant."

"I'm glad to hear that. The hospital alarm would have rung," he said in a stern tone.

"You need to stop. You have no idea the damage it does to your lungs."

"We each have our thing. I will stop mine. Will you…?"

"I will. I will," Alan said, interrupting me.

"I will too, not tonight, though," I said before sinking onto the couch, blowing smoke toward the ceiling, reaching for his hand, and kissing it, and mouthing the words *I love you.*

"I too am putting you on probation," Alan said.

"Agreed," I said smiling, holding his hand tightly.

I couldn't sleep that night. The conversation we had stirred up my mind. I analyzed every word and sentence we exchanged, Alan's nonverbal behavior, and the fact that he didn't pour himself a second drink.

At daybreak, Alan kissed my forehead. "I have to go to the hospital." We hugged and kissed again, before he left.

Despite all the positives, initiating a formal relationship while still married was not what I had anticipated. And one with a heavy drinker—even one who was trying to curb his drinking—worried me. I wasn't ready for such a relationship, and least of all for that issue. I had gone beyond what I had intended and felt comfortable doing.

My parents' relationship came to mind—her tirades, his denials. Not for me.

NEW YORK, NOVEMBER 3, 1983

Alan had controlled his drinking for a year. It had become social, except on one occasion when he got tipsy. After the slip, he grabbed a cup of coffee and skipped drinking the next day. Throughout the process, I monitored his progress, slowly hoping he would control his drinking permanently.

In any case, I needed to sort out my marital status before deciding about my relationship with Alan. As far as I was concerned, I was leaving Eddy because I didn't want to remain married to him—not because I wanted to be with Alan. That was crystal clear to me. Neither relationship was causally related to the other.

Most of all, I needed to protect my daughters. I was concerned about the impact of my separation from their father on them.

Eddy was arriving soon in New York. I had to plan our meeting. While waiting for him to arrive, I practiced what I would say to him and how I would say it. I was ready to separate and needed to be on point. The lines I devised years ago were just as relevant in 1983 as they were in 1967: We can no longer live together. We need to separate. Please leave. For the sake of our two daughters, let's remain cordial.

The statements seemed candid and considerate. The significant difference between 1983 and 1967: I was finally ready in 1983 to say what budded in my mind in 1967.

NEW YORK, NOVEMBER 4, 1983

Eddy was arriving in the late afternoon to spend a few days in New York. Good timing to address our marriage. It was imperative to prepare myself for a divorce.

As I mulled over the upcoming meeting, my daughters' laughter interrupted my thought. I opened their bedroom door. They were having fun with their activities. Joelle was drawing. She showed me the intricate design she just completed. Sabrina was building a tower with blocks and looked pleased with her accomplishment. Both smiled and came running when they saw me.

I commended them and said, "Let's read a book."

"Yeah. Mom, please continue reading *Treasure Island*," Joelle asked.

"Splendid idea."

We sat on the floor. Joelle sat by my side while I read a chapter of *Treasure Island* and then *Goldilocks* to Sabrina sitting on my lap. After hugging and kissing both, I said, "I'm stepping out for a while. When I come back, I'll put you to bed."

The early November evening was beautiful. A brisk walk seemed perfect. After a few steps, I found myself in front of St. Patrick's Cathedral and went in. I went in and lit five candles, one for each of my daughters, myself, Alan, and Eddy, and said a quick prayer for each of them. After leaving the cathedral, I felt calm and at peace with my decision to separate from Eddy.

As I got home, I heard the telephone ring and ran to pick it up. A friend of my parents was calling me from Paris. "Hi," she said.

"Hi. Good to hear you."

"I hesitated before calling you, but as your parents' friend, I thought I should. I wanted to let you know personally."

"What's the matter?"

"Well, I'm sorry, but one of the women with whom your husband is having an affair is pregnant."

"How do you know?"

"She's blabbering about it and flaunting her belly."

"Oh, that one."

"I'm sorry, but felt I needed to let you know. Your parents were close friends of mine."

"I am leaving Eddy."

"And leave the door open for other women to walk in?"

"Eddy is only faithful to himself. He has many women and there will be many more. I know the man. I'm done."

"Are you sure? Think twice."

"I did, much more than twice."

"I'm sorry. I'm so sorry, but you needed to know, to be aware."

"I understand. Thank you for telling me. It took courage."

When I hung up the phone, I ran to my room, threw myself on my bed, and buried my head in a pillow.

Eddy's impulsive behavior had escalated. I wished I didn't have to deal with this at the exit door. I didn't expect my days in the hospital to have a child to be rewarded in kind.

How come he didn't ask for a divorce? How fair was it to our daughters? How appropriate was it for the unborn child? Eddy was not about making things right. Unbridled behavior was his way of being. Murky was his style.

It was only in this situation that I was grateful my parents were not alive. They would have been mortified to discover this. Even my father would have lost his cool. No wonder they guided my steps to the church. I prayed to speak my mind, be up to their legacy, and be done with this capharnaum of a relationship—too crowded, too cluttered, too convoluted. Alan, too, was in my thoughts, but I didn't want to implicate him in this episode, at this junction in my life.

I lay in bed for about an hour, curling my knees and holding my head with my two hands, and finally mustered enough energy to step into the shower. Splashing warm water on my head and body released some tension and cleared my mind. I put clothes on, brushed my hair, and gazed at myself in the mirror. I looked pale, distraught. The Ombre Rose I sprayed all over did little to uplift my mood.

I sat by the floor-to-ceiling window in my bedroom and reflected on my marriage. First and foremost, Eddy had given me two daughters, and I was grateful for them. They were the most successful outcome of our marriage. My primary love was for them. Second, Eddy kept me in the dark about his business deals. Third, we had an attractive social life. We wined and dined with notable people—that was interesting.

Searching for a sweet memory, only one came close. Eddy removed his socks on the day Joelle was born and put them on my feet—one tender gesture in twenty years of marriage. Not much.

It was all about him for twenty years. I could have said, "No, no more!" But I stayed with him. Was it a matter of upbringing? Was it religion? Or were my parents the role models with their intact marriage? Was it for my daughters? It was in essence all the above and latterly about finding an efficient way out. Now I trusted I could do it. Today, Eddy gave me the ultimate free pass to leave him.

Short of providing my daughters an intact family, I decided to show them what it meant to be a woman, a wife, a mother, standing on her own two feet, finally declaring, "Enough! No more. I'm out," and become who I am today.

108

NEW YORK, NOVEMBER 5, 1983

The soft rustling of the front door closing brought me back to the present. Eddy had become a master at making no sound, closing the door at night so I wouldn't wake up and realize what time he was returning home.

"Hi, how are you? How are the girls?" Eddy said.

"Fine, sleeping," I said. "Please sit down. We need to talk."

"Woo, I'm scared," he said, trying to be funny.

"I'm serious. Sit down."

He looked at me without uttering a word.

"I got a phone call from a friend in Paris who told me one of your women is pregnant."

"It wasn't planned. There is no relationship there."

"It doesn't matter. I'm done."

"What do you mean?"

"I'm out."

"I don't love her."

"It's worse if you don't."

"…"

"Whether you love her or not is not the issue. Dedication is. Dignity is. Decency is long gone," I said in a staccato tone.

"You are my wife, the mother of our daughters."

"Too late. I want out. I was planning to ask you for a divorce before I found out about the pregnancy."

"There is nothing there."

"Yes, there is. A child is there."

"It wasn't planned."

"Planned or not planned, you have a child. Did you think about the child?"

"It wasn't planned," he repeated.

"That's it. I'm out. There's nothing you can say or do that would make me change my mind about divorcing you. I am overdone."

"You can't do this to me."

"I can't do that to you. Are you serious?" I yelled from the top of my lungs.

"Please don't leave me," he whimpered as he kneeled, holding on to my right knee, tearing up (a first), and putting his head in my lap.

Eddy's behavior made me wince. I held the two sides of the armless chair, lifting myself up and pulling my leg away. Eddy knelt, weeping, and grabbed my shoe to kiss it.

I looked at him in disbelief. Life is a merry-go-round. It takes twists and turns. I didn't expect that one. Eighteen years earlier he bent his knee and flaunted his then Oxford shoe on the coffee table in front of me, asking me for money from my father. Wearing tasseled loafers now, he was kneeling to kiss my right ballerina slipper, crying, begging me not to leave him.

"I love you. Don't leave me."

"You love me! You love me!" I yelled again from the top of my lungs.

"You are my life partner."

"What kind of partner are you?"

"The kind who can't be without you."

"I wish you well. I wish you far."

"You don't love me anymore?"

"What was there to love, except Joelle and Sabrina?"

"You are my social image. My business will collapse if you leave me."

"You, You, You … all about you. You should have thought about it earlier."

"Bobby, your childhood best friend will stop working with me."

"I trust Bobby is conducting business based on merit, not on friendship."

"We are married. We are Catholic. You will die carrying my name."

"Suddenly, you're Catholic? Are you living in a fantasy world?"

"We will be buried side by side."

"You too?" *Was he parroting my father?*

"What do you mean?

"Forget it. That's it. It's the end of the road."

"You wouldn't have behaved this way if your parents were still alive."

I almost laughed and said, "Leave my parents out of this. This is between me and you." I refrained from saying my parents would have said, "At last!"

"We need to speak to the girls. It's the right thing to do."

"Out of the question. I won't do it. I have nothing to do with the nonsense of this evening."

"Nonsense! Please leave," I yelled one more time.

"Where shall I sleep?"

"You have another place. Sleep wherever you want. I don't want you to sleep here, ever again. We are separated. Send me a letter stating you're responsible for the girls' upbringing. That's all I want from you, for now."

Eddy looked at me in disbelief, realizing I was serious. I stood up and led him to the door. Incredulous, he followed me.

I opened the main door. Eddy took a step toward the door, paused, looked at me, hesitated to say something, but stopped and stepped out.

I closed the door slowly. Silence.

I leaned against the door and took a deep breath, poking my chin forward.

The doorbell rang two seconds later. I looked through the peephole. Eddy was back. I opened the door.

"I forgot my coat in the closet."

"You have your wallet and briefcase?"

"Yes."

"You have credit cards. You can buy a coat on your way."

Finally, I pulled the plug. I closed the door on my relationship with Eddy. It was not so difficult after all. How come it took me so long?

The silence was deafening. My parents' eighteenth-century turquoise enamel pendulum clock tolled the bell of my marriage at exactly 10:30 p.m.— six years after its death at Mom's bedside.

I sat on the floor, folded my head against my knees, and held my back against the door. Unbridled emotions ran free. Every time I lifted my head, a mantra played out in my mind over and over again.

What just happened was my experience—not who I am.

I lifted my head, unaware of how long I sat on the floor. I might have dozed for a while. When I stood up, the apartment was pitch dark. I went to see the girls. They were fast asleep—unaware of the 180-degree turn our lives had taken.

Then, I stepped into my bedroom and looked around. For the first time in twenty years, I slipped into my bed and stretched my arms at my sides in a tree position. The bed was mine; all mine. I stared at the white ceiling and felt a sense of accomplishment, of freedom.

As far as I was concerned, the separation was done, sealed, and delivered that day. No regrets. We were over. Our marriage was done.

It was the right time to get a divorce and move on, but emotionally I wasn't ready. I felt completely drained and needed a break to gain some perspective, particularly on the impact of what happened between Eddy and me on Joelle and Sabrina.

My daughters needed to know what took place between their father and me. I needed to take in what had just happened. I wished I could share the breakup with my parents. Thoughts of Alan came to mind, but I pushed them away. Another talk didn't appeal to me, not now. I didn't want to mix the past, present, and possible future. I considered calling Bobby, then decided to spare him. His plate was full, and I didn't want to disrupt his settled, traditional lifestyle.

The landscape of my life had significantly changed. I had to take a step back to reassess and possibly reconfigure the path of my journey, my life.

109

NEW YORK, NOVEMBER 6, 1983

Eddy's reaction to my leaving him was a significant departure from his usual behavior. Never had I seen him cry, let alone kneel and beg. What was the reason behind his behavior? Was he burdened by it all? Perhaps. Most people would be.

Eddy argued all the points that came to his mind but avoided the core issues—commitment and candor. The reality he perceived was designed for his convenience and filtered through his lenses. He had a hard time understanding or perhaps conveniently ignored that what worked or pleased him wasn't the same for me. In his view, what made him happy must also make me happy. He behaved as if I were an extension of himself, as if I didn't exist on my own, or even worse, as if I would tolerate, if not condone, his actions. Wrong!

Eddy enjoyed his social status as a married man. He was pleased, proud to have me as his wife and mother of his daughters whom he said he loved but for whom he had no time and didn't curb his behavior. He was also glad to come home and take refuge with his family under the same roof.

My presence next to Eddy enhanced his personal and professional status. I was protecting him in an unwilling, convoluted way from the women he seduced. I was the unwitting enabler. Since we got married, I had given my input for him to pursue his work and thrive. I also took on the role of an aircraft refueling another in midair through personal and business contacts. Some funded him, others partnered with him. Altogether, my significant contributions helped him follow his course as high and as far as possible and succeed.

"If Djenane is still there, Eddy can't be that bad," was the social consensus. And Eddy was aware of it.

Eddy had faulty psychological brakes and an ability to delay gratification of impulses, compounded by the illusion of invincibility. He followed his whims, living his experience, consumed by self-gratification—without considering the consequences of his behavior or the people involved in his life, including his born children and unborn child.

His intention was not to hurt me. Eddy was oblivious to my feelings—too busy being himself. Success in business and finances had been exceptional, sudden, and hard to manage, triggering excessive, scattered energy to expend and money to spend. He was paying for the ride, the thrill. So, the more cheers the better it was. I had to enjoy it too.

Eddy was playing a complex chess game, where each piece served his master plan, which only he knew. His game plan worked well, except for one chess piece—the Queen. Eddy didn't account for the Queen's moves in his chess game.

110

NEW YORK, NOVEMBER 7, 1983

The following day, I woke up with ten-year-old Joelle standing by my side, and eighteen-month-old Sabrina trotting behind her, a heart-warming wake-up. I hugged them and kissed them both and hopped out of bed to get ready to drop off my older daughter at school and organize the day for my toddler. Then I remembered I needed to speak with the girls about our new normal. I felt a twist in my heart and deferred the talk to after school.

Identifying a suitable time for such a discussion is difficult.

When I came back from school, I noticed my phone light blinking. Alan had called me several times and left me voicemails.

"I haven't heard from you in two days," he said.

"Only yesterday."

"You don't sound your usual self?"

"Yesterday was a long, hectic day."

"What's going on?"

"I'll tell you when I see you."

"When do I see you?"

"This evening, if you're not on call."

"I'll be there by eight."

I felt comforted knowing Alan was coming over in the evening—though I was somewhat concerned about our conversation.

Eddy called me a few minutes later. He wondered how I was and threaded toward whether I was in the same frame of mind. I repeated what I had said the night before, only adding, "Let's remain cordial for the girls' and our sake. I want them to see you. We will come to Paris for a month in the summer as usual. We will stay in the apartment. You will stay elsewhere at that time."

"Fine. Will you send them to Mykonos afterwards?"

"Not this summer."

Eddy groaned and mumbled unclear words.

"You can visit them at home in New York."

Eddy mumbled again, then said, "I will send you the letter you requested via messenger."

"Thank you. I will send you all your stuff tomorrow."

"My stuff stays ..." He started and stopped in mid-sentence.

We both left it at that and ended the call.

As soon as Joelle returned from school, I put Sabrina on my lap, and said, "I am sorry to tell you that your father and I will no longer be living together. I tried for a long time and exerted my best effort, but I am unable and unwilling to remain married. Your father and I will always be Dad and Mom for you. That biological fact will never change."

Both girls stared at me.

"We will go to Paris and stay in our apartment in the summer, and I offered to have your father visit you at home when he is in New York. I prefer it this way for you and me. The two of you must maintain a positive relationship with your Dad."

Joelle and Sabrina continued staring at me.

"Both your father and I love you and always will."

I stopped, out of breath, having expressed the most supportive words I could utter. Joelle remained pensive.

"A penny for your thoughts?" I asked.

She looked at me and said, "I understand."

I nodded. I didn't have it in me to ask further. I knew full well that what I shared was incomplete, but I had done my best—more wasn't in me, not on that day.

When the evening came, I was pacing around the apartment, waiting for Alan to arrive. He came earlier than stated. He must have sensed something unusual in my voice. The minute he walked into the apartment, he said, "What's up?"

I told him what had happened.

"The man has no boundaries."

"I guess not."

"And you said?"

"I asked him to leave, saying, "We are separated.""

"Separated. How about divorce?"

"I paved the way toward divorce."

"What more do you need to dump him?"

"I'm doing it my way—one step at a time."

Alan sighed and said, "How many steps are we from your divorce?"

"It's my divorce. It will take me the time I need. As you know, I need to protect my daughters and myself."

Alan gave me the Band-Aid analogy. "It's better to remove it quickly."

"We're discussing my life—not an imaginary wound."

In a sudden shift of mood, he hugged me, saying, "I want to host a party at my place with all your friends and mine. I want everyone to meet you, the lady in my life, the lady I want to marry."

I reached for his hand, pressed my fingers against his palm. "So sweet. Thank you. Not now. I need to defer everything for a year. My heart is pounding, my breath scant, my feet wobbling. Let me get back to myself."

Alan nodded and bent to hug me. "I understand," he said.

The relationship we shared was new to me. Alan made me feel connected and supported. I closed my eyes, feeling grateful for having him in my life, showing me another way of being, of relating.

111

NEW YORK, NOVEMBER 9, 1983

Eddy sent me his commitment letter two days later. It consisted of one-and-a-half-lines written and signed by Mike, stating Eddy would attempt to maintain our daughters' upkeep if his financial conditions allowed.

The letter was inconsequential. It was not legally binding. It allowed a way out at any time. The letter protected Eddy and supported his belief that alimony and childcare laws did not apply to him—even though Family Law required him to pay child support.

So far, Eddy had been maintaining the household budget and most of the family's day-to-day upkeep. That brief note, and my knowledge of Eddy, warranted a thorough revision of my financial plan. I needed to review and cut expenses to prepare for a worst-case scenario. That is, Eddy using finances as the pressure point to control my behavior.

I brushed off the commitment letter from my mind. Ruminating about it was pointless. The content matched the author's spirit. As soon as I packed Eddy's belongings in suitcases and sent them to his office, I felt relieved.

112

NEW YORK, NOVEMBER 10, 1983

My life was finally in my own two hands. It had been from the get-go—but I didn't fully exercise its ownership. I acted on my long-held thoughts and felt gratified. I was ready to start my own journey, free of marital ties. It was the dawn of a new era. Before me lay a blank canvas.

So, I thought.

The significant change in our family constellation and, most of all, its impact on Joelle and Sabrina, was massive. As a wife, I separated from my husband—with solid reasons, after much consideration and delay. Having said that, I had also separated from my daughters' father. Eddy was still the father of my two daughters.

Joelle and Sabrina no longer had an intact family. Did they ever have an intact or seemingly intact family? Was Eddy present in our daily lives? Or did he have a whimsical access to our family?

The visitations I offered allowed me to know where Joelle and Sabrina were and with whom. My intention was to create a transition easier for my daughters and for me to direct the course of my new life. My offer required that I present myself in an affable manner when I felt exhausted and short of social graces to dispense. It may have also created a fake reality. A few days in the year and a month in the summer, we were to relate as a family despite living separately. Some would say a dysfunctional one. I would say a family attempting to be socially cordial.

What I didn't expect was my sudden near-breakdown. Pent up emotions burst out. I experienced an emotional flood. It was as if the losses, bereavement, and sorrow I experienced screamed to the forefront of my mind. It started with embarking on that Swissair flight from Cairo to Geneva and culminated with my confronting Eddy about extramarital procreation—all together a twenty-year block.

In the meantime, I mistook Eddy's behavior as a reflection of who I was rather than who he was. Acute pain came from feeling invisible and immaterial, bruising my self-esteem. And that made a significant difference in my self-misperception. Nonetheless, the notion that I didn't matter, that I was not visible, seeped through my mind and affected my behavior with everyone, including my daughters.

Due to our family situation and my commitment to being financially responsible, I took on the role of the sole earner, which often made me unavailable. I used the energy I had left to prioritize my daughters' well-being. While I was physically present, I was often on autopilot, overseeing things without consistently being hands-on with them.

Letty was there and Marie often there. Neither of them was Mom. That much I knew. The Mom in me adored her daughters and was responsible for their well-being and keeping their lifestyle intact, as it was when their father was around. Everything else needed to be whole, except for their father's absence.

113

NEW YORK, END OF NOVEMBER 1983

I couldn't stop thinking about how to deal with the apartment next door, as we called it. At first, I considered relocating. After evaluating a few options, I felt hesitant about it. We had already undergone so many changes, and I wasn't sure if the girls and I could handle one more. Besides, the initial apartment held a lot of sentimental value for me. It was the gift from my father during our last conversation.

Next, I considered connecting the two apartments and consulted with an architect. He sent me a pricey estimate that included the permits, breakthrough, and side work needed. I had to decline it. It was too expensive and would substantially deplete my funds.

Neither of these two options was sustainable from a sentimental and financial standpoint, especially if Eddy were to stop paying for the household budget.

A third option was to keep the two apartments separate. This option posed a significant family issue. I was sleeping next door—just five steps away, but not under the same roof as Joelle and Sabrina. Joelle had her own room, and Sabrina had hers, with Letty sleeping in the other twin bed. Marie slept in a folding bed in the apartment next door, when she was around.

At that time, financial considerations came first. Having two apartments allowed me the flexibility to rent one and make do, if necessary, one day. Of course, there were more options. Under pressure, while I was reorganizing my life, the third option seemed to be the financially secure one.

On a personal level, the apartment next door initially served mostly as my crying room, where I sobbed to no end, where I didn't want to be seen or heard. It also served as my work and family space. It was where the children would come to play and spend time with me after school or on weekends.

Alan and I also met there in the evening once a week, rarely twice. In those days, he gave me his ongoing loving support and challenged the invisibility misperception I carried within. Understandably, I was not in a romantic mood. I needed to put order in my life. I wanted to be self-reliant, enjoy his company, and put my head on his shoulder, knowing things would be OK .

114

NEW YORK, EARLY DECEMBER 1983

What took me so long? How come I stayed? How come I endured an overdone marriage—beyond salvation even for a born and raised Catholic woman? How come I settled for a marriage I wouldn't wish for my daughters?

That realization spoke more about me than anything else. I had no one to blame but myself for my decision.

My decision. My responsibility.

I stayed married for complex factors that changed over time. Instability was a core factor affecting my life and relationships. Country changed; events changed; people changed too. I sought stability. Following my family role model and having fought with my parents to marry Eddy, I was committed to my marriage and didn't want to quit before giving it a reasonable run. Having children was an essential dynamic aspect of my life, compounded by challenges in conceiving.

Once Joelle was born, I wanted another child, and had Sabrina. Then I wanted my daughters to enjoy an intact family, as I did. In between the two, life happened with its share of loss and bereavement, leading to insight.

The day I met Alan, I discovered new potential and possibilities within myself. He showed me and gave me love. I saw myself differently through him and gradually learned to know myself accurately with my own two eyes.

115

NEW YORK, MID-DECEMBER 1983

My next goal was to reduce the budget. A friend of mine introduced me to a notable auction house. I needed to plan to liquefy the assets I had to bridge a potential funding gap. Reversals of fortune were familiar to me. My parents had once lived in lavish luxury until politics seized their wealth. Material goods needed to be saved and, if necessary, used—not hoarded.

Separated from Eddy at age thirty-nine, I had two daughters whom I loved and were the center of my life. I also had by my side a man who loved me and wanted to marry me, and I loved him too—though getting married didn't rise to the top of my wish list. Once was enough.

With two daughters in school and preschool and me attending NYU, living in the apartment my father gifted me in my city of choice, along with the savings account my parents left me, was a blessing. I was grateful for having my head bolted on my two shoulders to deal with life's challenges. I was thankful to my parents for giving me the privilege of having options.

The pieces of the puzzle would fall into place. Money comes and goes. To secure our monthly expenses, I needed to create another source of income until I could earn a living. I trusted I could achieve a break—an even balance sheet by selling personal belongings.

I looked at my bedroom ceiling and the New York skyline and said aloud, "Thank you, God."

I will make it. I am a responsible mom. *I will survive this stretch*, I said out loud, playing Gloria Gaynor's "I Will Survive" as I collapsed on my bed.

116

NEW YORK, 1984

The longest, most challenging year was 1984. It drained my energy day by day. I struggled inch by inch to feel better, exerting all effort to regain my vitality. I knew the girls were having a hard time too. I kept my eyes on them. Neither of them spoke or complained. Both were doing well in school and preschool and seemed fine.

Some days, in the morning, I had a hard time getting out of bed. I tried, but soon after I put the sheet over my head *a la Oblomov*, Goncharov's title character. He too had difficulty getting out of bed. A smile spread across my face thinking about him. I don't think Oblomov's issues were like mine.

To top it all off, I felt guilty. I knew and wanted to do more, but I had limited ability to fulfill my wants and was petrified to fall apart—the ultimate failure in my view.

To heal myself, at the recommendation and observation of friends, I tried different modalities: transcendental meditation, acupuncture, and homeopathy. Each modality had a limited positive effect, for a limited period.

The turning point came the day I looked at myself in the mirror and said, "You did your best. Pick yourself up." And I did. I held my chin up and bit the bullet, one day at a time, one nano-step at a time. Although painful, that day, followed later by a five-year analysis, gave me the fortitude to overcome the twenty-year block.

117

NEW YORK, EARLY NOVEMBER 1984

Day by day, I felt more and more confident about the decisions I made. As a woman, a married woman, my decisions were self-evident and long overdue, but as a mother, I had an occasional twist in my heart for not having been able to provide for my daughters what I had lived at home—though I knew I had done the best I could and was half of the parental duo.

One day, during a one-on-one conversation with Joelle, I shared with her, "Sweetie, I considered staying married to your father so that you and Sab would live with both parents at home and regret I couldn't provide you a complete family. Now, I am separating from your father and showing you how to be a woman with fortitude, moving forward."

"Mom, do whatever you think is best."

I hugged her tightly and teared up inwardly.

My ground needed to be solid before starting a divorce proceeding. I wanted to do it the right way and prepare myself ahead of time. I knew not to fight Eddy in his professional realms: finances and legalities. The last thing I wanted was a lengthy, contentious divorce.

My marital separation status would remain until I identified a reliable exit strategy that caused the least disruption in my daughters' lives. Possible exits were churning in my head.

What if I said I didn't want child support? That might be the efficient option. It would work. Did I want Eddy's money? No! A no-brawl or argument-proof, without headache (a *bala dawcha*) exit was what I wanted. With that in mind, I had to stop demanding something Eddy wouldn't do.

I told Marie my latest life developments over the phone. Her only comment was to ask, "How are you coping with the separation?" She paused and without waiting for an answer added, "You put in your all to make your marriage work."

Given the circumstances, she offered to spend as much time as possible with us in New York. I felt relieved that she did.

The prospect of being single was a nonissue for me. I had stopped relying on Eddy for a long time. My two daughters were at the center of my life. Alan was eager to move the relationship forward. Perhaps being an only child fostered my resilience and ability to cope with aloneness. My internal theater filled with ideas, and projects kept me busy planning and deciding.

Close friends who knew the headlines of my life thought I should drag Eddy into court. They were appalled I would not and did not.

Independence comes at a cost.

NEW YORK, NOVEMBER 4, 1984

One evening after dinner, Alan sat close to me on the couch and spoke softly, repeating what he had said a year earlier: "It's been a year. I want to host the party I wanted to host a year ago. I want everyone to meet you, the lady in my life, the lady I want to marry."

"You're so sweet."

"Please don't serve me the sweet talk."

I had known Alan for over two years, and he had been containing his drinking. "Yes, do it. I can't wait," I said wholeheartedly.

NEW YORK, NOVEMBER 11, 1984

Alan hosted his party that evening. Meeting his friends, mainly physicians, marked a significant step forward for us. I fixed my hair and makeup and chose my outfit carefully. I wore a short black dress tight around the waist and hips with a loose, swirling skirt. I also wore drop silver shining earrings. My look was elegant and fun. I wanted to make a lasting impression. Vanity never hurts a woman.

I arrived on time and rang Alan's doorbell with a touch of anxiety. His medical associate welcomed me at the door; I gave him a hug and looked for Alan, surprised not to see him at the door. The associate told me Alan was in the kitchen, then bent his head and whispered in my ear, "He is eager for the party to be a success so you can enjoy it."

When I entered the kitchen, Alan was tipsy. He looked at me with an "Oh, well" expression. He struggled to maintain his balance while mixing sauce in a pan with his right hand and holding a glass of vodka with his left. As he leaned down to hug me, he bumped into me and slurred his words. I only understood, "Sorry." Alan tried to kiss me and almost fell over. Trying to regain his balance, he jiggled his drink and attempted another gulp but missed his mouth. The glass slipped out of his hand and shattered into a thousand pieces on the kitchen floor, leaving an imprint in my mind, etched into my memory.

Is this where our relationship is headed?

I came back to myself and rushed toward Alan, staggering on wobbling legs. I feared he would fall and hurt himself with the broken glass. I held him by his waist and helped him walk to his bedroom and sit down in an armchair. He first resisted but then heeded what I was asking him to do. "Put your head against the back of the chair with your arms by your sides."

I stepped into the living room, seeking help from his physician friends who were chatting and laughing. They asked me to join them. As I said, "Alan is not well," I heard a bang. We rushed to the bedroom. Alan had fallen on the floor, inanimate. I knelt beside him to hold his head and ran to the bath-room to wet a towel with alcohol to put it under his nose and on his forehead.

Alan's associate followed me and lifted him from the floor with another male guest. They put Alan on his bed. One friend told me he would take care of Alan while the other was making coffee and boiling water for pasta. Then his associate asked the guests to leave and said, "I will take care of him." Then he looked at me and gave me a hug, saying, "Don't worry about Alan. You can go home."

My eyes must have spoken for me.

"He will be OK," the associate said and added softly, escorting me to the door, "Please take my business card. He so much wanted the party to succeed. He got himself worked up."

"Does he often drink that much?" I asked, looking at him.

"He does sometimes when he gets stressed out," he murmured, looking down.

Alan's associate and I hugged without saying a word. My chest was tight, my throat knotted. Silent tears burst forth as my hopes for a future together came crashing down.

I left without saying goodbye to Alan. I felt angry, mortified with myself and Alan on the ride home. Stoli stood omnipresent, while I thought he had achieved a milestone. Once at home, I felt restless, paced in my bedroom, tossed and turned in bed all night. I didn't want to believe what I had seen.

I knew what I had to do and loathed having to do it. I hugged my knees to my chest and spent most of the night crying in silence. I didn't want to wake up my daughters.

120

NEW YORK, NOVEMBER 12, 1984

Alan called early the next morning and muttered, "I'm sorry, very sorry."

"..."

"Will you ever forgive me?"

"We need to talk."

"When can we meet?" he said. "I can come right now. I haven't gone to the hospital today. I took a sick day."

"Let's talk tomorrow."

Alan called me later that evening, slurring, "I need you. Could you come over?" he mumbled, sounding drunk.

"I'm on my way."

I ran to my desk, pulled Alan's associate's number, asked him to meet me at Alan's place, and dashed out.

The front door was open. I walked in. Alan had passed out in the living room; I shook him to wake him up and put my finger under his nose. He breathed. His body was warm but wouldn't move. I rushed to the kitchen to make coffee. When I returned to the living room, Alan's associate walked in. He looked at Alan, then at me, and said, "I'll take care of him. This is not a situation for a lady like you."

I nodded.

I had heard this one before. What was I supposed to learn?

121

NEW YORK, NOVEMBER 13, 1984

Alan called me the following afternoon. "I need to see you."

"How about this evening, 7:30 p.m.? The girls will be asleep."

"Fine."

"See you then."

"I love you. You know I do."

"I love you too. Love is not the issue."

"Let's talk."

"See you tonight."

I was apprehensive about our meeting, anticipating it would be dicey. Something needed to be done. We were no longer in our twenties. Alan was a prominent professional. I aspired to become one. He was also a fine man, but a fine man with an issue, a serious one for me.

Alan had left me with no option—as a mother and as a woman. I was unwilling to have a man with such an issue in my household. I didn't leave Eddy to associate with a man with a different problem. I was also unwilling to commit to a relationship where I would have to monitor or take care of a man's behavior from the get-go, even if Alan were that man.

Would Alan agree with my decision? These thoughts tormented me. I made a pragmatic decision—not a judgment call. I hoped I could convey my resolve with calm and clarity. He had been the turning point. He made a significant impact in my life. I had been patient and understanding with Alan as he was there with me and for me throughout my pregnancy. He was by my side when I was about to go to sleep the evening of my Caesarean section and when I woke up from it. He showed me understanding and compassion. He showed me love and made me feel loved. Our personalities fit well together. We talked, laughed, were happy, intimate, shared comfortable silences, and understood each other.

Yet I had to say goodbye.

Conflicting thoughts and feelings were bouncing in my head. I felt frustrated and restless. I took deep breaths, a cold shower, and went for a brisk walk. I stepped into St. Patrick's Cathedral this time to pray and light a few candles at the chapel of St. Anthony, who Marie believed had miracle powers. I sought inspiration and guidance toward the right path.

When I recalled what my spiritual counselor had said about mothering, I wondered: Would my daughters choose me as their mother? Reflecting on his words, what I had to do for them became crystal clear. My prayer had been answered. I signed myself on the forehead, genuflected, and left the church.

God, thank you so much.

My steps led me to Central Park. Sitting on a bench, I watched the pigeons fly around me. They were unappealing. I turned my head and focused on the trees. I raised my head. The gorgeous autumn sky welcomed me with a glimpse of infinity.

NEW YORK, NOVEMBER 17, 1984

By the time I put my key in the door, the house phone was ringing. Alan was calling me to let me know he was on his way. Alan looked pale and tired when he came in wearing a sweatshirt and worn-out jeans. As he wrapped his arms around me and wouldn't let go, I felt he knew exactly what I would say. I hugged him back and planted a kiss on his neck.

Alan held my hand as we sat down on the living room couch. He leaned toward me and said, "I apologize for what I did. I'm going to a rehabilitation center tomorrow morning. It's supposed to be the best in the country. I have admitted myself. I will overcome this issue. I want to do it for me, for you, for us. Please give me a chance. Please wait for me. I love you."

I was tongue-tied. I ran my hand across the couch's armrest. I did not expect Alan to make such a decision so fast and me to say, "I will. Yes, I will. I love you too. Still, I will not tolerate your inability to control Stoli. It is the breaking point."

"Understood. I won't. I promise. I won't. I want you to be proud of me."

We spent the rest of the evening talking about the center where he was heading, the treatment involved, and addressing his concerns and expectations. Before we knew it, midnight came about—time for Alan to go.

"Thanksgiving is close. We won't be together," Alan said.

"For a worthy reason."

"Any plans?"

"Re-Entry Program related."

We exchanged another long-lasting hug, both understanding nonverbally he would go back to his place. As Alan was stepping outside the door, he said, "I will write to you and keep you posted."

"Please do."

"Phone calls are not allowed. I will miss you tons."

"I'll miss you too," I whispered as I gave him a last hug and kiss.

When the door closed, I found myself one more time sitting on the floor, leaning against the front door, hugging my knees to my chest. Alan's decision to enter rehabilitation was both commendable and troubling. He showed courage to kick an alcohol addiction—a tough disease to overcome.

What Alan had told me at the hospital popped into my mind. Was he thinking about Stoli when he told me, "Nakhle, learn how to deal"?

I had dealt but was unwilling to deal with alcohol abuse, especially at the beginning of a relationship. It was beyond my limits. Some topics I would be willing to negotiate, and some I wouldn't—not for lack of love, but for the principle and experience, and most of all for my daughters, for me. No way.

I went to see my daughters asleep and kissed their foreheads. They were both my love and security blankets.

My body ached all over. I went to bed and curled up, thinking of Alan. The two hands of the maxi clock on the other side of the bed seemed still. Twice I stood to check whether it had stopped. I stretched. I paced. I lifted my head and looked at the New York City skyline one more time. The city that had given me so much.

123

NEW YORK, NOVEMBER 18, 1984

I forced myself to get out of bed and got scared when I saw myself in the mirror. My eyes were blood red, my lids were swollen, and my hair was messy. As I wondered what to do about my appearance, I hopped in the shower—my immediate solution to many tight spots.

As I started to get dressed, I heard Marie's and my daughters' voices. They had fun and were eager to let me know all about it. That allowed for a relaxing afternoon, dinner, and bedtime. Afterward, Marie found me in the living room. She looked at me while I looked through her. She sat on the couch and said, "What's going on? Talk to me."

I wiped my eyes with the tissue she handed me before saying, "You know the story. It's tough."

"Yes, it is," she said and continued saying, "Remember you're a mother with duties."

"I know."

"You can't afford to be broken. You need to keep your chin up."

"You too, Marie. I will. Today I'm feeling so sad and angry. We were getting along so well."

"He went for treatment. It's huge."

"Whatever the outcome, it will be a tenuous situation. I refuse to monitor and supervise him and worry constantly about his relapse. I'm no warden."

"Don't worry. Things will clear up," Marie said with a nod.

Marie, a loving, upbeat, nonjudgmental woman, had herself been through thick and thin. Her heart was filled with compassion and understanding. I felt comfortable and at ease with her. Her motherly stance enabled her to have open exchanges with me. Even though sometimes I didn't like what I heard, it matched what I already knew and felt.

After chatting for a while, I decided I needed to be by myself. Silence settled in the living room. I was alone, but the room was packed with memories, with people who had been in my life, who were now in my mind.

A fierce mind game went on between what I knew I had to do and what I wished I could do.

124

NEW YORK, NOVEMBER 19, 1984

My stance with Eddy and Alan was right, except that I longed for Alan and feared losing him. I hadn't anticipated how much I would miss him.

Eddy and Alan betrayed me. How come neither one of them spoke up? Was it for Eddy's unbridled entitlement? Was it for Alan's denial of alcohol excesses?

Faced with my dilemma, sleep and calm faded away. Changes and revisions whirled in my mind all night long. To unravel my peace of mind, I had to explore the depths of my soul. I wanted insight as I gazed at one New York skyscraper and projected my inner conflicts onto it. Thick smoke billowing from its chimneys matched my feelings.

I heard sirens. Were they warning me to be cautious, courageous, and follow my path? An hour later, smoke was still billowing out of chimney tops. I could almost smell the burn. I crossed my fingers over my hands and massaged them robotically. I was shaken, shaking. The faint sound of Hayno's tune seeping through the closed window rocked me to sleep.

I held my head in both hands. The solution was in me. By dawn, my decision won over fleeting moments of wish fulfillment, dangling the thought Alan and I might be together. I pushed the idea away, took a deep breath, and hopped out of bed to make do with everyday life.

My willpower will prevail. It must. I had to bite the bullet. Time to buckle up. I had two daughters to raise and protect. And I had twenty years to make up. So upward and forward, I had to get moving, chin up.

125

NEW YORK, NOVEMBER 20, 1984

My daughters were growing up. Joelle, a diligent student, took pride in her academic excellence and her growing independence. Sabrina, an enthusiastic preschooler, started her days with an engaging grin. The girls were both loving, sensitive, and thoughtful. The older one was reflective and reserved, whereas the younger one was vivacious and cheerful.

My daughters and I formed a strong trio. A friend of mine told me, "Together, you deploy the power of the Spanish Armada." She thought we carried formidable energy, stating it several times, also adding, "No one can go in between the three of you. You're an insuperable force."

With that mindset, I was concerned about whether my daughters had enough family support. Based on my offer, Eddy visited them at home when he was in New York—though not regularly. I wanted the girls to be with me during vacations. If they were with him, I didn't know with whom they would be.

Marie was the confidante who witnessed my joy, heard my sorrow, and understood the steeplechase I was running. My daughters enjoyed having her around. She continued to be with us in New York as often as possible.

Letty was very close to our trio in several ways. As the chosen grandmother, she was near and dear. Above all, she was there for my daughters, whom she cared for and loved, and who loved her too. I trusted her wholeheartedly.

I had a small immediate family. Loulou's travel range and our strained relationship prevented her from visiting us across the Mediterranean and Atlantic. Prim came to see me but had a family and profession that required her constant presence in Lebanon.

Eddy's parents lived in Egypt and Lebanon. As sedentary people, they were reluctant to travel to see us in the US, at the other end of the globe. Our separation also upset them. They wished I hadn't paid attention to their son's behavior and had stayed with him for his well-being. This would have spared them from dealing with his issues over which they had no control and appetite. They were therefore less likely to cross the Atlantic to visit us.

Socially, I wanted to create connections with a diverse group of caring individuals. Classmates and friends from Cairo who immigrated to New York were close to us. Several other friends from all over the world visited us regularly as well. My New York friends became my family of choice over time.

My recently trimmed budget was foremost in my mind. It was necessary for me to review and be mindful of expenses. I continued to ignore a close friend's advice about private schools. Staying within the budget was as important as keeping the girls' lifestyle comparable to when their father lived at home. The only way I could fund my monthly expenses was to sell more items. And I did and trusted it would work.

A review of my goals followed. My long-term goal was clear. I wanted to become a licensed psychologist. My life experience enabled me to put myself in other people's shoes easily. I was inclined to analyze situations or events from a pragmatic perspective. My short-term goals were ambitious. I wanted to be a single mother there for her daughters, a student trying to make up for lost time and get high grades, and a social being seeing friends.

My days were filled with children, classes, and household chores. In the evening, after kissing my daughters goodnight, I would go to my room, do my work, prepare for the next day, read for a while, and go to sleep by midnight, sometimes later if I was writing a paper. I also enjoyed having dinner with my chosen New York family, generally over the weekend.

Education was a priority, both for the girls and for me. It was what I wanted to pursue. What I wanted for myself. Education would allow me to earn a living and become financially independent. A dissertation would be a better investment than a divorce. I would be proud of myself if I achieved the former at NYU, but not if I argued the latter in court.

New York symbolized my harbor, my chosen home. The apartment played a pivotal role because of its legacy and essential function. I found inspiration and peace there, an anchor with a view of the New York skyline, my source of reflection and meditation.

My awareness and determination to put our trio first had reached its apex. I had to take care of myself. Exercise became an integral part of my everyday life. I went on the treadmill when the girls were asleep, generally reading or reviewing a work document.

When Alan went to rehab, I contacted my social network for support. Friends introduced me to eligible bachelors. My mind was not on dating. I was dealing with two broken relationships and wasn't in that state of mind.

I did not use drugs or antidepressants or overuse alcohol during the tough times. It was imperative for me to experience psychological difficulties without coating and know how to handle them. It was equally imperative for me to know myself without cosmetics and build psychological muscles. How would I be able to toughen up and overcome experiences unless I struggled through them with full awareness?

126

NEW YORK, NOVEMBER 21, 1984

Few days had passed since Alan left. Even though I focused my attention on my daughters and NYU, I was becoming impatient and checking my mail twice a day. The concierge noticed my nonverbal cues when I entered the elevator empty-handed and offered me a few kind words. The day before Thanksgiving, I saw him waving an envelope as I passed through the revolving door. After snatching the item out of his hands, I nodded and ran into the elevator and through the hallway. I searched for my keys frantically to open the front door and ran to my bedroom to tear the envelope and read Alan's letter.

He wrote it with a thick, black marker and pressured handwriting, the precursor of the letter content. The inpatient conditions were challenging, therapy intense, and his mood a mixture of fogginess and explosions. "Thank you for being there, for getting to know me. I can't wait to hug you and more at the end of my treatment," he concluded in his letter.

I sat at my desk, drumming my fingers, trying to make sense of Alan's text, trembling when I finished rereading it for the nth time. Recovery was arduous. I was not disregarding his effort, but the treatment was more rigorous and extensive than anticipated.

With a pounding heart, I hid the letter in my desk drawer and wiped tears with the back of my hand. I took a deep breath to pick myself up and release inner tension and rushed to the shower to calm myself down. When I came out of the shower, I looked in the mirror. Some color was coming back to my face. I smiled at myself and took another deep breath. I gave myself a mental $B+$ and smiled even more in the mirror. I felt a chill and looked for something to wrap around my neck. I opened a drawer and dug my hand in without looking.

I froze when I saw what I had retrieved from the drawer. The Hermes scarf Mom had gifted me was in my right hand. *How come I pulled that scarf now?* It had been in that drawer for more than eight years. I caressed it softly.

Mom had asked me to meet her at a coffee shop on Rue de Bourg in Lausanne. Then we walked down the steep street and stopped in front of Hermes. Mom said, "Let's look at the scarves."

"I like this one. Its colors will match what you like to wear."

"It's yours," Mom said.

A beaming smile spread across my face as I said, "Thank you."

Mom was delighted to see how enthusiastic I was about her gift.

I pushed the thought from my mind and wrapped the scarf around my neck, experiencing an incredible feeling of warmth and protection. The scarf was the comfort I was looking for that evening. It came from Mom. She must have sensed I needed support. The thought pinched my heart. I continued to hold the scarf and caress it until I went to bed and fell asleep holding it.

127

NEW YORK, NOVEMBER 22, 1984

In New York City, the holiday season begins on Columbus Day and ends on January 6, Three Kings Day. This is the time when New York shows off its best. Christmas trees are everywhere, from the celebrated Rockefeller Center tree to those at the Metropolitan Museum and Public Library. Store windows are decked out in glittering lights with different themes every year.

Santa Claus visits department stores to meet with children and take their wish lists. Lincoln Center is also home to the world-famous *Nutcracker* ballet. One gloats about being a New Yorker, especially during that season.

In honor of Thanksgiving, NYU's Director of Re-Entry Program hosted my daughters and me at her home. Marie was also invited since the Director's mother attended the brunch. Our quartet was delighted to be included for the first time in a traditional Thanksgiving celebration.

Marie baked a superb Lebanese dessert, *konafa,* made of shredded wheat stuffed with thick cream. Its aroma spoke for itself, sharpening our appetite. I wanted to express my regards and appreciation to the Director, who had initially supported my academic career—an aspect of my life remaining pristine despite the upheavals in my personal life.

We made it to the Director's lobby by 3:25 p.m. on Thanksgiving Day. We had enough time to be announced, take the elevator, and ring the doorbell on time. The Director greeted us at the door, saying, "Happy Thanksgiving! So nice to see you and meet Marie, Joelle, and Sabrina."

"Happy Thanksgiving to you too! Marie baked a Lebanese dessert for you."

We stepped into the living room, basking in the November sun with Beethoven's "Moonlight Sonata" welcoming us, sounding different than when I heard it at the memorable dinner in Paris.

The Director introduced us to her boyfriend, a gregarious lawyer who offered me a drink. "I will have an apple cider, please."

"An apple cider! Have something else. It's Thanksgiving."

I said, "A prosecco then ...," feeling put on the spot, experiencing the culture of alcohol and the subtle pressure to drink.

I thought of Alan. *Abstinence was challenged even at small friendly gatherings. The refusal of a drink was questioned, not the other way around.*

Warm, friendly energy filled the living room, allowing us to enjoy our first Thanksgiving and savor the succulent feast.

NEW YORK, NOVEMBER 29, 1984

Classes for the Re-Entry Program were held at the West 43rd Street location in Midtown. Discussions led to various topics, including a chosen writing assignment. My first paper for the Re-Entry Program was a production. and a challenge. Not only was it my first paper in a long time, but also my first in English.

A neighbor and friend from Mexico City, Lorenza, offered emotional and technical support. Her method of listening to me read the paper aloud helped me improve my writing efficiency. I can still see us both on all fours in the living room, editing and cutting segments to rearrange them before I retyped the whole document.

This experience led me to purchase my first computer, a Macintosh, a significant improvement from the typewriter even at the early computer stage. Editing text or rearranging paragraphs became a quick process. During the computer setup, the system asked for my name. As I pronounced my first name, it paused, then said, "I'll call you Juanita," which made me laugh. Even the computer couldn't pronounce my name.

Too often I felt exhausted at the end of my days. I tossed and turned in my bed with memories of Alan stirring mixed feelings. The voice of reason escalated to a struggle taking a course of its own, at its own pace. Sweet memories triggered pangs in my heart, seeing Alan in my mind's eye walking into my living room with Frank Sinatra singing "New York, New York." I dismissed that thought and focused on what I needed to do next.

In the morning at around 5:30 a.m., I would wake up groggy and levitate to kiss and hug the girls until school started. Then I rushed to get ready, and off I headed to NYU to focus on my studies.

NEW YORK, DECEMBER 1984

The following week I kept myself busy preparing for my final exam, the first in a long time, and signing up for my upcoming spring semester classes.

Christmas was on my mind. We were celebrating it at home as usual. I invited close friends to ensure they wouldn't make other commitments. This year I wanted the girls to have a joyful Christmas like those they had in previous years.

Right after my final, the girls and I bought a Christmas tree and added two ornaments to our stockpile, one for each of them. Marie was there to encourage and provide feedback.

The girls didn't ask about their father during the holiday season. I wondered about their reserve. It might have been adjusting to his limited presence, especially over the past eighteen months.

Caution was warranted. Children intuit situations. Their imagination can be wilder than reality. Divorce and parenting are separate issues. I separated from my husband, but my daughters needed to stay connected to their father. I encouraged them to call him. Joelle's shyness refrained her from initiating the call. Sabrina was too young to dial his number.

I took the initiative and called Eddy, then gave the receiver to Joelle who spoke briefly with him. Sabrina engaged with her father in her own words, "Daddy? Daddy? Miss you."

Her spontaneous language made me smile. She had the knack of expressing her feelings with the words she knew—an ability few people possess. Several minutes later, she called me from the top of her lungs, handed me the phone, and said, "Daddy wants to talk."

"Did you tell them what to say?" Eddy asked me.

"Of course not, I was in another room."

"I'm impressed by our daughters' communication skills."

"So am I."

Seasonal frenzy carried me forward in the days ahead. We enjoyed every Christmas event I planned. Dinners at home with friends were the most memorable. Despite all this, I thought of Alan constantly. He was fighting an uphill battle, and I worried whether he would succeed. Each condition bore different consequences. I knew what I had to do in either case.

When I received Alan's second letter, I hesitated to read it. My reaction to it lacked the excitement of the first. I waited for the girls to be fast asleep and was alone in my room.

Marie stuck her head through the door without uttering a word. She picked up my vibrations and left the room saying, "You know where I am."

I nodded and opened the envelope as my bedroom door closed.

The tone of the letter was more impatient than the first one. "I've had it with the program. I want to come back, be with you, go back to work," Alan wrote.

I pressed his letter against my heart and immediately wrote back. "Alan please complete the program. It's the best way to achieve your stated goals." I took a deep breath and turned off the light. I dug my head in my pillow and went to sleep.

Marie spontaneously extended her stay. Her intuition and presence were spot-on for the girls and me. She symbolized family. We felt the Christmas spirit having her around.

The 1984 Christmas holiday celebrations flew by. As planned, friends came over for Christmas Eve and New Year's Eve. They brought along animation and laughter and paid much attention to the girls who seemed to enjoy it.

The beginning of 1985 rolled in. We were back to our usual schedule. I still had a few days before the spring semester started. As Marie planned to return to Canada, she suggested we have one more gathering with friends, and we decided on a date before her departure, and I started school.

130

NEW YORK, JANUARY 1985

I picked up the phone and was startled to hear Alan say in one breath, "Hi. It's me. I am at the airport. My plane should take off soon and land at LaGuardia at 2:30 p.m. I'll call you when I land."

"You graduated? You're done?"

"Yes. Yes. I'm done. I'm overdone."

"You didn't leave? Did you?"

"Yes. I did. See you soon."

"Alan…"

My short tone reflected my surprise and frustration. Alan discharged himself and was returning based on his annoyance. I had invited ten friends for dinner that evening. I would not rearrange my plan to suit him or adjust to his impulses, creating ripples in my life. I needed stability and to reaffirm my boundaries. Perhaps Alan would join us for dinner. Everyone would be happy to see him, including me.

Alan called again a couple of hours later. "I am at LaGuardia," he said before even saying hello and continued, "I'll hop in a cab and see you at my place. Ok?" And hung up without giving me the chance to tell him about my dinner plans.

"Ok," I said to myself, and added a place setting to the table. I told Marie where I was going and who else might come for dinner. "Great," she said.

131

NEW YORK, JANUARY 1985

Alan opened the door. "I'm so happy to see you," he said, lifting me off the floor, hugging me and kissing me.

"I missed you too," I said, raising my voice as he blasted Michael Jackson's "Billie Jean."

Alan extended his arm, took my hand, and we danced, harmonizing to the hit song. When the music stopped, my disheveled reflection in the mirror by the couch shocked me. I glanced at my watch, already 5:30 p.m.

"I must go. Please come over for dinner. I didn't have the time to tell you when you called. I invited friends tonight. You know them all."

"I'm not in the mood. Cancel the dinner."

"I don't want to cancel it. I would like to host them before Marie returns to Canada."

"Stay with me."

"I didn't know you were coming back today."

"I told you."

"This morning. I must go. They're coming at 6:30 p.m."

Alan went to the kitchen and returned with a glass of Stoli, filled to the brim.

"What are you doing? You just came back from rehab."

"They told me one drink a day is fine," he said guzzling his drink.

"They did?"

"You don't believe me?"

"No. Not that kind of drink," I said, shaking my head.

He didn't answer.

I continued, "Not on the first day. I don't believe you. What you're saying is nonsense. I'm leaving." I stared at him and left, slamming the door behind me.

All it took was saying "No" and being self-confident about my appropriate stance.

Once outside, I felt proud of standing up for my beliefs. Alan's drinking incensed me. It would not compromise my standards or commitments. I was trembling in the cab on my way home and must have looked distraught when Marie opened the door. She looked at me with question marks in her worried gaze.

I told her, "Don't ask."

She got it.

I hopped in the shower and came out looking refreshed. I was glad my friends were coming over and hugged them tighter when I saw them. "So glad to see you," I said with enthusiasm.

"What's up with you?" said Marco.

"Someone tried to push my boundaries. I stood firm and said no."

"You seem pleased."

"I am," I said, laughing out loud.

"Let's sit down," I continued, and managed to enjoy the rest of the evening.

"Are your friends gone?" I heard Alan say as I lifted the phone.

"Yes."

"Can we talk?"

"Yes."

"What I did was silly."

"Much more than silly."

"I was fed up with being told what to do. It's been a long time since I had been held on such a tight leash."

"You needed it."

"It won't happen again," he said.

"It's a statement I've already heard, more than once."

"I'm telling you it won't happen again."

And he started playing Jennifer Holliday's "And I Am Telling You."

I bent my head backward and ran my fingers in my hair. Tears were spilling down my face, my lips trembling.

"It won't happen," he repeated.

"You said it many times."

"See you tomorrow."

"Call me when you're done."

I sat on the edge of the bed, holding my head with my hands, and pulled my head back. "We shall see," I repeated, doubting what he maintained.

Marie startled me. I had not heard her coming into my room. I shook my head from side to side and raised my right hand, signing 'stop' with my index. She got it and left, understanding I needed to be alone. I would apologize later.

That freezing February evening was emblematic of my mood. I gazed out. Dim light filtered through the floor-to-ceiling window. The New York skyline didn't seem as bright as usual. It was noisy. I heard the screeching sound of a firetruck's siren mixed with the melancholic sound of the saxophone.

One more time, I knew what I had to do but hated having to do it. Exhausted, I threw myself in bed and held my pillow one more time, thinking of Alan, hugging my damp pillow.

132

NEW YORK, FEBRUARY 1985

While riding the bus to NYU, I recalled I hadn't checked my messages. Was I avoiding more voicemails? Or was I getting some distance from Alan?

The bus driver's loud voice asking the passengers to back up captured my attention, and I squeezed myself to the back of the bus. A sudden stop jolting the crowd got most of us destabilized. I bumped against a hefty man, apologized, and directed my attention to the upcoming logic class. The topic was interesting, and the instructor knowledgeable with a good sense of humor.

I made a concerted effort not to think about Alan until I got back home, then rushed to the phone, and found the red light seemingly flickering faster than usual. He had left me four voicemails: "Hi it's me. Please call me back." "Where are you? I've called you twice." "I want to see you." "I called you so many times—when you will be home?"

▲▲▲

Alan came that same evening with a big brown shopping bag. "I hope you like prawns. I'll prepare them for dinner," Alan said.

"Great, I love your preparation. Cooking is not my favorite activity."

"I love it."

I stood by Alan, handing him items while he prepared a tray with all the ingredients he had brought with him. He lined them up in perfect order of use. Soon, the garlic and tomatoes' aroma made me salivate.

I set the table, taking particular care, choosing the placemats and napkins. By the time I was done, so was Alan. He gazed at me with an endearing look in his eyes. I was melting inside but found enough resilience to think twice about what I would say or do.

We sat down to eat and interjected "hmm," savoring the dinner. The various ingredients blended very well together. The prawns were delicious, the sauce spicy. We finished fast, tidied up, and moved to the living room. Alan put music on and smiled when Jennifer Holliday's, "And I Am Telling

You" resonated in the living room. He sang along and said, "It was on. I didn't plan it."

Joelle came to spend some time with us. The two chatted about how to identify math calculations and solutions. I tucked her into bed and kissed Sabrina, almost asleep with her teddy bear in her arms.

We sat on the living room couch. Alan took my hand and caressed it, saying, "What happened yesterday will not happen again."

"Stop saying it. I've heard this one so many times."

"I will do it."

"Shall I believe you?"

"Yes," he said, using an affirmative tone.

A fuzzy feeling ran through my spinal cord. I put my head on the cushion. The fabric was smooth. I held myself back from hugging Alan. Apart from my doubts about our future, we had a wonderful evening. We chatted without addressing the prior evening or drinking. We were in the now and cherishing it.

133

NEW YORK, APRIL 4, 1985

The girls and I had made plans to go away the second week of spring break. We were looking forward to it and happy to be the three of us together for a few days.

I asked Alan to come for an early dinner to see the girls before they slept. After I tucked them in their beds, he put music on and sat close to me on the living room couch. Sergio Mendes's "I Will Never Let You Go" was playing.

We both chuckled, "Good timing."

He sat close to me and held my hand. "You are separated from your husband. I am sober. When are you committing to me?"

Alan's statement didn't surprise me. He hardly drank alcohol in recent weeks. We rekindled our intimacy and tender-loving relationship—everything I wanted.

"I am not ready to commit yet. Sobriety takes time."

"More monitoring?"

"Yes. I have two daughters. I can't take a chance."

"You must give me an answer. I need to know," Alan said, raising his voice.

"You're waking up the girls."

"You get me off my rocker."

"I have to tell you things as they are."

"Me too. You'll have time to think and give me an answer upon your return."

"I will, but I'm afraid it won't be much different," I said with a tremor in my voice.

"You know what mine will be," Alan said with a dry tone.

We hugged each other, mumbling see you soon.

BAHAMAS, APRIL 1985

The vacation flew by. Joelle and Sabrina's company was uplifting. I did my best to make their days enjoyable and succeeded by offering possibilities, such as asking, "Ready for swimming?" or suggesting, "Let's search for seashells." They looked happy, and I was happy to see them smiling.

In our daily conversations, Alan and I only discussed our individual activities and our plans to meet up when I returned.

The anticipation of what lay ahead clouded our upcoming trip to New York. I managed to lessen my internal concerns for my daughters' sake and mine by focusing on the best decision for us. Before we knew it, Joelle, Sabrina and I were in the plane on our way back home. I held their hands tightly when the plane took off.

The prospect of another talk was unappealing.

135

NEW YORK, APRIL 15, 1985

Without paying much attention to what I was doing, I prepared myself for dinner thinking about our conversation. It gave me stomach cramps. My mind was set on what I had to do and what I wanted to say. I loved Alan and was attracted to him, but I had to let him go. His drinking had become a source of ongoing discord and anxiety. I was unwilling to carry the daily weight despite my feelings for him.

Alan called me to say he was on his way to pick me up. I waited for him downstairs and saw him walking at the other end of the street, lost in thought. I walked toward him. He raised his head, ran toward me, and lifted me off the ground to hug me. We hailed a cab and made out in a cab for the first time.

We went downtown on the East Side and walked into a long, narrow, trendy seafood restaurant. The bar on the left side had below the counter an aquarium with small multicolored fish chasing each other in bubbly water. The host greeted us and escorted us to our table, just three steps away from the bar.

Contemporary music and boisterous conversations, along with occasional raucous laughter, contributed to the lively atmosphere. A loud group of people at the table next to us added a din of voices to the service's clamor, making me wish I had requested a secluded restaurant where we could have had a private conversation. The high energy compounded my feeling discombobulated when we sat down at our table.

Unfazed by the decibel level, Alan stretched his arm to hold my hand. I gave it to him. Our hands were touching, holding, caressing. Before we could speak, a waiter came to take our orders. I ordered a glass of white wine and Alan a double shot of Grey Goose on the rocks.

"I thought you were not drinking," I said, looking at him in disbelief.

"I'm not drinking Stoli; I'm drinking Grey Goose," he answered.

"Please…"

"I will only have one drink. You will blow everything away for one drink?"

The waiter came back with our orders.

"Cheers," Alan said, guzzling his drink. I took a sip of mine.

"Did you have time to think and decide while you were on vacation?"

"I did."

I had a hard time breathing. My throat tightened. My heart thumped. I was at a loss for words. When I met Alan's gaze, my eyes filled with tears.

"I can't say yes," I said, my voice cracking as I pointed to his drink.

"There is no issue. I told you."

"Yes. There is a serious one. I had asked you for one year of sobriety or control over vodka. You recently came back from rehab, and here you are." I closed my eyes to prevent my tears from streaming.

"You must decide. We have known each other for three years. I love you. I want to marry you. Say yes."

"I love you, but I can't be with you. I will not tolerate your drinking."

Alan's brows creased into a frown. He lifted his arm and gulped his vodka in a straight swallow, called the waiter and ordered another double Grey Goose on the rocks. His defiance mixed with denial did it for me. I gasped.

My decision was irreversible. I felt numb from head to toe. My mind went blank. I stared at the fish in the aquarium. *The orange one with stripes, the clownfish, so pretty.*

Alan kept on talking. I heard him speaking, but I didn't follow what he said. I didn't want to follow. I was drained, completely drained. I twisted my napkin, hoping some motor activity would alleviate the numbness. I could hear police and fire truck sirens in the street nearby. I couldn't integrate my surroundings into a meaningful whole.

Alan saying, "Djenane," captured my attention. "So, I've been talking for ten minutes. Do you have anything to add?"

I shook my head. "No," and mustered the energy to say, "I cannot marry you because you're a heavy drinker. I won't do it for my two daughters. I won't do it for me."

Alan gazed at me but didn't say a word until the waiter brought the double Grey Goose, along with our food orders. I stared at the crab salad in my plate. Alan raised his drink up, saying "This is to the two of us," and gulped half of the drink.

I abstained from answering or drinking.

Then he said, "You don't love me."

"If I didn't, I wouldn't be here."

"I don't have a drinking issue."

"You're in denial."

"You don't want to be with me. Fine. I'll make sure you won't ever forget me—never forget me," Alan said forcefully, gazing at me.

"Your words hurt. I love you. Yet, despite my love for you, I will do what I must do for my daughters, for myself."

"You don't love me," Alan repeated.

"…"

I crossed my hands on the table, trying to stand straight.

Upon hearing my silence, Alan gulped his drink, held his arm straight, and with a defiant stare broke the glass singlehandedly with his dominant right fist. The pieces of the shattered glass dropped on the table, triggering a *déjà vu* in my mind. Blood ran from his palm, his fingers. He turned his hand down, keeping his bloody fingers separated, cringing and frowning.

I screamed and handed him a napkin, sobbing. Without looking at Alan, I pushed my chair and ran out of the busy restaurant, bumping into people on my way. I dashed into the street. I ran. I ran fast, panting.

I was done. So were we.

By the time I got to 34th street, I was out of breath, wiped out. Time to go home and shelter myself. I had been wailing for too long. Time to stop. I thought of my daughters. I wanted to be with them, for them. I remembered my spiritual counselor. His insight and synthesis had withstood the test of time.

I hailed a cab, curled up in the back seat, almost in a fetal position, and made my way home.

I rang the doorbell of the main apartment looking for Marie. She opened the door. She looked concerned by my looks and sounds. I bawled and ran to put a kitchen towel in front of my face. I howled in the living room. I couldn't stop myself. Despite the towel quieting my voice, I must have sounded like a wounded animal.

Looking alarmed, Marie gave me a throw pillow. I put it against my face, holding it with my two hands, bending forward. I didn't want to wake up my daughters. I didn't want to upset them, upset their lives. They came first.

I was Eloa, unwilling to jump in the pit of my disillusions, of my wounds. I was spewing the horror within. The pain. An unacceptable reality I could no longer contain. I fell on my side and dug my face in the cushion, gasping for air.

Marie kneeled on the floor next to me. She had a small wet towel sprayed with her Jean Naté fragrance and pressed it on my forehead.

"What am I going to do? I love him."

She didn't answer, bending to help me.

"You will hurt your back."

"My back has already been hurt, broken, and operated on several times."

Marie touched my shoulder and gently said, "Stand up. Get to bed."

I shook my head. The thought of standing up was beyond me, let alone doing it.

"I'll help you."

I almost smiled. How kind of her with her broken back.

I reviewed the evening play-by-play but couldn't play back one word of the ten-minute monologue. I spaced out in the restaurant. My head sank deeper into the cushion.

I thought of Dad. What would he have said?

He would have said, "You have known it for a while. Why are you getting upset now? You did the right thing. Shake it off—chin up." When I fathomed what Mom would say, all I got was, "I told you so." She wouldn't have held back her thoughts in such a situation.

I felt energized and soothed after the internal dialogue with my parents. I lifted my head from the cushion and turned around on the floor. Marie sighed. So, did I.

"Slowly," she breathed in my ear.

"I'll try." I rose to my knees, held on to a chair with my left hand, put my right foot on the floor, and attempted to stand up. I did. And quivered my way to bed. I collapsed in it, and before I knew it, I was fast asleep.

136

NEW YORK, APRIL 16, 1985

The telephone rang the next morning at 6:45 a.m., while Joelle was getting ready to go to school. Marie picked it up. Although still foggy, I snatched the phone from her.

"It's him," she whispered, pointing to the phone.

"Hi, I wanted to check how you are."

"How do you think I am?"

"No guessing games."

"Lousy. I feel lousy."

"Your decision?"

"Same as yesterday, more so because of yesterday."

"I will stop drinking if you marry me."

"I just woke up. I need to sort things out," I said, unwilling to repeat this dialogue.

"I will stop drinking," he repeated.

"Let's take a break. Let's talk in three months."

"I'll make sure you won't ever forget me. Ever, hear me...EVER," Alan said, raising his voice, sounding angry.

"I'll call you in three months," I said, feeling I was lacking enough air to breathe and unable to withstand the intensity of our conversation.

He hung up.

I felt drained.

"I did the right thing. Now I must live up to it," I told Marie.

She stared at me with questions in her eyes. "Deal with today first. You'll deal with the rest of your life later."

"It's a standstill," I said. "There is nothing I can do."

"Yes, there is. You can pick yourself up and go to your classes."

The idea of going to NYU seemed beyond my reach for the first and only time, but I needed to gather enough energy to make it to class. I knew if I could muster the strength on that dark day there's not a class I would miss, moving forward. So, I pulled myself together, took a deep breath, and stepped into the shower.

Classes worked well for me. They materialized a purpose, a priority. I managed to engage in discussions and enjoyed the topics at hand.

The day went by.

The time came to go home. As I put my key in the door, I heard the girls giggling with Marie. They were enjoying themselves and came running to hug me.

After they went to bed, I sat at the kitchen table, cupping my head in my hands. I looked at Marie and told her, "I don't have the energy to talk about it. I have two daughters. He wants to marry me, but he doesn't control his drinking. I can't say yes. I won't say yes. We broke up."

Marie frowned, moving her head from left to right, and remained quiet.

"Our relationship was too intense, too passionate to withstand everyday life."

I went to my room. I needed to be alone.

The New York skyline didn't inspire me that evening. It appeared surprisingly still. Silence resonated in my head. I dragged myself into bed and tossed and turned, feeling restless. I sat by the window and zoomed in on a skyscraper's top to get through the evening.

Hayno's languorous street music disrupted the numbness, interrupted the silence, the stillness I so desperately needed. No happy ending to my relationship with Alan in sight. I had to move on, letting go of my feelings for him, holding dear what he had done for me.

137

NEW YORK, APRIL 22, 1985

Alan's letter came one week after the infamous dinner. The sharp, pointy handwriting and black ink made my heart palpitate wildly. Once in my room, I opened the letter. I didn't know what to expect. I was happy to have a sliver of him. Alan stated the same arguments about controlling alcohol and revising my perspective. He questioned my feelings for him. The content frustrated me. Our viewpoints were still vastly apart.

Marie knocked at my door before entering. She gazed at me, "What did he say?"

"I am happy he wrote, but nothing has changed. We are still at a standstill."

"He loves you."

"I love him too, but we are done."

"What does he say?"

"He still says drinking is not an issue. I think it is a serious one. He says he's going to stop. I no longer believe him. We have opposing standpoints."

"You do. It's a tough decision."

"I know. It's tough for me. My decision is irreversible. I will not marry a man with that preexisting condition. I will not be the monitor or caretaker of a man from the get-go—not for me, not for my daughters."

"Too bad. He's such a wonderful man. You get along so well. You are so close."

"Alan is entrenched in his denial."

Marie looked at me with sadness in her eyes and added, "I wanted you to have an honorable man by your side to shoulder you."

"My shoulders are strong. I can shoulder myself," I said, patting my two shoulders.

NEW YORK, MAY 1985

The time-out was somewhat of a relief. We had an intermission, not a split. I didn't have the drinking issue churning in my mind, and I also didn't have to mourn our relationship. Schrödinger's quantum paradox seemed to be playing out in my life. Two seemingly disparate conditions—"in the relationship" and "out of the relationship"—coexisted while I had a respite to regain myself.

For a long time, I lived with different levels of grief. Losing Alan made me deeply sad, but it didn't crush me. I had experienced love and personal affirmation. Those feelings would live within me forever. They would replenish me in days of drought.

I had done the right thing. My daughters were my priority, and so was my wellbeing.

The spring semester ended well. Eager to complete my AA degree, I had signed up for summer classes. Academic life was becoming familiar. Excelling was my goal. I worked very hard and earned top grades.

Beyond the grey, I could perceive light on the horizon.

NEW YORK, JULY 15, 1985

nxiety about the approach of our phone call surfaced. I had said three months but hadn't been specific. I was too overwhelmed to pinpoint details. Catching myself becoming overly anxious, I verified the date of our infamous dinner date and approximated the date of our phone call.

I will call him next week.

For several days, I dragged myself from one activity to the next. I felt as if I was going to sit through a significant exam. I was also concerned about opening a now-dormant wound. Several times, I had my hand over the phone and removed it.

Enough—I was done agonizing over calling Alan. I waited for my daughters to fall asleep. To have privacy without the girls overhearing me, I went to the bathroom and placed the phone on a cushion for soundproofing. I glanced at my watch once more. It seemed still. A sigh escaped me as I pondered what to say. I mentally rehearsed what I would say to prepare myself for the call.

My anxiety percolated. With my hands shaking, I picked up the receiver to dial Alan's number then put back the phone on speaker, fearing the phone would slip out of my hands in the middle of the call.

Alan answered after one ring. I trembled when I heard him say, "Hello." It felt so good to hear his voice. *It's wonderful* raced through my mind. I stopped it. His somber voice betrayed the intensity of the exchange. I almost forgot what I had planned to say.

"I missed you," Alan said.

"I missed you too."

"Did you? It doesn't seem like it. You didn't ask about me."

"You didn't either. Besides, we needed time to sort things out."

"Did you ask for the divorce?"

"Not yet, but I will."

"I'm in control over my drinking."

"I wish I could believe you. I really wish I could," I said with a strangled voice.

I wanted to say *you love vodka more than you love me*, but I didn't. Instead,

I said, curling the phone cord around my index finger, "I need to go to therapy. Do you know someone?"

Alan gave me a name and a number. "Then nothing has changed?"

"No."

"I'll make sure you won't ever forget me. EVER, EVER," he restated in a loud tone.

I don't remember what we said afterwards or how we hung up the phone. I was numb. I knelt forward, grabbed my pillow, stuffed my face in it, and marinated in my sorrow for a couple of hours. By midnight, the sound of Hayno's saxophone brought me back from my daze.

I rolled on my back, thinking I couldn't do this to myself, cry about issues over which I had no control.

My tears would dry. I would move on with Joelle and Sabrina and the life I had created for ourselves, in the apartment Dad gave me, in my city of choice.

I had it all. Most of all, *I have my family's will of steel*, I said to myself.

140

NEW YORK, EARLY AUGUST 1985

When I answered the phone, I heard, "It's me again," from my parents' friend who had previously told me about Eddy's upcoming fatherhood.

"Hi. How are you?"

"She's pregnant again!"

"Who?"

"The boy's mother."

"I'm no longer in the picture."

"What do you mean?"

"We're separated."

"You haven't told me. When did this happen?"

I walked the caller through our recent history, relaying the saga that was no longer in my mind.

Much had changed, and I had changed so much in two years.

Hallelujah.

141

NEW YORK, LATE AUGUST 1985

As I entered the living room, I plopped down on the couch. The soft touch of a pale green silk pillow with embroidered palm trees transported me to the banks of the Nile, where they softly swayed. I squeezed the pillow and then let it go, reminding myself that the present moment needed my attention.

I contacted the psychiatrist. He knew the reason for my call. Alan had spoken with him. We scheduled an appointment for the following week. Before meeting him, I wanted to regain my new normal. He was a link to Alan, a colleague he recommended over the phone. The psychiatrist served as a transitional object, a facet of Alan when I wanted to live without him.

His private practice was in an Upper East Side townhouse. The spiral staircase led to the first floor. As I approached his office door, he greeted me with a nod. He looked about the same age as Alan, but his Freudian beard made him appear austere. His first statement was, "Alan called me and asked me to make sure you wouldn't forget him. I told him this is irreconcilable with the work we will be doing."

Alan's request was idiosyncratic, if not grandiose. It fit well with his personality, and I should add his boastful sense of self. Self-preservation was my priority.

The rest of the session I teared up, staring at a marble bust of Freud and wondering what he would have said. Therapy brought up many questions already at the forefront. Was I looking for a man in the image of my father? Was I also looking to differentiate myself from my mother? Did I want to stop the cycle of men with issues before it became my issue?

Mom and Dad were married for many years, and they were committed to one another. She didn't start her marriage with a heavy drinker. It happened later. His drinking was situational and somewhat controlled. Then he stopped drinking, and I absolved Dad in this way.

"We each wanted the other to be different and designed according to our wishes. If that had been the case, the story would have been different. We wouldn't have had a story. We would have lived a good, loving life together," I shared with the psychiatrist.

I needed to let Alan go. We broke up even though we loved each other—a sour reality. It was not a question of love. It was a question of who I fell in love with. It was, in essence, a question of putting my daughters and my well-being first.

142

NEW YORK, JULY 1986

Therapy lasted for one year. It mainly focused on my coping with the loss of my relationship with Alan and, to a lesser extent, my separation from Eddy. Along the way, I felt at ease with my decisions and gained self-confidence. At the end of therapy, I reached a point where I had said everything I needed or wanted to say and had dried my eyes and let go of the sorrow I experienced for a long while.

Therapy was, overall, a healing relationship. I saw the big picture and made my own diagnosis: Post-Traumatic Stress Disorder (PTSD). A cascade of events challenged my ability to cope with consecutive losses and protect myself from overwhelming emotions.

Loss began when I left my birth country, followed by an unsuccessful marriage against my parents' wishes, diminished procreation, my mother's agonizing death, Eddy's affairs, the intrusion into my Paris apartment, the loss of my Beirut apartment, the feuds between my father and Eddy, the sudden death of my father, my precarious pregnancies, the tribulations to obtain my green card, Eddy's out-of-wedlock procreations, my separation from Eddy, and my break-up with Alan.

I was out of breath but survived it all and was on my way to overcome it as well. Difficulties can break us or make us stronger. I chose the latter. I chose to let go of the pain and hold on to the learning.

The PTSD diagnosis helped me better understand my condition and decisions over the years. It framed my behavior and experience since we left Egypt. I wasn't always right, but I have persistently aimed at doing the right thing—and that made me feel good.

Could I have done anything else? Despite all my reading, studying, and learning, I still came to the same conclusion. I did my very best with the knowledge and skills I had at the time those events happened.

Life gave me plenty, starting with a solid head on my shoulders, loving, supportive parents, and two wonderful daughters. For more than two decades,

I had dedicated my life to others. The time had come to focus on my two daughters and myself.

At this point, I stood up and replayed Gloria Gaynor's "I Will Survive."

I had indeed survived.

143

NEW YORK, 1986

Free from chaos and emotional entanglement, I focused even more on my daughters and myself. Seeing them grow and develop their respective personalities was an insightful joy. My goal for Joelle and Sabrina was to see them become free-spirited beings with a mind of their own, capable of sharing their thoughts and feelings with me and telling me off if need be. I voiced my intention one evening over dinner to Marco, who shook his head, saying, "You don't know what you're getting yourself into."

Joelle was in the seventh grade. She was earning strong grades in all subjects with an aptitude for language and writing. Her teachers raved unanimously about her demeanor and academic distinction. She took her studies seriously and had genuine intellectual interest and curiosity. I never told her to do her homework or prepare for an exam.

As her school held massive ambition for her future, the head of her school scheduled a meeting to discuss Joelle's academic career, stating at the end of our meeting, "Joelle has huge academic potential. We need to be there for her to help her reach it."

When I got home, I informed Joelle of the raving comments I had heard about her and the immense pride I felt about her. She smiled. "That's nice," she said, half bashful and half seemingly aware of her performance and the hard work she put into it.

While Sabrina completed her preschool program, I applied for independent schools on her behalf. As part of the kindergarten enrollment process, the Educational Records Bureau (ERB) administered the Wechsler Preschool and Primary Scale of Intelligence, Third Edition (WPPSI-III). I told her on test day, "Do your best and ask questions if you're unclear."

She replied, "OK, Mama."

That was it—no preparation, no mediating interference. Unadulterated data was all I wanted. I waited for her to be done, and we went for hot chocolate. Sipping our hot chocolate, I asked her, "How was it?"

"Fine."

"Great," I said, taking a deep breath.

As a mother, I took on the role of a responsible provider rather than a hands-on caretaker. I was concerned for their well-being and feeling depleted of physical resources. I monitored and supervised everything that happened but did not read to them as I should. As a student, I focused on my studies and professional development. My academic results boosted my self-confidence and helped me cope with lingering flashbacks and numbing effects from the past years.

In the early Fall, the Director of the Re-Entry Program and I scheduled a meeting to discuss my academic plans. I sat in an armchair opposite her desk. The late October sun shone on her face. The rays emphasized the contrast between her alabaster skin complexion and her short, curly salt and pepper hair, matching her professional dark grey suit and white silk shirt.

"You're about to receive your AA. It's time to initiate your transfer to another department of NYU and consider graduate studies," she said, tilting her head slightly and shuffling gently through my academic transcript.

"I would like to continue my studies in psychology."

"I strongly recommend that you transfer to the NYU Department of Arts and Science. You have the aptitude and earn the grades. I will write you a letter of recommendation."

The Director listed the steps I had to take and shook my hand with a smile. I left her office beaming.

I leaped, walking through West 4th Street, humming Sinatra's "New York, New York," heading toward 32 Waverly Place to pick up enrollment paperwork at the School of Arts & Science for September 1986 admission to the Psychology Department.

The broad selection of psychology classes stimulated my brain. I perused the psychology bulletin, savoring the class directory and course descriptions—each quenched a thirst in my mind.

At age forty, I filled in my application and enrolled in the undergraduate department full of recently graduated high school students bustling through the hallways with youthful and often loud energy. It suited me well. I enjoyed it. I was curious to see whether they would notice the age difference. No one did. Or I should write, no one made me feel out of place. Undergraduates' compliments boosted my ego. I had the time of my life when, for the first time, a student asked me on a date. I smiled and said, "Thank you," which might have revealed my age group, and continued to say, "I have a boyfriend." *A white lie is innocuous.*

That student made my day, my week. I was chuckling on my way home for not mimicking Mrs. Robinson's behavior, the lead character in *The Graduate*, and blasted the Simon and Garfunkel song named after her.

By mid-November, Sabrina's preschool head called to schedule a meeting. I walked in anxious. It was a first in her three years of preschool. As soon as we sat down, she said, "I wanted to see you because of your daughter's extraordinary results on the ERB."

"Oh, wonderful," I said with shining eyes.

"Your daughter is intellectually gifted."

"Sab…" I said, moved to tears.

"She can do everything she wants."

"Which subjects would be her best fit?"

"Later in her professional life, architecture would be an excellent discipline for her. She could pull on her right- and left-brain exceptional talents and do extremely well."

I left the meeting elated and wondered about sharing the information with Sabrina. By the time I saw her, I had answered my rhetorical question. "I met with the head of your preschool, who told me you performed very well in the work you did a few weeks ago."

"Ok, Mama," she said, seemingly unfazed by what I was saying.

"Do you like architecture?"

"Building buildings?"

"Yes."

"I do it with Legos."

"Yes, you do," I said, lifting her in my arms and wrapping her in a warm hug.

144

NEW YORK, 1987

By the second half of 1987, one milestone followed another. Events started to fall into place and line up as intended. In September, Joelle, now an eighth grader, continued earning straight A's thanks to her intellectual curiosity and hard work. Sabrina started kindergarten at one of the most prestigious schools for girls in New York City, some would say in the States. I didn't enroll her in Joelle's excellent school because I wanted them to be their own people and enjoy their own academic settings. Joelle's school didn't appreciate my decision; my perspective didn't match theirs.

My college senior year progressed steadily. Determined to continue my studies to an MA level and seriously considering a PhD, I gave my senior thesis full attention. As it required complex statistical analysis, I connected with the NYU mainframe for my data and results. I also asked Eddy's NY office manager for computer support. She directed me to Rafik, a Lebanese gentleman, programmer, and technology expert.

From the get-go, I felt comfortable with him. Rafik was laid-back and easygoing. He soon became my go-to person for all computer issues, designing the programs I used for my psychology and accounting work. He also helped me develop my computer and technology skills. Reliable and levelheaded, he also became a family friend. As a divorced father with two daughters, I empathized with him. It couldn't be a better fit.

Marie continued to visit us in New York as often as possible. The three of us appreciated her contagious *joie de vivre*. She had a knack for seeing things from a realistic, yet optimistic, angle. Positive energy zipped through the minute she stepped into a room.

Analyzing my relationship with them, I realized Marie and Rafik were mother and father substitutes. They gave my family the tender loving care we missed. They helped me through challenging times of my life. Both were also talented in the culinary arts and turned my home into a relished spot for dining and relaxing. My guests enjoyed their home-cooked meals and their witty sense of humor, which lightened the after-dinner conversation and made everyone laugh.

145

NEW YORK, LATE NOVEMBER 1987

Eddy suddenly stopped maintaining the household budget and our daughters' upkeep toward the end of November. It happened suddenly with him just saying, "I can't send money anymore."

My first reaction was a mix of surprise and disbelief. What happened? I left a very successful, affluent man who said he couldn't pay for the maintenance and his daughters' schools? It was perplexing.

Was Eddy attempting to control my behavior by stopping payment? No way to find out. No need to expend energy over an issue where I had no control and a man who was out of control. If indeed he was so money tight, where did the investments, funds, and businesses go? Who were those around him during the downfall? Who had been ill-advising him?

I felt both overwhelmed and relieved: overwhelmed that I suddenly had to face all the household expenses, but relieved that I had planned for that possibility and was also cutting ties with Eddy.

Relief won. I chose not to lock horns with Eddy regarding our daughters' financial obligations. My decision was based on multiple counts: A lawsuit would have been pointless. Eddy had no money to his name. Nothing. In any case, I wouldn't squander my funds and psychological energy pursuing him legally. And I wouldn't wrestle with my daughters' father in an endless legal battle. I wanted to conserve my energy. On all counts, I was unwilling to barter morals for materials and deeds for goods.

Born and raised in a non-legal society, I considered legal feuds the last resort. My dissertation was my priority—not a divorce battle.

My goal was to seal the past hermetically as quickly as possible. Being financially independent made me feel confident and proud. My initial decision to prepare myself to be the sole independent provider from one day to the next proved to be solid. I almost boasted about it. I had planned to be self-sufficient by investing well the funds I received from my parents and selling personal belongings.

An itemized inventory of my sellable belongings came next. I listed all my possessions by category and order of sale—furniture and jewelry—along with the telephone numbers of two auction houses I knew would be interested in selling my items.

My mind raced through the memories of the circumstances under which my parents purchased these valuables and others when they too had to sell a few after Egypt. I stopped the melancholic recall. It was a moot meandering. I could not afford it.

A close friend worked with one of the two auction houses I had listed and gave me a solid recommendation. The initial meeting was difficult. I felt both conflicted about selling my parents' property and grateful for their support. The following meeting was productive. The representative and I built a positive working relationship. We came up with a schedule for listing items for sale biannually. The sale exceeded my expectations, while also making me feel secure that I wouldn't have a budget gap.

Despite this context, I was still adamant about maintaining my daughters' lifestyle. Growing up without their Dad was enough for them. Their lives didn't need to be further destabilized.

A friend called me, frustrated with my behavior, saying, "Stop taking all the parenting responsibility. Stop putting your daughters in private schools. They are his children too. Drag him to court. That's the only way he will understand, and your children will understand what their father has done."

"Home and school are their stability platforms. I will not disrupt my daughters' lives any further. They should not pay for either of their parents' behavior. Private schools will remain in the budget."

"You will find yourself without money."

"My daughters first. I'm an adult. I will fend for myself."

I gained freedom and took control of my life by disregarding alimony and child support. I could do it with some effort and grit. And I felt invigorated. Except for Joelle and Sabrina, I had no one to answer to. My inner compass guided my decision without hesitation.

Money managers would find my plan more than flimsy. They would even cringe at the thought. In my gut, I knew it would work. What mattered to me was protecting my daughters and cutting marital ties.

Rafik offered to work pro bono and Letty volunteered to take a reduction in her remuneration— until I created sufficient cash flow or earned a living. I was deeply grateful to these two loyal, dedicated people, and committed to compensate both once my financial situation stabilized.

It came sooner than expected. My self-confidence increased when the first sale at the auction house was more successful than expected. I allocated funds for the essentials and spent the surplus compensating Rafik and Letty and traveling with my daughters as usual to Paris for a month in the summer.

I sighed and stood up. I looked out at my bedroom view of the New York City skyline. That evening the skyscrapers emanated powerful energy, bolstering the eternal resilient spirit of the city. I took it in by osmosis. The view inspired me, comforted me. I experienced formidable support. I knew success lay ahead.

Starting on December 1, 1987, I took on the sole, independent financial responsibility for my daughters, Joelle (fourteen years old) and Sabrina (five years old), and continued to do so until their respective college graduation. This is a genuine source of pride for me. I felt grateful and privileged to maintain their standard of living close to what it was when their father was present in the household. I wanted my daughters to know that we were OK, that everything remained the same, except Dad wasn't around.

Their mother and father splitting was enough for them to bear.

146

NEW YORK, MID-DECEMBER 1987

I received a letter from the immigration department informing me that Joelle and I would be naturalized in February 1988—coinciding with my mother's death anniversary. The letter evoked deep emotions.

On the set day, Joelle and I went to the assigned courthouse. The judge made us swear to abide by the Constitution and spoke to us briefly about our rights. Given my internal trepidation, I only retained: *You are US citizens standing equal to someone born in the country. Don't let anyone ever tell you otherwise.*

Joelle and I were moved by the ceremony and the experience we shared. We were home, at last—a landmark date. Twenty-six years after leaving Egypt, I chose an adoptive country that welcomed us and lived in a city we cherished and called home.

We skipped down the sidewalks for a few blocks to savor a deep feeling of shared gratitude, perhaps only understood by millions around the globe who have been estranged from their country of birth.

147

NEW YORK, MID-DECEMBER 1987

While I was halfway through my senior year, my psychology advisor organized a meeting to plan my graduate career. He recommended I apply to an MA in psychology, exactly what I wanted to do. A doctoral degree was looming in my mind, but I elected to take it in strides. Enrollment at an MA program was as seamless as at the BA program.

I was a graduate student. I couldn't contain my joy.

For the last semester of my senior year, I sat for the Honors seminar, researching and writing my Honors thesis: aspects of Atkinson's Theory of Achievement Motivation. The topic was totally up my alley. Results supported my thesis about high and low need for achievement. Individuals who chose difficult tasks scored significantly higher on the assertiveness comfort scale than those who chose easy tasks. Personality characteristics influence task difficulty choice. I derived pure joy and validation from researching this subject and writing my findings.

The Honors Psychology Program's graduation ceremony came late, but it's never too late to do the right thing. I attended the ceremony with my two daughters and went down the podium steps, petrified I would trip taking my degree from the department's head (I had the bad idea of wearing high heels—a legacy of my previous life). Upon receiving my degree, I savored the achievement and regained my seat without incident.

Achievements, I should write, as in the five I had set for myself—having a second child, living in NYC with my two daughters, breaking free from marital ties, earning a college degree, and enrolling in a graduate program. These were of utmost importance. And they all came through. Pure blessing.

I felt beyond thankful and grateful. My parents came to mind. The completion of these milestones would have been a joy for them.

Gloria Gaynor's song, "I Will Survive" came back to mind. I blasted it and felt invigorated, dancing and twirling in my bedroom.

It was time to take a break. Joelle and I could travel with Sabrina. We had recently received our citizenships and passports. I planned to go to Europe with the girls. First, I wanted to stop in Switzerland to put flowers on my parents' graves and introduce the girls to the country where their grandparents and I had lived. Next, we would go to Paris as we used to do every summer.

I wanted to maintain the same structure and schedule for the girls.

148

LAUSANNE, PARIS, AND MONACO,
SUMMER OF 1988

My daughters and I stood in front of my parents' grave in Lausanne. Sabrina didn't know them. Joelle did. I prayed with my eyes closed and my fingers crossed. During my parents' lifetimes, I didn't always listen to them. Yet, I was hoping they would help me in their afterlife.

Mom and Dad, I earned a college degree and applied to a graduate program. Please help me complete my divorce honorably.

We spent our time in Lausanne visiting family landmark spots, such as the building where my parents lived and the playground where I took Joelle and strolled by the lake, admiring the scenic views.

We flew to Paris two days later, planning to stay in the apartment where Eddy and I lived before I moved to New York. The apartment was in my name. Eddy had done it with the clear understanding that it was a savings account for the girls. I told him I would stay there with them. He was away for the summer and rarely stayed at that address. I invited Marie to join us in Paris for the duration of our stay.

Paris welcomed us with glorious weather. We had an amazing time sightseeing. Museums and parks were easily accessible. Seeing the girls explore Paris was great fun for me.

We adjusted to our Parisian life. Friends flooded the apartment. They were happy to see Joelle and Sabrina. We shared memories, hugs, laughter, and French cuisine. Joelle, a native French speaker, enjoyed seeing her classmates, who reciprocated by inviting her for lunch and special outings. Sabrina was ecstatic to meet new friends and discover different parks.

Eddy asked me to take the girls to Mykonos for a week. I declined the offer, again, feeling uncomfortable about the company they would keep on vacation.

"You can vacation in Mykonos but cannot contribute to your daughters' education?"

"Someone is inviting me."

"…" I ended the conversation there, knowing Eddy would go in circles. I took a deep breath and, with effort, dismissed the thought.

At the end of July, close friends were going to the south of France for their summer vacation and insisted I join them. They were staying at the Hotel de Paris in Monaco, where I spent summers with my parents. Lodging at that hotel was no longer possible with my current budget. I declined the invitation—not keen on having anyone pick up my bill. My friends urged me to go, insisting on inviting me. As a compromise, I agreed to stay only for a weekend and pay for my expenses.

Joelle and Sabrina stayed with Marie, and off I flew to Nice, rented a car, and drove to Monaco. Long-distance driving was well known to me from the days I lived in Europe and went around France, Switzerland, and Italy, driving my car at full speed.

149

MONACO, JULY 1988

Friday afternoon, I arrived at the Hotel de Paris. A tap on the shoulder caught my attention as I checked in. I jumped, shouting, "Bobby!" My heart pounded. We fell in each other's arms and remained enlaced for a while. We were both moved and happy to see each other. He looked more handsome than ever, with his gorgeous salt and pepper hair, and seductive, playful smile. We maintained through the years a deep connection unaffected by time and space. We could pick up right where we left off after going one or two years without speaking or seeing each other.

"How are you? Please tell me you're well," he said.

"I am."

"Let's sit and chat."

We did for over two hours. I told him with enthusiasm about the recent developments, the girls, the graduation, and the graduate program. He filled me in on his wife and three daughters.

While speaking, I felt he hadn't tuned into my energy. He looked at me unconvinced, and said, "When are you coming back to Paris? Your life is here. You have so many friends. You know everyone, and everyone knows you. You have roots here."

"Who's everyone?"

"Your friends."

"Where was everyone when I was in trouble or in need?"

"Did you tell anyone?"

I shook my head. "I prefer to handle things myself."

"You'll be forgotten in Paris if you stay in the States," he said, shaking his head, seemingly unconvinced.

"Sometimes it's better to be forgotten. I'm no longer able to keep pace with most of my friends."

"What do you mean?"

I didn't respond. Money is a sensitive topic for the have-been (those who had but no longer have affluence) in general, and for me in particular. My parents did not discuss religion, politics, and money, except with close ones.

"What are your plans for tonight?" he asked.

As it turned out, we were invited to the same dinner hosted by close friends at the terrace restaurant of the Hotel de Paris. We were thrilled. Then I caught myself being not-so-thrilled. I didn't want to slip back into my pre-New York life, a life I could no longer afford. Most of all, I didn't want to get myself in another unviable romantic situation.

Back in my room, I focused on my evening look. I wore a dress I had bought the summer before Sabrina was born. It was a very elegant tulle strapless dress with sparkling silver and gold sequins on the bottom part. The top was tight, while the skirt had ruffles and a slit to the mid-thigh on the left side. I paired it with black satin stilettos. When I finished, I swirled to see the skirt twirl with me. I had my hair loose to mid-shoulder. Make-up and dangling earrings completed the look. I held my head upside-down and swung my hair side to side to give it a natural look as if the two-hour preparation hadn't taken place. Pleased with the result, I smiled at my reflection in the mirror.

Just as I was about to step outside, the phone rang. It was Bobby asking about picking me up from my room. I suggested we meet in the lobby.

Our hostess and her husband, well-known socialites, were meeting us at Le Bar Americain for pre-dinner cocktails. She was a beautiful woman with a head-turning sense of style, and he was an eloquent and sophisticated industrialist. The two of them welcomed me with compliments and bear hugs.

Bar Americain was alive with contemporary music, loud conversations, and occasional laughter. Couples danced. "L'Italiano," Toto Cutugno's summer song, filled the air with its liveliness.

Bobby sat to my right and a gentleman I didn't know to my left. He stood up to introduce himself. "Good evening, I'm Smiley. My friends gave me this nickname. It stuck with me." He kissed my hand and told me he was from the Middle East.

"Who's the dude?" (*C'est qui le mec?*) Bobby whispered in my ear, pushing the chair behind me, and reminding me of his presence.

"Just met him."

The hostess winked at me as soon as I was seated at the table. So did her husband, signaling the seating arrangement was not random. They were friends on a mission.

Bobby took my hand as slow romantic music began to play, and we danced. He held me close with one hand around my waist and the other holding my hand. My head rested on his shoulder. When the song ended, he held my shoulders and said, "If I didn't have my three daughters..."

I stopped him by saying, "You would have longed to have a child," and then held his hand and smiled, leading us back to our table.

Our hostess stood up and asked me to accompany her to the ladies' room. Some women stay in teenage mode. She was eager to hear how pleased I was with my dinner companions. She raised her eyes and eyebrows about my cozy dance with Bobby. "It was hot," she said. "He loves you."

"He's married."

"So?"

"So, I won't do to another what caused me pain when I was a committed wife."

"He has always loved you."

"That was ages ago."

"You couldn't see his look when he was dancing with you. He still does. Decide for yourself. You have a choice. You have two dinner companions," she said, smiling with an air of double entendre.

"Bobby and I were supposed to be with each other. It didn't happen."

"It's not too late."

I looked at her without answering. I didn't want to exacerbate my dilemma.

Upon returning, our group went to the terrace restaurant where dim, soft lighting filled the room. Each guest had their name on a napkin ring. My seating arrangement remained the same. Soft breezes blew through my hair. Bobby guided my steps to our table and kissed my neck while helping me with my chair.

My left-side dinner companion started talking to me as soon as I sat down. He spoke with gusto in impeccable French. He told me he lived in Los Angeles and frequently went to New York, and he would love to see me on his next trip. Without missing a beat, he said, "I hope you can join me for dinner tomorrow evening. Our hosts will attend it."

"Yes. Thank you."

"I look forward to seeing you tomorrow," he replied, evidently pleased to have covered the points he felt comfortable addressing in our first meeting.

The dinner conversation was split between my left- and right-side companions. Toward the end of the evening, Bobby said, "I'm supposed to fly back tomorrow midday. I will reschedule my trip for Sunday evening. We could be on the same flight?"

I froze on the outside, with my heart palpitating and my breath halting inside. "Please don't change your schedule."

"Why not? Are you interested in the guy on the other side?"

"No."

"I'm flying to Beirut Monday morning. I'm not sure I'll see you in Paris. I'll see you in New York. I should come before Christmas."

"Great. I'll see you there."

At the end of the dinner, Bobby walked me to the elevator and looked at me as the door opened. I hesitated for a second and bent forward, hugging him. He pulled me closer. We hugged again.

"See you in New York," I said.

He nodded.

MONACO, JULY 1988

The dinner the next evening was elegant, and a touch stuck-up. The men were wearing tuxedos; the women had white orchid corsages at the dinner plate's side. The host sat me to his left. At his right was a Middle Eastern princess sparkling from head to toe with her embroidered dress and jewelry. The setup starched the conversation and mood—though everyone was exchanging pleasantries and chatting away. The host danced with me. It had nothing to do with Bobby's tight embrace from the day before, but we were getting to know each other. He was divorced and the father of two sons. That seemed fine.

151

PARIS, AUGUST 1988

The girls and I enjoyed the last ten days of our stay in Paris. A member of Eddy's executive team called the day before we left for New York and asked to visit us. We spent a pleasant hour reminiscing about the past and contemplating the future. As we parted ways, the officer handed me a large yellow envelope and said, "Hold on to this. You may need it someday."

"What is it?" I asked.

"You'll see. Please don't open it now. Open it at home in New York."

"Thank you."

The executive stepped toward the door and stopped, saying out of nowhere, "Eddy comes up with an idea, repeats it enough times to take it for real and have others believe him, and then…" The executive shrugged, hugged me, and left without finishing the sentence.

The scene intrigued me. As soon as the officer left, I opened the envelope in my bedroom, curious to see what I was carrying. Eddy's signature in blue ink was at the bottom of two blank, undated letterheads. The first note was written on his personal stationery, while the second note was written on his holding company's stationery.

The documents left me speechless.

In my call to the officer, I expressed my thanks and gratitude, and said, "I hope I will not have to use them."

Sometimes things happen when you least expect them.

The fall was going to be busy.

152

NEW YORK, AUGUST 1988

As soon as I returned to New York, I put the yellow envelope in the safe, trusting I wouldn't use its contents.

Now a high schooler, Joelle continued her hard work, earning straight A's. She joined the New York Junior Academy of Science, where she looked forward to making her imprint in the upcoming program. In first grade, Sabrina thrived with her friends and seemed to enjoy the experience. Her outlook on life was consistently positive.

I registered for three psychology courses in Arts and Science, including statistics. The subject resonated with me. Its applications in all industries and aspects of life were evident. The student reviews unanimously stated that the professor was brilliant, articulate, and concise. Her ability to simplify complex concepts made them crystal clear.

153

NEW YORK, SEPTEMBER 1988

By mid-September, Smiley left me a voicemail telling me he was coming to New York and wanted to have dinner with me. We scheduled it for the day after his arrival.

On the set evening, he picked me up from the lobby of my building. He had reserved a table in the preferred seating area at La Grenouille, a notable French restaurant. My compliment on his choice appeared to please him. His smile was wide and contagious. We were two adults trying to determine if we were compatible.

After ordering drinks, we shared backstories. Our conversation became transactional. No romantic energy emerged for me. The exchange felt like a business exchange with a social relationship component. We were checking each other out. In addition to being attractive, elegant, and well-spoken, Smiley was also a bit loud and grandiose. No one is perfect. His interaction was prim and proper—no vibrations, no heartaches.

At the end of our second dinner, Smiley invited my daughters and me to spend Thanksgiving with him and his sons in Los Angeles. He offered us to stay in his home, which he said could accommodate us. I expressed my appreciation and told him, "We would be more comfortable staying in a hotel."

"I understand. I will take care of the reservation and organize a schedule based on our conversation," he said.

"We'll keep in touch."

"Yes."

As we turned the last corner to my building, he gave me a bear hug. No way comparable to Alan's or Bobby's. Nevertheless, it felt vigorous and was greatly appreciated. That's what I needed. Then he encircled my arm and kissed my hand in front of the canopy, showing off his posh European style. I leaned toward him and kissed him on his cheek.

Smiley left the following day. To find out more about him, I called my friend in Paris who had introduced us. She reiterated what he had told me about himself. He was a successful, divorced businessman, with two sons, who wished to remarry. I told her he had invited me and the girls to celebrate

Thanksgiving with him and his family in Los Angeles.

"My husband and I are coming to the wedding," she said, laughing loudly and not listening to what I said.

"You're pushing things too fast. Let me see what this is all about."

Midday, I received a gorgeous bouquet of fuchsia roses with a note that read, "I'm looking forward to seeing you in LA and introducing my sons to you."

This is a good sign—though the roses are not red yet.

154

NEW YORK, OCTOBER 1988

A couple of weeks later, I sat for my statistics midterm. Toward the end of the session, I could hear the professor's footsteps coming closer behind me. Did I turn my head? I couldn't tell. Statistics don't work well with distraction. "Are you done?" she said.

I nodded.

"Please come meet with me in my office at the end of class."

My heart began to beat faster and faster. How come my statistics professor needed to talk to me? She had only glanced at my exam booklet—without having enough time to assess it. After class, I walked into the professor's office. She gestured for me to sit down and asked, "What are your plans for psychology?"

"I'm working toward an MA."

"Go for a PhD. Don't waste your time and money on anything else in psychology."

I choked.

"Go meet with Dr. Cohen at NYU Graduate School of Clinical Psychology."

"Thank you," I mumbled. I had no idea my statistics professor was affiliated with the Graduate Clinical Psychology Department until she verbalized and materialized my intention.

On my way out, I stuck my head in the psychology advisor's office. "Hi. What's the relationship between the statistics professor and the Graduate School?"

"She is the Chair."

"She's what?"

"The Chairwoman."

How did that information escape me?

"And who is Dr. Cohen?"

"She's the Clinical Director."

Upon returning home, I called the Graduate School to schedule an appointment with Professor Cohen, emphasizing that the statistics professor had recommended it. The admission department gave me an appointment a week later.

The following week, I arrived early at school to see the Chairperson, the statistics professor, before class. She was working at her desk when I stood outside her office.

"Hi. Thank you for paving my way to the Graduate School. I did not know your position."

"I know."

"I have an appointment on Wednesday."

"I know."

"Thank you."

She nodded.

I left.

155

NEW YORK, EARLY NOVEMBER 1988

In preparation for my meeting with Professor Cohen, I practiced answering questions she might ask. To ensure a seamless interview, I took a cab. The cab driver drove like a maniac, so I arrived slightly ahead of schedule.

The interview consisted of two parts. First, I met with an ABD (all but dissertation) doctoral candidate. With long, ebony hair, she spoke monotonously, like an airport announcer delivering emotionless messages, a tone often used by psychologists at the time. Her delivery sedated me, distracting me from her message.

After our meeting, the graduate student led me to the Clinical Director's waiting room. Five minutes later, the Director opened her door to greet me. She started the meeting by saying, "Your statistics professor's recommendation brought you to this office," and then asked me, "Tell me about yourself?"

With a squeaky voice and unassertive body language pointing to my inexperience introducing myself professionally, I became self-conscious about my subpar presentation. I had difficulty concentrating. The powerful introduction landing the interview weighed heavily on my mind. A noncommittal "We'll keep in touch" concluded the meeting.

Disheartened, I returned home. I flunked my first interview at a very prestigious doctoral psychology program.

NEW YORK, MID-NOVEMBER 1988

Soon after I made it home, Smiley called me to go over the details of our stay in California and got my mind off the interview. I thought the girls would enjoy going to Disneyland, visiting the Getty Museum, and having some West Coast experience and knowledge. The trip seemed fun. I asked Letty to join us because I wanted the girls to have a safety net if Smiley and I ventured out at night.

After we hung up, my mind went back to doctoral programs. I needed to prepare myself and get my act together. I reviewed all the graduate psychology programs in the New York area, found eight, and had no time to waste. Applications were nearing their deadlines. I filled them out and mailed them on time. Next, I researched other requirements and letters of recommendation.

My graduate school applications were completed the day before I left for Los Angeles. Living in Manhattan and with two children in school, NYU was my first choice.

I pondered over an acceptance letter and our Thanksgiving break with Smiley and his sons while flying to Los Angeles with Joelle, Sabrina, and Letty. The possibility of a meaningful relationship and providing my daughters with a sustainable family life was on my mind, especially before starting a doctoral program.

LOS ANGELES, CA, NOVEMBER 22, 1988

Smiley picked us up at the airport on the Tuesday before Thanksgiving. He drove us to the Beverly Wilshire Hotel, where he had already made reservations for our stay. He left us in the lobby and said he would pick us up at 5 p.m. to meet his sons and have dinner at their home.

Upon entering our rooms, I was shocked to find a three-bedroom suite with a large living room and a kitchen. I called reception and told them a suite wasn't what I had in mind. Smiley had requested and paid for it according to the receptionist. On the night table in each of our rooms was a printed copy of our Los Angeles schedule. Everything was organized to perfection.

"I would like to change rooms and pay for them," I said as a greeting when he met us in the afternoon.

"I invited you and your family to Los Angeles. That's the very least I could do."

"We would do very well in two rooms. No need for a huge suite."

"No worries. The cost of the suite is equivalent to two rooms. I have a special arrangement with the hotel."

"I don't know if I can believe you, but I insist on paying for our rooms," I said, determined to settle my bill before leaving.

Smiley's home was a mansion close to the beach in Santa Monica. I mainly remember its brightness, not much else. Smiley's sons were waiting for us at the door of their house and greeted us formally. The boys were between my daughters' ages. The children's respective nannies made them feel comfortable and eased social interaction.

Smiley and I sat by the pool with the kids nearby. We could hear their laughter. He poured me a drink and helped himself. "Thank you for coming to LA and meeting my sons," he said, clinking my glass with his as a 'cheers'.

I smiled and nodded, not sure what I wanted to say. A smile was plenty for now.

LOS ANGELES, NOVEMBER 23, 1988

Disneyland was the focus of the following day. I told Smiley I wanted to spend it alone with the girls to give them my full attention and follow their whims. We visited one attraction after another and marveled at the well-known characters we saw along the way. "It's a Small World" was our favorite ride. We enjoyed the animated world tour filled with lively music. My girls and I had a great time exploring and laughing together.

That evening, Smiley and I had a one-on-one dinner. The restaurant was one-third on a terrace and two-thirds inside. It was hard to hear each other and have a conversation, though I'm not sure we had much to share.

159

LOS ANGELES, NOVEMBER 24, 1988

Smiley kept Thanksgiving intimate with two other couples and their children. My daughters enjoyed being with peers and jumping in the kids' swimming pool under Letty's close supervision. Parents sat nearby, munching appetizers on the sheltered patio in front of the pool.

"I would like to show you the house," said Smiley.

"Thank you," I said, standing up. We walked side by side to a bay window leading to a spacious and well-designed house. It was aesthetically pleasing and didn't appear ostentatious. All along, Smiley took the time to provide me with background information to describe details of the house. He introjected in the conversation that he had not lived in the house with his ex-wife. He moved in right after the divorce.

During the walkthrough, I thought *I could live here*. Yet, when the following question came to mind, I hesitated. *How would the girls like to have a stepfather and two stepbrothers?*

Smiley's sons' suite was the last stop. His older son had already joined my daughters and other guests. His younger son was pulling a belt from his closet when he saw us walking in. His eyes widened in surprise. I stepped closer to him and engaged him in conversation. He looked at me and then toward the right side of the closet. I turned my head to see what veered his gaze. A passport-sized photograph of a good-looking, smiling woman hung in the back. The boy and the woman in the picture bore an uncanny resemblance. The boy frowned and lifted his eyebrows, mouthing, "Mom."

The scene made me feel uncomfortable. I stayed quiet. Smiley told me he had divorced because of incompatibility, but I wanted to explore the topic. Questions popped into my mind. How come the boy was so anxious? Why did he hide the picture of his mother deep inside his closet?

Thanksgiving dinner was delicious. Everyone savored it. Smiley's friends welcomed me and made me feel at ease. At the end of the evening, they offered to drop me off at the hotel, but Smiley protested, saying, "I'll take Djenane and her family back."

I agreed, not wishing to make a fuss in his home with the surrounding audience. The drive to the hotel was not conducive to serious conversation. Letty and my children were in the car. The next opportunity would be Friday evening before leaving for New York.

160

LOS ANGELES, NOVEMBER 25, 1988

The Getty Museum was a phenomenal experience. My greatest surprise was how much information the girls absorbed and how interested they both were in art.

By midafternoon, we returned to the hotel. After a daylong outing, the girls were exhausted and ready for their evening schedule. I wouldn't miss the last dinner and anticipated conversation with Smiley.

He came to pick me up at 7 p.m. We drove to another busy restaurant where he was also known, as the host rushed to greet us at the door and give us a preferred table. Smiley was pleased with the welcome and the waiter running to take our orders.

As soon as the drinks came, I said, "Smiley, thank you for a wonderful stay. My daughters and I appreciate it. Still, I feel I don't know you and would like to know you better."

Smiley seemed pleased with my request and said, "What would you like to know?"

"How come you're raising your two sons alone?"

He stated the incompatibility script. I asked how his sons handled the divorce and how often they saw their mother. My questions seemed to agitate Smiley. "They see her when I give them permission."

"What do you mean, 'when'?"

"When I decide."

"How often do you decide?"

"When I take the boys to Europe twice a year."

"That's all?" I said, stunned.

He nodded.

"Their Mom doesn't come to LA?"

"Not really."

"Don't the boys miss their mother?"

"They have their father."

"Children have two parents for a reason. They should have access to both."

"They do, but one parent has more access than the other."

Smiley's answer was insightful. I stopped asking. *My daughters were in a similar situation.*

"I'll be in New York before Christmas and would love to see you again and get to know you better," Smiley said.

"Smiley, I have goals to achieve. I don't think I have the latitude to start a long-distance relationship with respective children involved."

"I hope the kids' visitation issue did not concern you."

"Divorce is complicated. Children must see the noncustodial parent, regardless of our feelings toward them," I said calmly.

"If you knew all the details, you would do the same."

"We have our reasons. Kids have their feelings. We must remember that." He remained silent.

"Smiley, you've been great, but I don't think we'll move beyond friends." He nodded and said, "I'll drive you to the airport."

After my morning coffee, I headed downstairs to settle my account. The receptionist told me Smiley had paid my bill in full. Nothing was due. Smiley was already on his way to pick us up at the hotel when I called him. As soon as he arrived, I brought up the hotel bill question. Inflexible, he repeated sternly, "It's done."

Unwilling to get into a last-minute argument, I said, "Thank you."

We hugged goodbye at the airport. We didn't speak to or see each other after that. Both of us knew there was no future in the relationship.

I can summarize my trip to Los Angeles in four sentences: We enjoyed it. I tried to give my daughters a traditional family. I left aware that Smiley was not for me. It wasn't meant to be.

Were my standards too high for my own good?

I wasn't disappointed that a relationship did not develop. We weren't a match—just a social encounter, incompatible in the long run. I was glad I found out early on. In other words, I tried to have a stepfather beside me. It didn't materialize.

My thoughts swirled as I reviewed my conversation with Smiley. I stated that children's feelings toward the "other" parent must be respected. I also stated that children need to have access to both parents while I denied my daughters' trip to Mykonos with their father based on concerns about the company they would keep.

My script needed revision. I must give Joelle and Sabrina comparable exposure to both parents. A mother can dismiss her husband but cannot change her children's father. I accepted my updated perspective before we landed at JFK.

161

NEW YORK, MID-DECEMBER 1988

Just two weeks remained until Christmas! New York was busy during the holiday season. We had a plan in place. *The Nutcracker* was a week away. We had two extra tickets to invite friends to St. Patrick's Cathedral Grand Mass on Christmas Eve. A New Year's Eve gathering was organized. Close friends agreed to join us, a much-appreciated solution for those without family in the city. Each year the group increased, through word of mouth and culinary treats prepared by Marie and Rafik.

The phone rang ten days before Christmas.

"Hello, I'm here," Bobby said joyfully.

"In New York?"

"Yes, in New York. I told you I would be coming."

"Great," I said with enthusiasm.

"I can't wait to see you. Thirty minutes, OK ?"

"That long," I said laughing.

"Thirty minutes, *illico presto*. I'm happy to see you."

"I'm happy to see you too."

Happy was an understatement. Elated, I bolted off my desk chair. My house dress flew away. I felt my heart pounding, my breathing getting faster. I dashed into the shower, came out as fast as I could, and grabbed the first jogging outfit from the nearby drawer. I put it on and emerged from my room disheveled, yet with a beaming smile. I brushed my hair, put some lip gloss on, sprayed Ombre Rose, looked at myself in the mirror, and said, "Yes."

My winter coat flew from its hanger as I sprinted down the hallway, raced to the elevator, then held myself back.

What am I doing? I need to remember: Bobby is married. I won't do to others what was done to me.

My internal lecture slowed my breath and anchored me in the now, away from dreaming, from impulse dyscontrol. I landed in the lobby breathless, sat on a couch, trying to appear calm.

By the time Bobby arrived, my breathing was under control. Seeing him made my heart race. He looked disarming with his bashful smile and swept me in a huge bear hug.

"I have a surprise for you," he said.

"Tell me."

"No, let's walk."

We walked, making a right turn to reach Fifth Avenue, and walked toward Central Park South.

"Where are we going?"

"You'll see."

"It's cold. Are we walking for long?"

"No. We're almost there."

A few minutes later, we stood in front of a skyscraper in midtown Manhattan. I stared at him, puzzled. He held my hand to make a right on 56th Street and smiled as he led me to enter the building's residential side.

"Hello," the concierge said, handing him a key with a formal salutation.

We walked into the elevator. "Where are we going?" I asked again.

"Soon, you'll see," he whispered in the elevator, landing us on a high floor. He took my hand and led me with determination, knowing where he was heading, and turned the key in the door, saying, "Voilà!"

We entered a bright apartment with a magnificent view of Central Park South. I looked at him.

"I bought it," he said.

"You bought it? Congratulations! It's stunning."

"I'm glad you like it. I bought it to come to New York to work and see you."

I threw myself in his arms and then held myself back.

What am I doing?

"Let me show you around," he said as he sensed my ambivalence.

He showed me every room of the beautiful, well laid out, two-bedroom apartment.

"And it's already furnished."

"Yes, I did it all to size, based on the floor plan."

"Beautiful."

"We have to make up for the lost time."

"That's what I'm concerned about."

"Concerned about what?"

"There are other people in our lives."

"You mean your husband?"

"No. We are separated. We'll divorce soon. I'm thinking about you, married with three children."

"I told you in Monaco. If it weren't for my three children…"

"But you have three children."

"We should have been together. You know that."

"But we're not."

"My feelings haven't changed."

"Our lives have."

Bobby held me tighter and tighter. The attraction overcame my better judgment. We lost track of time. Past midnight we were still in the living room. He looked at me and said, "As I always fantasized it would be and more."

I hugged him.

The view was magical at night. The Metropolitan Museum stood out as a bright spot amidst the dimly lit surroundings of Central Park.

"I have to go."

"You're not staying over?"

"No. I rarely go out at night and come back home so late."

"I'll take you back home."

"Better not."

"Let's have dinner tomorrow. If it's OK with you, I'll come by and see the girls before we go out."

"That's fine."

"I'll walk back with you."

We ambled home together, holding arms. Every few minutes, he held my arm tighter and pulled me closer to him.

What have I done?

At home, I reflected on what had just happened. Bobby was and consistently had been a wonderful man, dear to me, so very close. As Bobby had said, our intimacy felt natural and overdue—the way it should have been from the beginning. I was happy we had become intimate, and I felt it was the missing connection in our relationship.

Despite the above, Bobby and I had started a connection that I wouldn't allow to bloom. For me and him, I wouldn't do it. He would resent me for his guilt if he disrupted his family commitment. Bobby was a kind man. He didn't have built-in wiring for pulling plugs.

I was also concerned I was getting myself into another sticky situation. Again, I wouldn't do to others what was done to me. Twenty-five years later, we were somewhat back to where we started, except now Bobby had family commitments. And I was still legally married.

That night I wondered *how come I married Eddy, instead of Bobby*. Bobby would have been a great life partner, still I doubt I would have accomplished much in a cozy environment. I wouldn't have become who I am today.

Did I say no when I should have said yes? Was I saying yes when I should say no?

162

NEW YORK, MID-DECEMBER 1988

The girls were thrilled to see Bobby the following day. Joelle had known him since she was born. His oldest daughter was her best friend. With the gifts he brought for the girls, pure frenzy was in the air the moment he stepped inside the apartment. He chatted and giggled with them. His ways of interacting with his daughters were also effective with mine.

Seeing my daughters happy made me happy. We tucked the girls in bed and went out for dinner. He held my shoulder and lifted me to hug me. *So, this is how our relationship would feel.*

I liked it. I basked in his tender love. I would put my head on his shoulder, feel calm, and enjoy it forever. It was a sweet and sour realization—he wasn't mine. He was someone else's. I gathered my composure and braved the situation as I knew I should.

We walked to the 21 Club, his favorite New York restaurant. We were seated at a corner table, gazing into each other's eyes. He bent to squeeze my hand and kiss my neck. I took the lead and said, "We go a long way back. When I see you, you come accompanied by an entire village, my children, your children, my parents, your parents, Lausanne, Beirut, and I can go on. These memories are extremely meaningful to me. You know it. I care about you a lot, but I don't want to be entangled in a dead-end situation for me or cause any disruption in the lives of others, especially in the lives of children."

"I have always loved you."

"Me too, but let's stop here," I said, looking at him intensely. "We can't go further without hurting someone emotionally."

Bobby nodded.

We chatted for the rest of the dinner. We had known each other forever. None of us would disappear. We knew it. We would be in each other's lives until the end—no need for more. More was not feasible.

We walked out of the restaurant with our arms enlaced, our palms clasped, our fingers interlaced. How much closer could we be? He pulled me toward him, telling me sweet nothings. Nonverbally, I nudged him toward my home rather than his.

"Do you mind if we go to look at the Rockefeller Center Christmas tree?" he asked.

"Not at all."

We both needed to spend more time together. We strolled and bantered, his arm embracing my shoulder, window shopping. Fifth Avenue was lively, as it usually is during the holiday season. Masses of people were sprawling around as we were. We occasionally had to struggle through the crowd, enticed to walk around in the cool but not freezing evening. I told him the little I knew about the first twenty-foot balsam Christmas tree in 1931 during the construction of Rockefeller Center at the time of the Great Depression.

I held Bobby's hand tightly and hugged him in front of the tree. We were just the two of us embracing each other in the middle of the Christmas multitude, careful not to slip on the icy ground. I pressed my lips against his neck and asked him to part there. He wouldn't hear of it and walked me back home. We kissed goodbye. While brushing away burning tears, I saw him mouthing "I love you," from a distance.

163

NEW YORK, JANUARY 1989

The midnight between1988 and 1989 brought clarity.

I am ready. I must divorce this year and become a free woman.

Eddy and I had been separated for over four years. I reviewed the essential aspects of my upcoming independent life. Everything was in place, including my revised balanced budget. The doctoral program started in September. I didn't wish to be distracted by divorce hassles. The timing was right.

I had become the protagonist of my own story, in control of the center stage. My relationship with Eddy slid into the background, a tangential relationship about to split off, already estranged. We saw each other occasionally around the girls and were both keen on maintaining social courtesy for our daughters' sake as well as ours.

My daughters and my doctoral degree in preparation for my upcoming professional career required my undivided attention. No longer did I have the time or appetite for time-consuming romantic relationships.

Neither of the two men I wanted to be close to would be my life partner. One had alcohol-related issues, and the other had family obligations. Yet I longed for and loved them both for different reasons. Alan was an essential counterpart of a major turning point in my life history; Bobby was an integral part of my history. Neither was meant to be. Positive vibes flew to both men across time and distance. I trusted they received them on some level.

Enough wishing. It was time for action—divorce action.

164

NEW YORK, JANUARY 1989

Joelle and Sabrina were back in school. I was still on semester break, enjoying a few relaxing days. Spending time in the New York University bookstore was one of my favorite extracurricular activities. I enjoyed browsing through all the recent publications, wishing I could x-ray the information straight into my brain without spending time reading and assimilating it word for word or concept by concept.

At the end of my book browsing, I was still looking for a book to read and went to La Librairie de France at Rockefeller Center to browse French psychology books. The library atmosphere was stimulating. I looked around and stepped in front of the psychoanalysis section. Didier Anzieu's *Le Moi-Peau* captured my attention. I pulled the book, perused the first couple of pages, and stepped up to the cashier to pay for it. The subject matter spoke to me. Life experiences changed the make-up of my cells. I was no longer the same woman.

On that sunny day in January, I went to the payphone before sitting by the skating rink and ordering coffee to call home and ensure all was well. Letty answered, telling me Eddy's cousin had called to let me know he was in New York on business and wished to meet with me. The cousin was a fine family man, a father of two sons. His younger son, my godchild, a year older than Joelle, shared her spunky personality and red hair.

I dialed the number the cousin had left with Letty. We agreed to meet at my place at 6:30 p.m. to catch up and for him to have time to see the girls before they went to bed.

The cousin had not changed. His years in the Lebanese navy had maintained his stature and disposition. Tall, slim, with a thin mustache, he still carried the energy and stamina of the navy officer he once was before working with Eddy. Endowed with a radiant smile and loud laughter, he emanated cheerful verve and managed to be liked and appreciated by all. We had dinner with the girls in the kitchen and, once I kissed them good night, we sat in the living room to chat.

"Your husband is in a terrible spot."

"What's going on?"

"You know him. He doesn't consistently put the brakes on. He is in deep debt. He may ask you to finance him, to loan him some money."

"We are separated."

"Pardon me. I am a navy man. I say what is important without using diplomatic terminology."

"We have a prenup. We haven't lived together for almost five years. I won't be Eddy's wife when it's convenient and not his wife when it's not."

"He needs you."

"I needed a committed husband so many times and he wasn't there. I don't have any extra funds to give him, and if I had, I wouldn't get involved with him financially or otherwise. He has a father, a mother, a brother, other women, and one with two other children. He can get help from them. I am the sole caregiver and provider for my two daughters."

"I wanted to see you and pass on the latest update, so you won't be surprised when he asks you for money."

"I appreciate the delivery, but not its content. What led Eddy to that dire spot?"

With a somber expression, the cousin described his belief that Eddy's involvement in banking and politics, combined with struggles with impulse control, led him to take risks and suffer significant financial losses.

The scenario didn't seem impossible to me; I had been part of the core circle for so long. Still, I expressed my resistance to helping Eddy as I no longer trusted or believed in him.

"I have no idea what his business deals are, let alone the details."

"I know. I don't know the details either. No one does."

"Eddy made money. He can choose to lose it if he wishes. As his wife, I played a significant role in his journey to wealth and fame. I left an affluent, successful husband who believed he could control everything. Let the people who contributed to his financial downfall step up and support him."

The officer nodded politely, and we chatted until late at night. My decision to stay out of the latest issues was irreversible.

I was sad to see the cousin leave and thanked him for forewarning me.

Will the chaos ever stop?

165

NEW YORK, FEBRUARY 15, 1989

The second semester of my MA in psychology started well. My classes provided me with a reference point and background knowledge in psychology. The professors were excellent, but sometimes idiosyncratic. I remember asking the physiological psychology professor whether there was a way to excel at his subject without obsessing about it. He looked surprised, paused, then looked at me and said, "I don't think there is. Keep obsessing."

I chuckled and said, "I will. I'm good at it."

Intellectual stimulation and knowledge were my daily frame of mind. In the evenings and weekends, I studied and spent time with my daughters, occasionally with friends. Due to lack of time and sleep, social life took a back seat. The girls and I followed a schedule. It made life predictable—a welcomed change after a hectic past.

In my mind, I was eager to receive my doctoral admission response letters. The due date was approaching. Was it going to be a slim envelope received ahead of the chunky acceptance letters?

A week later, I received fantastic news. Two doctoral programs accepted me in the fall of 1989, and two others placed me on the waitlist. I accepted New York University's offer immediately—my top choice. My doctoral journey was to begin in September 1989.

166

NEW YORK, FEBRUARY 19, 1989

The girls and I enjoyed relaxing during Presidents' Weekend. We went to Central Park and the baby zoo on Sunday. The temperature was dropping. We rushed back home for an early Sunday dinner.

We were just done with dinner at about 6:30 p.m. when the telephone rang. "Your husband is in trouble, big trouble," said his executive administrative assistant.

"What kind of trouble?"

"Bankruptcy. It's serious. They want to arrest him. They are asking for one million dollars in bail to let him out on parole."

"One million dollars!"

"Yes, and he is asking you to pay."

"Where will I get the money from? I don't have a million dollars, and if I had a million dollars, I wouldn't pay for him."

"Eddy needs money."

"Where did all his funds go?"

"..."

"I am accountable for my two daughters and myself first," I said, and reiterated the line I had given Eddy's cousin. "We have a prenup. We have been separated for over four years. Let Eddy's family and entourage pay for him, loan him. I am no longer part of that saga."

"He needs you."

"Where was he when I needed him? I don't have the money—end of the conversation. I am hanging up the phone."

She called again an hour later, saying, "If you don't pay, they will arrest him."

"Who are they?"

"..."

"It's his problem."

She called one more time. "If they arrest him, you're going to be in trouble because you're his wife."

"Are you threatening me? Hear me: Our assets are legally separated based on the prenup he required twenty-five years ago. I have no idea what he has done all this time and don't want to be involved in his transactions. Let him go to jail if he deserves it."

She called again twenty minutes later. "How would your daughters feel if they knew about your decision?"

"I was instrumental in his rise to glory and left him when he reached the peak of his career. Summon those who contributed to his downfall. They ought to be there for him."

"Eddy needs you."

"Are you taking cues from him? I can hear him through your words. Every time you call me, you have a new line, a different tune."

"…"

"One more time, I know nothing and wish to know nothing about his business deals. I do not have a million dollars to donate. What belongs to me is mine."

"You can sell your apartment in NYC. Please do it for your children. Do you want them to have a father who went to jail?"

"Sell my apartment? The apartment my father gave me. No way."

"Mortgage your apartment. We could help you get a mortgage, a quick deal."

"Are you kidding me? No mortgage. No quick deal. No million dollars for my apartment."

"Please do it for the girls. I beg you. He begs you."

"I am keeping the apartment for Joelle and Sabrina, and for me. I am hanging up."

I put down the receiver, kissed the girls goodnight, and curled into bed, shaking from head to toe.

Will I ever, ever be done with this messy, manic nightmare?

167

NEW YORK, FEBRUARY 20, 1989

The phone started ringing at 5 a.m. There is a seven-hour time difference between New York and Beirut. The executive assistant called again. "Your husband has been kidnapped. They want one million and a half dollars ransom."

"Yesterday, he was going to be arrested and needed one-million-dollars in bail. Today he's kidnapped and needs one million and a half. Tomorrow what? What kind of story is this?"

Every fifteen to thirty minutes, she called me again and again. She wanted me to pawn everything I owned, begging me for my help and Bobby's help.

I called Bobby to get a realistic version of what was going on. "Stay out of this," he said without hearing anything further.

"What's going on?"

"I'll tell you at another time. Why don't you come to Paris?"

"Let me think about it."

I stopped answering the phone. I took a few deep breaths to calm myself down, hopped in the shower, and went for a brisk walk. Again, my steps took me to St. Patrick's Cathedral. I knelt in front of St. Anthony's Chapel and lit a few candles.

Walking back home, I decided on an approach to the situation. The first step was to get an airline ticket. I rushed to the phone. "Rafik, please find and book me on the cheapest same-day flight to Paris and meet me at home."

"Fine."

The concierge was a very knowledgeable, efficient man. I asked for paper and pencil and wrote the following Telex to Eddy: "I will try to help if you agree to give me your irrevocable unconditional commitment to divorce and full custody of our two daughters via this Telex."

Eddy answered back, "I agree."

I asked him to rewrite what I had written in the Telex, clarifying his agreement.

Eddy spelled out his agreement and resent the Telex.

How come Eddy had easy access to a Telex while being kidnapped?

His story didn't add up.

Rafik walked in. Seeing me shaken, he wondered what was going on. I told him. He didn't seem surprised. He shook his head quietly.

I went to see Joelle and Sabrina who were getting ready to go to school.

"I have to fly on business." A puzzled look appeared on Sabrina's face. A frown spread across Joelle's face. We sat down, as I said, "I wanted both of you to have an intact family, a household where your parents lived together. I tried my best, waited long enough. I cannot continue being married to your father. Our differences are irreconcilable. I will divorce your father. I would like to inform you and get your approval, if possible."

"Mom, do what you think you need to do," Joelle said.

"Thank you, sweetie." I gave her a huge hug and kissed her forehead and did the same with Sabrina.

Then, I said, "Mom and Dad will always love you."

Unable to conceal my trembling voice, I told the girls, "You have one biological father and one biological mother. You must maintain a good relationship with your father, not for him but for yourselves, for the father image you have within you that is part of you."

I hugged them again and went to the living room to call Bobby in Paris. "I'll catch the first plane I can get. The story makes no sense. It's getting mind-boggling."

"Please tell me which flight you're taking; I'll pick you up at Charles de Gaulle."

168

PARIS, FEBRUARY 21, 1989

Bobby waited for me at the arrival gate the following morning. He looked very pale and seemed not to have slept much. The minute he saw me, he said, "You have nothing to do with this. I'll see what can be done."

"Please don't put yourself in trouble."

"No worries."

"I would like to see a lawyer."

"I'll set up an appointment for you with a top lawyer."

He drove me to my apartment. As I was opening the door of his car, I said, "I also want to sell this apartment. It's in my name."

"I'll help you find a buyer. I must go to the office. Let's have dinner tonight."

"Sounds good."

Bobby called an hour later, "You have an appointment with an eminent lawyer tomorrow at 10 a.m."

"Thank you."

"Café Flandrin tonight at 8 p.m. sound good?"

"Very good."

"I'll pick you up."

The phone rang nonstop all day long. Karl, and executive members of the office, called me relentlessly, pressuring me to give money to Eddy. I threw the ball back in their corner, reiterating what I told Eddy's cousin and his executive administrative assistant.

Karl resented my resistance to help his brother financially. "Djenane, the family and I count on you to help Eddy."

"How come?"

"You are his wife."

"Now, I'm his wife? Only when it's convenient? Eddy has his entire family and other people in his life who could pay for him."

"Sell the apartment in New York."

"I will not. Hear me. I will not. My father gifted me the apartment. I am responsible for Joelle and Sabrina and for myself."

"You have to sell New York."

"I will not."

"You have to…"

Karl, I am hanging up."

"Djenane…"

"Please don't call me ever again about this matter!" I yelled at him and slammed the phone, shaking uncontrollably.

Bobby and I enjoyed catching up over dinner at Le Flandrin, a neighborhood restaurant we both liked and that was close to where we lived. He told me about the lawyer I would meet in the morning and veered to Eddy's crisis. I updated him about my conversation with Karl and said, "I know nothing about the crisis. As you know, Eddy hardly ever shared the details of the business with me, especially since he knew I didn't see eye to eye with his business style. And I wasn't around and hardly saw him in the last five years."

Bobby nodded.

"I'd like to be helpful without being pulled into his saga. One can lose a husband or partner, but it is much more difficult to lose the other parent of one's children," I said.

"Understood," he said and then asked me, "Who do you think would be willing or able to help?"

"Eddy's family—though they too are reluctant to get involved. They tried to put me in the forefront to protect themselves financially and emotionally. They don't want to get into a rabbit hole. Besides his family, other relation-ships perhaps, business or romantic. I'm not about to guess who would be reliable or available to help Eddy at this time."

"Are you OK if Eddy ends up in jail?"

"If he deserves it."

"How about Joelle and Sabrina?"

"I will do my best."

We remained pensive for a moment.

"I considered several options. There is no better resource than his family," I said.

"I think so too."

We continued brainstorming and chatting until the late hours of the night, ultimately reaching the same conclusion.

"Let me know when you're done with the lawyer," Bobby said, hugging me good night.

Given the time difference, I was still able to call Joelle and felt comforted to hear her voice. The minute we hung up, I collapsed into bed to sleep for a couple of hours.

169

PARIS, FEBRUARY 22, 1989

At 10 a.m. sharp, I was ushered into the lawyer's office, which was as impressive as his address. Right away he said, "Please give me the reason that brought you to my office and seek legal advice."

When I was done, the lawyer nodded and without skipping a beat, he said, "Are you, Madame, a citizen of the United States?"

"Yes, I am."

"Then, Madame, kindly pack your bags and go back to the US right away. You have nothing to do with this *magouille*. Go back to New York and stay there."

"Ok," I said, stunned to hear him use that word—the exact word the man who had made an early house call had used. This time the word carried much more weight coming from an eminent Parisian lawyer.

As I was about to leave, I asked him for the name of a family lawyer in New York to initiate the divorce proceedings. He spoke with his assistant and asked her to give me the requested information.

I stopped by her desk on my way out to settle his fee and get the name and contact information of a New York City family lawyer. She handed me the information and asked if she could provide him with some contextual data. I gave her consent and asked for my bill. She told me the lawyer would not charge me. I insisted.

"There is no fee. The lawyer is already with another client," she said.

It was time for me to breathe and collect my thoughts. I loved driving, especially in Paris. My ten-year-old Pacer was still in the garage with its keys hidden in the same place. Someone must have kept it tuned up. When I put the key in, I was happy to hear the motor running. I pressed my foot on the gas and took advantage of the right of way rule prevalent there (*priorité de droite*), squeezing the Pacer in the often-narrow streets of Paris.

Paris's spectacular surroundings refreshed my perspective and rebooted my energy. When I returned to the apartment, I sent a thank-you note to the lawyer and put "For Sale" signs on the windows facing the street.

A couple called that very same day, expressing strong interest in buying the property. To secure the sale, I discounted the apartment's price by 10 percent, a copious real estate broker fee. My time and energy were too limited for hassles. Aside from the apartment, the buyers also wanted to purchase the curtains and most of the furniture, including Eddy's desk, given to him by his mother when she moved from Cairo to Beirut.

While I agreed to selling the furniture, I was unsuccessful in retaining or bartering the desk for other furniture. It became the deal breaker. I dropped the request. The apartment was sold in three days. The notary Bobby recommended sealed the deal.

Serendipitously, the final sale price amounted to what Eddy's corporate lawyer had told me Eddy owed my father on the day of my parents' funeral in Lausanne.

Life is a merry-go-round. I shook my head and smiled. *Dad, you'll get paid.* That was the end of the Paris apartment and my father's consultation fee, but not of my marital saga.

Bobby and I had dinner in the evening. I gave him my feedback about the lawyer, including *magouille*. He remained silent.

Then, he summarized what he had been able to accomplish with Eddy's family. We thought we had done our best.

We looked at each other. Silence followed. In my heart of hearts, I felt extremely grateful to have Bobby as a lifelong friend. It is possible that I did not tell him then and there my care and appreciation. We were both out of breath.

I flew back to New York the next morning.

The minute I arrived I settled my accounts with Letty and Rafik.

170

NEW YORK, EARLY MARCH 1989

A few days later, Mike called me from Paris. "Hi. Eddy is asking you for money."

"Again! He just got money from his family."

"He needs more."

"And you're calling?"

"Well, he asked me to call you."

"I have no money to give him."

"May I tell you what he's asking for?"

"Yes."

"He's asking you to mortgage the New York apartment and sell the furniture you have there."

I choked. "I have already discussed these matters with Karl and other colleagues and told them, "No. No way. Never. I'm selling items to fund my own budget."

"Are you sure?"

"Positive."

Mike paused, and whispered, "Good for you, Djenane. I am glad you made that decision. Take care of yourself and your daughters."

Taken aback, with a slightly raised heartbeat and unsteady voice, I said, "Thank you."

Under duress, Mike revealed he had a soul. I hadn't expected him to dissent with Eddy.

How come they're chasing the New York apartment and not the French one, which was already sold?

Later that day, the head of the New York office contacted me. A fine professional woman and electronic expert, she worked well with Rafik. I agreed to meet with her. An hour later, she arrived with a briefcase filled with documents. There was no cash at Eddy's New York office. Business accounts were in the red. His New York city apartment had screaming bills.

I reviewed the office bills, paid the office's utility, and covered two months' salaries for both her and Rafik. I declined to pay Eddy's bills. The head of the New York office thanked me and left.

As soon as she left, I contacted the New York lawyer the Paris lawyer recommended.

171

NEW YORK, EARLY MARCH 1989

Our next day's meeting began with the New York lawyer telling me the Parisian lawyer had briefed him. He also told me he would ask for a divorce lawyer to meet with me at his office. Before scheduling an appointment, he needed to decide who would be the best match. I felt comfortable with his approach. Our meeting was brief. I was getting tired of rehashing my own story.

A couple of days later, the New York lawyer called to tell me he had found two divorce lawyers he thought would be a good match for my case.

Wearing casual attire, I walked into the legal firm. My lawyer met me first, followed by two other lawyers. I appreciated the advantage of having two lawyers handling the case. As I listened to their presentation, I didn't see myself working well with them. In the first round, they would ruffle my feathers. After thanking them, I told my lawyer that I did not think they were a good match for me.

Dismayed, I returned home. Bobby called me as soon as I walked in. I updated him on the latest developments. He understood and said he would ask friends for a referral. An hour later, he called back with the name of a family lawyer.

The lawyer answered his phone. I appreciated that. I also liked his voice over the phone and met with him the next day. I felt comfortable with him right away, sharing my backstory and chatting for a while. He was interested in my case, and his retainer fee was reasonable. I had found my lawyer.

Wanting to expedite matters, I asked him for a divorce application. We filled in my part and took the whole application ready to be completed by Eddy. As we were speaking, I told him, "I want to write my divorce settlement. You will peruse it and add a few binding legal statements."

"You want to do that?" he said.

"Yes."

"It's an efficient idea. It will save you money along the way."

"No problem with that," I said. "I will get busy writing the divorce settlement and send you the draft."

"Sounds good."

The meeting was well suited to my needs. I felt even better about writing the settlement. No one knew the details of the settlement better than I did. It only made sense for me to write it.

My business experience enabled me to label each request and asset unequivocally, and I spent the entire day fine-tuning the write-up. I reread it in the morning, made a few minor changes, typed it on my Macintosh, and printed it. The document was placed in a large envelope, and I handed it down to the concierge.

"Please send it by express certified mail."

With a nod of understanding, he replied, "Of course."

"The settlement is on its way," I said to the lawyer over the phone.

"You get an A for efficiency."

"I hope to get another one for legal matters."

"I'll let you know."

When I hung up the phone, I knew I had moved things forward as much as possible. I needed to take it easy and prepare for the weeks ahead.

The chaos of the past few weeks settled down for ten days. I didn't hear from anyone—not even from my lawyer—and counted my blessings. I was under the illusion, or rather delusion, that I would no longer hear from the group.

The lawyer was the first one to call. He said my work earned an A-, he had made some minor revisions to make it binding, and he had sent it back to me via FedEx. I was thrilled and took a deep breath. I wrapped up the settlement in the most cost-efficient way.

NEW YORK, LATE MARCH 1989

Bobby called me to tell me that Eddy had emerged in Beirut and was flying to New York with his brother. A few minutes later, Karl called me to reiterate the same information. Eddy and Karl were landing in New York in forty-eight hours.

The doorbell buzzed at about 10 p.m. I was already in bed. I walked to the door but didn't open it. Letty followed me with an anxious look in her eyes. I gestured with my index finger to remain silent. Through the peephole, I saw Eddy and Karl. They buzzed again, longer the second time around. Then they left.

I sighed, relieved the girls hadn't woken up. Brawls in front of them were the last thing I wanted. Silence. I was fuming. Given the circumstances, the late house call was a breach of boundaries.

Still shaking, I called the concierge telling him that Eddy no longer had free access to me and needed to be announced.

I sat by my bedroom window and gazed at the New York skyline. I focused on the chimneys emitting smoke. They mirrored my thoughts and feelings. Needing to release some of the tension, I engaged in the first physical exercise I learned and the one I enjoyed the most. Stretching my back on the floor and rolling my legs over my head, I felt subtle tension relief.

I stood up—ready for the busy fortnight ahead of me.

NEW YORK, LATE MARCH 1989

Eddy called me early the following day, saying, "You didn't open the door last night and didn't pay for my maintenance and Con Edison."

"We're separated. Why would I do any of that?"

"Suddenly, you change."

"It has been that way for over four years. That's not sudden."

"I would like to see the girls."

"Yes, and I would like to see you too."

"See me?"

"Yes. We need to start the divorce proceedings."

"You are my wife, and we will die married to each other and be buried next to each other."

"Remember the Telex."

"I was under pressure."

"You agreed with the divorce in the Telex. Let's meet daytime tomorrow when the girls are at school."

I sighed. One step done. I pulled out of my home safe the two blank letterheads with Eddy's signature in blue ink at the bottom, hoping I wouldn't need to use them.

NEW YORK, LATE MARCH 1989

Eddy was punctual. He usually is.

"Karl is not with you?"

"He said you didn't want to see him."

"Not when he makes unreasonable demands."

"You didn't open the door last night."

"I didn't want to deal with the two of you when the girls were sleeping."

"…"

"Here is the divorce paperwork. I filled in my part. Please fill in yours."

"I don't want to divorce, so I won't fill out any forms."

"I want to."

"Your parents would have stopped you from doing this."

I laughed it off. Little did he know.

"I filled in your part. Read it."

"I'm not interested."

"I will read it to you."

Eddy looked at me, took the document, reviewed it.

"Sign it."

He looked at it again and signed, saying, "If this is what you want."

Letty witnessed his signature and signed after him.

I handed him the divorce settlement, saying, "Please review it."

"You know I won't pay you a dime," he said, perusing it.

"You know you will continue looking at your face in a mirror for the rest of your life. Oh, but you will see a different face—not the one I see."

"I'm broke."

"Not when I left you. You must have hooked up with the wrong people."

"Hmm…" he introjected, looking at me intensely.

"You were right to tell me: My business will collapse if you leave me."

"…"

"I married a student who had potential but no material possessions. That gave me a unique advantage that no future partner of yours can claim. Almost five years ago, I left a man who had everything: affluence and power. Now, I am about to divorce a man who says he lost everything. What happened in the interim? What kind of unfortunate company have you kept?"

"What happened, happened. Let's not recriminate about the past."

"The sour part is that you're paying the highest price."

"I don't want to divorce."

"I understand. If I were in your shoes, I wouldn't want to divorce me either."

"Your decision. You bear the responsibilities. You'll get nothing from me."

"Not even for your daughters?"

"..."

I stopped, not wanting to engage with Eddy. We could have debated this issue till the end of time.

"I won't pay for the divorce either. You want it. You pay for it," he continued.

"Fine."

"You may kiss your divorce goodbye if it isn't concluded before I leave in three weeks," Eddy said, becoming physically agitated, moving his body across the sofa.

"I'll work with your time frame," I said, concluding our divorce conversation.

Eddy's money was not something I wanted—even for our daughters' upkeep. I had reached a point where I didn't want a thing from him. I wanted out. My upbringing, standards, and my parents' values shaped my paradigm. All I wanted was to be free and out of the never-ending chaotic saga.

Karl and I didn't see each other again. We stood on opposite sides of the fence. Our paths diverged thereafter. Our estrangement stood as a significant loss for me. The last conversation we had in Paris cost me my relationship with Karl, a man I liked very much and considered a dear friend.

175

NEW YORK, APRIL 2, 1989

Letty photocopied the paperwork before putting it in a FedEx envelope and sending it to my lawyer to verify and proceed. Then I called him to let him know the divorce documents, including the settlement, were on their way. Once he received them, he could file the divorce proceedings. The lawyer was very impressed and said he would start right away.

I asked him, "How long will the divorce procedure take?"

"About a year."

"A year … It can't be that long. Eddy is leaving in three weeks. Any other way?"

"Not if you want to divorce in New York."

"The clock is ticking. Where else could we divorce?"

"I'll check and let you know."

I became antsy waiting for a divorce destination. There was no time to waste. Divorce would keep me busy and take away my attention from the doctoral program. The thought tormented me for the next couple of days until the lawyer phoned. "Santo Domingo expedites divorces. You could have one in two weeks. Your husband ... sorry, your soon-to-be ex-husband will have to agree to it. I'll let you know once I have found a lawyer to handle the divorce proceedings and finalize them in New York.

"It sounds good."

"Would Eddy go with you?"

"I doubt it."

"The lawyer can represent him. You need to have a witness. Would you be able to have a witness with you?"

"That can be arranged."

I called Eddy and asked him if he wanted to go with me to Santo Domingo. "No, I don't. You want to divorce. I don't."

I gave him an outline of the procedure.

"You're in such a rush to divorce me."

"You would be in a hurry too if I had done to you what you have done to me."

"Who doesn't trip in a lifetime?"

"Trip?" I gasped. "You call your chronic behavior a trip?" I said, fuming.

"Ok. Go ahead with the Dominican divorce. Who will you take with you?"

"Letty."

"Did you ask her? She's Catholic; she may disapprove of divorce."

"The Pope would bless my divorce. I will ask her right now."

Letty agreed.

I called Marie to ask her to stay with the girls. She agreed, too, after chuckling and saying, "You're doing it."

Ten days later, Letty and I were on a plane to Santo Domingo. My lawyer had organized everything to precision.

176

SANTO DOMINGO AND NEW YORK, APRIL 1989

"We must be ready by 8 a.m. The lawyer is picking us up to go to court."

Letty looked at me and asked again, "Are you alright?"

"Yes, I am fine. I have been waiting for this event for a long while."

"I know."

"Please let me know if there is anything you need." She sighed and padded to her room. Before closing the door, she stuck her head in again.

"Thank you. You're very kind," I said to reassure her. Before I knew it, I was fast asleep but woke up several times during the night.

Before I knew it, 4:30 a.m. ticked the end of my night. I visualized the day ahead and hoped everything would be alright. By 6 a.m. I showered, ordered breakfast, and called the girls as they were waking up. They were chirpy, getting ready to go to school. They cheered me up. I sat on the room's balcony, took deep, slow breaths, and prayed for a few minutes.

Letty and I were standing in the lobby by 7:55 a.m. We did some window shopping, waiting for the lawyer to arrive. He came at 8 a.m. sharp, driving his car. We went through the busy city center to get to the courthouse. On our way, he asked me if I needed to review the morning's plan. "No. Thank you," I said, feeling surreal and thinking, *I got this*.

We arrived at the courthouse by 8:30 a.m. The lawyer parked the car at his assigned space, looked at me, and asked me again if I was OK.

"Tense," I said.

"Everything will be fine."

I nodded. It was time to get over the last chore.

We walked into the courthouse. I felt I was an outside observer of the scene with tingling sensation in my lower legs. The chamber where the judge would preside carried an intense energy. The judge came in at 9 a.m.

We stood up and remained standing with the lawyer to my left and Letty to my right. There were a few motions the lawyer answered for me after getting my consent at each time. He asked me a question. I answered and Letty replicated my answer. About an hour later, the lawyer turned toward me and said, "Congratulations, I guess. You are divorced!"

"Really?" I looked at the clock. It was 10:15 a.m.

"Yes. I will get the documents stamped, signed, and notarized. You will have them at your hotel tomorrow first thing in the morning and I will file the divorce in New York. You'll be able to catch your early afternoon flight back home."

"Thank you."

The divorce took years to materialize and seventy-five minutes to finalize. I had visualized that outcome for years, but not quite this way. Walking like an automaton through the hotel lobby and up to my room, I got into bed with a stiff body and aching bones.

I looked at my watch. It was only 11 a.m. The girls were still at school, but Marie would be at home. I called her and shared with her the courthouse experience—divorce reality versus fantasy. "I can't believe it's done," I said.

She kept a sober voice and said, "Congratulations. You're free. You can do what you want."

"It will gradually settle in my mind."

"How long has it been? How long have you been waiting for it?"

"I'm not counting anymore."

We hung up. I needed to relax. I stayed in my room and closed my eyes.

I was a divorced woman, at last.

When I woke up, I asked Letty to join me for dinner at the hotel's better restaurant. We needed to celebrate. We chatted about the girls over our meals, reminiscing about my older and younger daughters when she joined our family. I thanked her for being a discreet ear and a warm heart to each of us, including Marie. Both of us wept and laughed, even chuckling when we recalled fun memories of the girls.

In the morning, the lawyer reviewed the divorce documents with me and handed me originals, saying he would file the divorce in New York. After paying his remaining fee, I placed the divorce documents in my briefcase. I thanked him, shook his hand, and we parted ways. Both the divorce process and the lawyer were surprisingly positive experiences.

Letty and I headed to the airport with merengue music blasting in the taxi. My foot tapped along to the rhythm until the car stopped.

On the flight back, I suddenly realized I had indeed paid for my divorce. It made me smile and feel great. And I got my divorce without having to use the blank signed letterheads. I took a deep breath and smiled even more, my heart and mind filled with gratitude.

When the plane landed in New York, I considered telling Bobby about the recent developments in my life. I chose not to do it to avoid putting myself in a difficult situation or disrupting his family life. I was happy to return home to my children in my apartment, finally living as an independent woman.

On the ride home, Alan suddenly came to mind. It had been four years since I last saw or spoke with him. I thought, *as soon as I walk into the apartment, I'll write to him and tell him I'm divorced and ask him how he's doing.*

What was I thinking?

I didn't want to resume the relationship. My decision hadn't changed. I wanted to reconnect with the counterpart of the amazing journey we shared, culminating in the divorce.

As soon as I entered the apartment, I rushed to my desk and wrote Alan a note letting him know I had divorced and was looking forward to seeing him. After stamping the envelope, I ran to the mailbox to drop it off myself. Then, I counted down the days until I heard from him.

NEW YORK, APRIL 1989

I met with Eddy the next day to give him the divorce papers. First, I showed him the documents, then put each copy in its own envelope and handed it to him.

"You know what I'm going to do with it," he said.

"It's up to you."

Eddy took the envelope, placed it in his briefcase without opening it, then looked at me and said, "All right, you got what you wanted. Let's remarry."

I chuckled. Only Eddy could have come up with such a line.

"Let's get remarried," he repeated.

I laughed out loud. "Why would I do such a thing?"

"If you don't, I will be forced to get married," Eddy said, ignoring what I said.

"You will be forced to get married? Who has ever forced you to do anything?"

"I will be forced to get married," he repeated.

"What a love story. Your latest passion, another pregnant woman?"

He shook his head.

I left it at that.

178

NEW YORK, APRIL 1989

Alan replied immediately.

I walked into my room and locked the door to unseal the envelope. His note wished me well and said he was glad I divorced when it was convenient for me. He also said he got married a year ago and was happy with his relationship. He was accepted by his wife as he was. Therefore, catching up was not possible.

I froze. Our relationship had reached a full stop.

Didn't I already know it was over?

I sat down on the floor against my window, holding my knees, cupping my head in my hands. I was about to cry but stopped myself. My tears had been flowing for a long time, too long a time. Countless days, months, years.

Enough. I was going to dry my tears and move on—chin up.

It was high time to let the past go, hold on to the experience, enjoy the present, and look forward to the future.

NEW YORK, JULY 1989

Eddy, now legally my ex-husband, came back to see me about two months after we divorced. He asked me to get back together and forewarned me that he would remarry if we didn't.

When I said, "No," he reiterated what he had told me the previous time and added, "We're married under the Catholic Church. You still carry my name. We need to be buried side-by-side."

"No," I repeated, shaking my head.

I wasn't sure what motivated him. It didn't matter anymore. At this stage of our relationship, I wasn't going to speculate. My Herculean labors had been completed. It was time for me to begin a new chapter, not to mention a new tome of my life, and live it by my set of rules.

Divorce was done. Education at last! Dissertation, your time has come.

180

CAMBRIDGE, SEPTEMBER 1991

I dropped off Joelle with a friend of hers at her freshman dorm at Harvard—a wrenching experience. One of my daughters was beginning to fly independently. I cried all the way from Cambridge to New York.

Upon arriving in New York, I purchased a new bed and rearranged my former bedroom in the main apartment. Sabrina stayed in her room adjacent to mine. Joelle could use my or Sabrina's room during college breaks. Letty was happy to transition to a day schedule.

Next, I put an ad in the *New York Times* to rent the apartment next door, furnished. I signed the contract two weeks later.

Change branded our lives, and as a result the flexibility to adjust to imperative circumstances and rebound. And I had twenty years to make up. So upward and forward, I had to get moving.

Nietzsche uplifted me. What didn't kill me made me stronger. It fortified my psychological muscles.

181

NEW YORK, SUMMER 1992

I let Joelle and Sabrina visit their father in Paris on their own in summer 1992. By then Joelle was nineteen and Sabrina ten. They traveled and came back together. I felt confident they would speak up and stand on their own.

When they returned from vacation with him and their paternal grandmother during that summer, they reported a conversation they had with her. I was surprised by what she told them three years after our divorce and two years after Eddy's remarriage, "Tell your Mom she is still married to my son. We are Catholic. Your mother is my son's first and only wife."

"Yes," they both chimed in.

Only Eddy's Mom had the prerogative and audacity to say such a thing.

NEW YORK, UP TO MAY 1996 AND BEYOND

Once I disentangled myself from the chaos, I achieved my professional and personal goals. Milestones lined up one after another. Goal-oriented actions became the most effective stimulants and energy channels.

From the Re-Entry Program to my upcoming doctoral graduation at Washington Square, NYU was my home away from home. On class days, I took the bus to Eighth Street and walked to the School of Continuing Education, next to the Department of Psychology, and finally to the Graduate School of Education.

In my third year of graduate school, Columbia-Presbyterian Medical Center (CPMC), Department of Pediatric Psychiatry, became my hub. As I rode a packed elevator to the Child Psychiatry floor two weeks after starting my internship, a white-coated MD said aloud, "Nakhle, you work like an animal. You have a job here after your internship, if you want it."

Stunned, I inquired about her. She was the Medical Director. Later that day, I knocked on her office door and said, "Thank you for the offer. I will accept it in June."

At CPMC, I developed my clinical expertise and honed my passion for psychology, understanding and helping others. There, I discovered my professional identity as a clinician who loves what she does and does it with compassion. Working with families and running between the emergency room and outpatient floor with unbridled motivation, I liked and enjoyed the vibrant atmosphere. I felt helpful. Feeling helpful was a two-way flow of vitality. It helped me restore my self-confidence.

On CPMC's outpatient floor and emergency room, I provided individual and family therapy to eighty, mainly Spanish-speaking, families. I communicated with them in broken Spanish using words from my native French and soon became known as a Spanish speaker, even though at the end of a long day, French words replaced Spanish. The families empathized with my developing proficiency, which paradoxically strengthened our relationship. As I provided therapy, they told me, "We will speak slowly so you will understand everything." (*Vamos a hablar despacio para que usted entienda todo.*) Thanks to their compassion, I became fluent in Spanish.

My most meaningful clinical experiences occurred in the emergency room. One student was struggling with self-harming psychotic delusions. I entered the cubicle and engaged with the student, who was pounding the wall with their bare fists, making them bleed. The student suddenly yelled, "Dr. Nakhle, step out. The voices tell me to punch you. I don't want to do it."

Although experiencing a psychotic episode, the student showed empathy and differentiated between controllable and uncontrollable commands. As two situationally connected humans with compassion for each other, the student owned all the merit.

Work at CPMC also included supervision and teaching. I developed a psychology externship program. Each extern saw two patients and discussed their clinical charges with me. Psychiatry residents and psychology interns attended seminars I taught on multicultural populations, family violence, and psychological evaluations.

Research fascinated me. My study on child abuse was sponsored at the New York Psychiatric Institute and the Columbia Presbyterian Medical Center and its related clinics, The Montefiore Medical Center, Queens Children's Psychiatric Center, and Westchester Jewish Community Services. The study earned two grants: The National Center on Child Abuse and Neglect (NCCAN) Graduate Research Fellowship within the US Department of Health and Human Services (DHHS), and The Viola Bernard Endowment Fund at Columbia Presbyterian Medical Center. With these grants, I was able to hire an interviewer and create a double-blind scoring system for my questionnaires, enhancing the validity of my research. Conducting the study and analyzing the results were both insightful and enjoyable experiences. Most of all, I was eager to draw conclusions based on the findings and recommend further research.

I completed the doctoral program and defended my dissertation in May 1995—two weeks after the deadline for graduation—and had to wait another year to receive my degree and sit for licensing. I had waited twenty years. What were twelve months?

The defense of the dissertation was successful and went smoothly. I exited the room following the oral presentation and discussion. The committee invited me back a minute later. For the first time in my life, I was called Doctor Nakhle. My daughters waited for me outside the door and cheered me and hugged me tightly when I stepped out. Marie and Rafik met us in Washington Square to celebrate the event.

We walked around the area, reminiscing about the graduate school years and cracking family jokes. After that, we hurried home to celebrate the event. I was hosting a party that night, gathering close friends, including grade school friends who were also living in the US.

At age fifty, I felt rejuvenated by my degree. Education rebuilt my ego, filled my intellectual tank, and expanded my horizons. Academic and professional success restored my self-confidence.

My goal was to do it all. I wanted to embrace education and work and be a hands-on Mom to my daughters. I almost did, but it wasn't enough. It's rarely enough. While studying and developing a professional career, I short-changed my daughters despite my deep love and dedication to them. As their sole provider, I worked very long hours. My daughters complained about my hectic schedule, and I realized they had a valid point. I struggled to maintain a balance between providing and mothering. I couldn't. I wanted to be more present. I wasn't.

It's my loss. I apologized to my daughters.

Another heavy price was my physical exhaustion given the busy schedule and workload. The pace at the hospital was accelerated, and it was hard to maintain the same pace outside of its premises.

Joelle graduated from Harvard with Honors in Social Studies and was awarded a grant for research in India. She is analytic and thorough in her work approach and can achieve any goal she sets for herself. Her diligence and dedication to excellence shine in the many recognitions she's received. The depth of her thought is expressed in her oral and written languages. Any topic or project she undertakes will be deconstructed, analyzed, and reconstructed with extraordinary ability.

Sabrina graduated from Georgetown with Honors in International Political Studies. She picked up Tae Kwon Do at age eight, earned her black belt at age fourteen, and continues to excel in her athletic prowess. Sabrina has the ability, talent, and discipline to climb the highest mountain if she sets her mind to it. A firecracker quick on her feet with an unwavering ability to solve problems efficiently, she expresses herself with precision. Most of all, Sabrina shows boundless love and empathy.

My daughters and I are very close. They are my most trusted confidants. I feel proud and rewarded by our relationship. It is our most significant accomplishment as mother and daughters.

Characters in my life have moved on too. Marie and Rafik, my two chosen family members, were very dear to me as they witnessed and encouraged me during the most vulnerable years and episodes of my life. Letty was a granny figure for Joelle and Sabrina, who loved her dearly. I am forever thankful to Marie, Letty, and Rafik.

New York City has played a crucial role in my life. It's where most significant events took place. It's the city I call home, where I feel at home after twenty-four moves across four continents. I hold a state license in psychology in New York and have an office in Manhattan. New York is where I became the woman I am today.

Eddy is the biological father of Joelle and Sabrina. This fact will always remain true, allowing forgiveness to arise despite our differing views and values. It took a long time and considerable psychological work, but I have ultimately reached a state of neutrality and peace.

Always cordial, if not praising and affectionate, Eddy initiates periodic contact with me. More than anyone, I am Eddy's connection to our youth and beginnings and a significant contributor to his ascension to success and power. No one forgets this, not even Eddy.

Eddy has two other children. A girl followed the boy—both born while he was legally married to me. Through unforeseen circumstances, his children sealed my decision to embrace marital freedom. I am grateful to them for that and glad that my daughters have half-siblings. Children have nothing to do with their parents' behavior.

After our divorce, Eddy remarried a year later, but not to the mother of his other children. He and his second wife (substantially younger than him) seem to share similar values and make a good match.

Bobby holds a special place in my heart. He is an intrinsic part of my life, my history. I felt close to him early on and continued to harbor that feeling through the years. Counting on him was a given. I knew he'd be there, and he was, but rarely here, except at exceptional times when he was unconditionally by my side. Bobby is my cherished friend and more. As such, I am grateful to him. I know I can contact him at any time, but I will not interfere with his personal and professional lives. He is dear and near despite the Atlantic Ocean between us and life siding with the ocean.

I am grateful to unforgiving, unforgettable Alan, only remembering the exquisite parts. He was an eye-opener, a life starter. He stayed near me during my hundred hospital days. I will never forget the way he made me feel, the uplift he gave me, and beyond. We couldn't have a life together, but he inspired me to create my life's launching pad. We shared significant moments encapsulated in a song. When I hear Frankie's "New York, New York," I see Alan entering my living room looking for me and me leaping toward him. I lived it once and relive it on demand.

For the past five years, I have been in a relationship with a notable professional. We get along well. He is incredibly tender and loving, exactly what I need. He proposed—though marriage doesn't sweep me off my feet—and I will decide based on what is best for both of us and our respective children.

Each central relationship carried unique elements and, overall, was insightful. I hold a kaleidoscope of them at the core of my being

From a cultural perspective, I was expected to live under the care of a male, my father or husband, and thrive in his shadow. I wasn't expected to exist, let alone survive on my own, in New York of all places. I wasn't expected to write my experience—without shielding men.

Separation and divorce gave me the freedom to materialize my belief that I am no one's half. I am whole on my own, carrying a surname I hadn't used in a quarter of a century. I earned a doctorate degree, built my backbone, and flexed my psychological muscles, finally grasping my sense of self, which echoed within me "I can do it," and did it.

After much delay, came the day I realized I had all I needed to believe in myself and trust myself to make it on my own. I am the post-divorce woman looking back at my pre-divorce self and giving her a pat on the shoulder. As

Didier Anzieu writes, the aggregated insights have permeated my cells and brought awareness to the table.

Following a long, roundabout way, I am grateful for the bumps on the road. Had they not been acute, I might not have implemented the warranted changes. The wake-up calls served a purpose. Life is a brilliant teacher—a practical post-graduate program—and time a master healer. I learned from them beyond books, theories, and seminars.

I am prepared to share and contribute my professional insights to benefit others. Spontaneously, I applied and will uphold the Golden Rule, which is to treat others the way I want others to treat me, both personally and professionally. The people I have known or worked with are dear to me. I did my best to assist them in any way I could, and in turn, I learned something valuable from each of them. Regardless of their backgrounds, everyone shares the same desires and aspirations. Everyone strives to love and be loved in return. Everyone hopes to learn and achieve in life.

My diverse and intricate life experiences have equipped me to understand and share the feelings of others. To echo the famous quote from Harper Lee's novel, *To Kill a Mockingbird*, I can virtually put myself in someone else's shoes.

Analysis helped put my history in perspective as well as grasp and cope with its elements. Writing this memoir helped me come to terms with its details. I revisited places and people I thought I couldn't live without, but survived, feeling liberated and mature. Today I am at peace with myself and say, "My life was full and blessed."

Kierkegaard's statement about how he understood his life by reflecting on it while living it forward resonates with me. I can look back with compassion at my younger self leaving Egypt and say, "You had it all along, but you didn't see it or feel it back then. You mistook Eddy's behavior to mirror who you were—not who he was, a psychologically costly misperception. If you trusted then what you could accomplish, I would have written a vastly different memoir. But I wouldn't have had Joelle and Sabrina. They made the difference. They validate my actions."

The pyramids taught me that mastery endures. The ripples on the Nile demonstrated that external and internal appearances could differ. Little did I know that the instability and disruption of my early childhood would be emblematic of years ahead. The love I experienced growing up fueled my spirit in times of dearth.

I remember Dad telling me more than once, and Mom chiming in nodding her head, "Choose the subject you like. And go for it."

Dad, Mom, I did it.

I am the first woman on both sides of the family to earn a doctoral degree, and I trust I won't be the last.

My journey began as a teenager searching for an identity and anchor out of Cairo and culminated as an independent sole provider of two daughters, a Doctor of Psychology, and a New York and Connecticut licensed psychologist with a private practice in Manhattan.

183

NEW YORK, MAY 1996

On May 16, 1996, my peers cheered me as Valedictorian and the Doctoral Class Representative at the Department of Applied Psychology, New York University School of Education's Valedictory Celebration.

The next day, May 17, 1996, I sat on the dais overlooking Washington Square Park as Valedictorian, the Doctoral Class Representative of the School of Education, at New York University's Commencement Exercises.

From that platform and first row position, my view was unobstructed. I looked up. The sky was bright blue and the sun sparkling gold. It was just like the sky I saw from my balcony in Cairo.

I came a long way. My life didn't turn out the way I expected—it turned out better.

The last two days were happy celebrations of events that led me to sit on the dais. It wasn't an efficient or solo climb. I meandered along my path. Then I pepped my step. I made it. We made it. A whole town helped me, starting with Joelle and Sabrina, who inspired me and believed in me.

Taking a deep breath, I gazed around. On the other side of the aisle, I spotted Robert De Niro and Steven Spielberg, about to receive their honorary doctoral degrees. They seemed to be old buddies, having a good time chatting and laughing. I wanted to stand, shake their hands, and say, "Hi." It was my once-in-a-lifetime opportunity to be on equal standing with both. I tried to stand, but my legs wouldn't move. I tried again, nothing. Nothing. These legs of mine refused to budge—two solid poles.

I'll save my energy for my degree acceptance.

I inhaled and exhaled deeply, slowly, and abandoned saluting Rob and Steve. On that day, I could call them by their first names. I looked at them and smiled.

Hey, they smiled back! That's a minor success.

Joelle and Sabrina came along to Washington Square. We would find each other at the end of the ceremony, fending off the crowds of family, friends, and well-wishers to go home together and celebrate. My boyfriend also attended the valedictory celebration and is among the audience today.

They raised the banner of the School of Education. I heard Chancellor L. Jay Oliva, the President of New York University, calling my name and new title, *Dr. Djenane Nakhle*, on his microphone amplified by loudspeakers throughout Washington Square.

I trembled, wobbled, but managed to stand up and take five steps. Chancellor Oliva handed me the symbolic doctoral degree in a light beige tube. It bore my name: *Djenane Nakhle, PhD*. I took it from him, and said, "Thank you." We shook hands.

I ambled to the front of the balcony. Never have I climbed so high on my own. Washington Square was covered with people. Crowds filled side streets. I elevated my voice and lifted my right hand holding the degree. "I, Djenane Nakhle, accept this doctoral degree for all students at the New York University School of Education," I said as I waved it.

Raising my doctoral degree high, I waved it for the second time. This time, I did it for my parents and my two daughters. I kept my promises to them and paved the way for Joelle and Sabrina.

With my head held high, I tightly clutched my doctoral degree in my right hand, owning every aspect of my accomplishment, my journey. Frank Sinatra's "My Way" came to mind, and I sang it quietly. I sat down. My eyes were again drawn to the sky. It was a sunny day with a clear blue sky in New York City—my city, my home, the home I chose. The home I love.

I, too, Frankie, kept my chin up from Cairo until, finally, finding home in New York.

Not all those who wander are lost.

— Tolkien

ACKNOWLEDGMENTS

Thank you with love to my daughter, Joelle Tamraz, author of *The Secret Practice*. I am forever grateful for your encouragement and guidance, which helped me bring this book to life. You read my memoir in its entirety and parts at various stages of completion, providing insightful feedback. Your generous allocation of time and patience answering my countless questions have kept me going. Joelle's husband, Trevor von Puttkammer, has my heartfelt appreciation for his care during my writing process.

Thank you with love to my daughter, Sabrina Tamraz. I am forever indebted to you and your husband, Robert Horn. You invited me with open hearts and arms to Houston, included me in your inner circle, and gave me the support I needed when I wrote this book in the time of Covid. Most of all, you gave me the joy of seeing my five grandchildren, Serena, Sierra, Samson, Lazer, and Zahra, grow up and be part of their everyday lives.

I have infinite love for my grandchildren. Serena, you read the first pages of my memoir and gave me thoughtful feedback; Sierra, you showed me your feelings by offering me a treat you knew I liked when you came back from school; Samson, you asked me to play Uno when you felt I had worked too much; Lazer, you sat on my lap and gave me bear hugs; Zahra, you followed my directions in French and made me smile. The five of you fueled my inspiration more than words can convey. Your giggles and sometimes high pitch brightened my days, especially when the words did not align themselves as I wished. I hope I showed you one way of initiating, working through, and completing a meaningful task or project.

Special thanks to Bobby for reading my memoir. You believed in it from the get-go, just as you believed in me decades ago. You encouraged me in my progress and were enthusiastic about the completion of my book. Most of all, you gave its content your full backing

I have a deep fondness for my godchild, Serge Akl. You read my story and were supportive. The characters you know matched your recollection of them.

My profound gratitude goes to Maria Daversa, author of Sweet Baby Mine. Maria read my manuscript and provided a thorough, professional review, including the psychologist's insight and the author's perspective. Thank you, Maria, for your significant contribution to my memoir. Your input has given it wings.

I immensely thank Rosie Pasi and Chelsea Salinas for their willing assistance, discerning feedback, and unwavering support in reading this book more than once.

My heartfelt gratitude for Denise Mabardi, my childhood friend and classmate from Sacred Heart School. Denise and I have known each other since we were three years old. She kindly agreed to read the manuscript and provided valuable pointers. Her keen attention to the text is a much-appreciated contribution to my memoir. Thank you, Denise.

I sincerely appreciate Gail Gilmore, author of *Solomon* and *Dog Church*, for generously agreeing to read my manuscript. Gail, I am thankful for your time and meaningful feedback.

Deep gratitude to my talented editors: Margaret Diehl, who had the foresight to see the silver lining through ink on paper; Amber Hatch, who identified the merit of restructuring the story presentation, as did Allison Williams just by perusing two chapters. Jennifer Duardo, I thank you wholeheartedly. You have cleared my voice, allowing it to rise and be heard, carrying various tones through the pages. Thanks to you, achieving a clean manuscript was close to a cinch.

I want to express my endless appreciation to the talented artists who have contributed to my memoir. Kari Brownlie created an eye-catching book cover that genuinely reflects my words, while Stuart Grant designed a striking website to promote it. Asya Blue kindly stepped in on short notice when I was in a bind and designed the book's interior with elegance and mastery. Rob Greer took a beautiful photograph of me for my book's back cover, adding a personal touch that complements the story. The four of you have my earnest thank you. Your artistry created a remarkable visual representation of my story.

A whole town walked along with me while I wrote this book. Special thanks to Cameron Hammon, author of *This Is My Body*, your seminars were my initiation to writing a memoir; Jessica Wilbanks, author of *When I Spoke In Tongues*, your consultation set me on the right track; D.J. MacPhee and Craig Moskowitz, your sample reading of my initial scribblings traced a writing path.

Thank you so much to you all and to those I may have inadvertently omitted.

AUTHOR BIO

DJENANE NAKHLE is an Egyptian-born, Lebanese-American psychologist. Due to political and economic upheaval in her birth country, she lived in Switzerland, Lebanon, and France before immigrating to the United States, making Manhattan her home and professional address.

Her travels and diverse life experiences across four continents have exposed her to multi-cultural environments and given her multilingual fluency (English, French, Spanish and Arabic) and an expanded worldview.

A licensed psychologist in New York and Connecticut with nearly thirty years of experience, Dr. Nakhle has, in addition to her private practice, served as the Director of Therapeutics at Columbia Presbyterian Medical Center (CPMC) for five years and taught a Graduate seminar, "Trauma: Theoretical and Clinical Perspectives," at New York University.

Dr. Nakhle's clinical focus includes anxiety, interpersonal relationships, and learning differences. She strives to use her clinical expertise and broad experience in a supportive and collaborative approach to help others achieve their goals.

Website: djenanenakhle.com

Facebook: @drdjenanenakhle

Instagram: @drdjenanenakhle

LinkedIn: linkedin.com/in/drdjenanenakhle/

X: @NakhleDr

REVIEWS

If you enjoyed this memoir, please share your thoughts on Amazon and Goodreads. Your reviews are crucial in helping authors have their books discovered by other readers.

Thank you!

Amazon.com

Goodreads.com

www.ingramcontent.com/pod-product-compliance
Lightning Source LLC
Chambersburg PA
CBHW061415160726
47995CB00003B/619